Pathologies of Paradise

Pathologies of Paradise

Caribbean Detours

Supriya M. Nair

University of Virginia Press
Charlottesville and London

University of Virginia Press

Printed in the United States of America on acid-free paper

First published 2013

9 8 7 6 5 4 3 2 1

Library of Congress Cataloging-in-Publication Data

Nair, Supriya, 1961-
Pathologies of paradise : Caribbean detours / Supriya M. Nair.
pages cm. — (New World Studies)
Includes bibliographical references and index.
ISBN 978-0-8139-3517-1 (cloth : alk. paper) — ISBN 978-0-8139-3518-8 (pbk. : alk. paper) — ISBN 978-0-8139-3519-5 (e-book)
1. Caribbean literature (English)—History and criticism. 2. Stereotypes (Social psychology) in literature. I. Title.
PR9205.05.N35 2013
810.9′9729—dc23

2013013059

In memory of A. P. Gopalan Nair and M. Rajan Nair

Contents

Acknowledgments

THE IDEAS for this book appeared in my research and conferences several years ago and have been germinating in different environments. I am grateful to all the people who sustained the process along the way. Papers related to the book were delivered at the American Tropics Conference, the College English Association, the Caribbean Philosophical Association, the Caribbean Studies Association, the Modern Language Association, the Society for Caribbean Studies Conference, Dartmouth College, University of Texas at Austin, and University of the West Indies, Mona, among other places. I am grateful to all the organizers, colleagues, and audiences across hemispheres that helped me hone my arguments and nudged me toward paths I would not have taken. None of this travel would have been possible without research and travel support from Tulane University and the School of Liberal Arts, which enabled me to visit England, the Caribbean, and Latin America. The Clare Hall fellowship supported a crucial and charming summer of research at the University of Cambridge. My thanks also to Rosanne Adderley, Tony Bogues, Janice Carlisle, Carolyn Cooper, Lewis Gordon, Barbara Harlow, Ann Hawkins, Paget Henry, Peter Hulme, Amy Koritz, Rebecca Mark, Brinda Mehta, Marilyn Miller, Angel Parham, Sandra Pouchet Paquet, Mimi Sheller, Felipe Smith, and Molly Travis for their support, feedback or encouragement at conferences and other collegial venues. George Lamming, the writer whose work first directed me toward the field of Caribbean literature, continues to be an inspiration.

Colleagues at Tulane University, particularly in the Department of English, the programs in African and African Diaspora Studies, Gender and Sexuality Studies, the Stone Center, and Newcomb College Institute provided a supportive network. During the aftermath of Katrina, they showed me how a fierce sense of community can help a city and a university rise to a challenge. The students in my various classes were icing on the cake. I am grateful to my editor, Cathie Brettschneider; my copyeditor, Colleen Romick Clark; my project editor, Morgan Myers and the anonymous readers whose incisive feedback was instrumental in pruning my unruly manuscript. Paige Bailey, Samantha Bruner, and Amber Gafur conducted valuable research and made many a trip to the library on my behalf.

My extended family and friends on another continent continue to be a solid firewall despite the irrecoverable loss of my father and my eldest brother. For persuading me to take the detours en route to this book, and for making that longer road delightful, I thank Gaurav Desai and Sameer Nair-Desai.

My thanks to George Lamming and Esther Phillips for permission to reprint portions of my article "Toxic Domesticity: Home, Family, and Indo-Caribbean Women," which first appeared in *BIM* 2, no. 3 (May–October 2008): 62–75.

Pathologies of Paradise

Introduction

tink yu in heaven . but yu livin in h. ell
tink you in heaven but yu livin in hell.

—Kamau Brathwaite, *Born to Slow Horses*

Diversion *leads nowhere* when the original trickster strategy does not encounter any real potential for development.

(We cannot underestimate the universal malaise that drives Europeans, dissatisfied with their world, toward those 'warm lands' that are deserted by unemployment as well as subjected to intolerable pressures of survival, to seek in the *Other's World* a temporary respite.)

—Édouard Glissant, *Caribbean Discourse: Selected Essays*

THIS BOOK was conceived in the serendipitous moments when teaching and research fuse in a lightening flash, illuminating thorny debates about the literary archaeology of the Caribbean and the discursive regimes by which it is enunciated in contemporary anglophone literature. My readings of the texts under discussion are haunted by classroom questions about the way the literature helps "articulate the past historically."[1] In one iteration of a frequently taught course on anglophone Caribbean literature, we read Edwidge Danticat's short story cycle *Krik? Krak!* during the final week of class. One student who found the stories particularly wrenching wondered aloud if I had deliberately chosen the text as a kind of last word on the *tristes* tropics, our terminal seizure of the perpetually smiling sun, beach, and service of the Caribbean that saturates popular imagery in the United States. Indeed, students in various Caribbean literature classes have consistently pointed out the incongruence of the insouciant tourist package that defines their immediate perception of the Caribbean here and the painful excavation of the literary texts that reveal a daunting history of genocide, slavery, servitude, colonial settlement, plantation regimes, economic exploitation, sexual violence, ethnic conflict, and other upheavals. The works seem invested in the premeditated murder of the ubiquitous paradise motif that frames the reinvention of the Caribbean from Columbus to contemporary times.

I once asked a friend if she had enjoyed reading Shani Mootoo's *Cereus Blooms at Night*. Despite her obvious admiration for the novel, she responded thoughtfully, "I don't know if 'enjoy' is the right word for it." Those who have read the book know that the flowery title presages a nightmarish chronicle, and readers are just as perturbed by Danticat's work, which relates shattering events in exquisite prose. Students echo my friend's unease when they claim that the literary texts "ruined" the Caribbean for them, not petulantly but seriously acknowledging the inadequacy of the relaxation they envisioned in brochures or experienced in cruises and holiday resorts.[2] Contemporary anglophone Caribbean literature, which is my focus here, often deliberately halts the gratification one may expect from an "enjoyable" reading experience where one mentally vacations in the Caribbean through the text.

As paradise critiques of the Caribbean note, its diverting utility in recreating the overstressed life cycles of metropolitan late capitalism exploits the prelapsarian idyll of the garden in Genesis.[3] The etymology of "resort" has suggestive links with "recourse" and "retreat," all derived from Old French. Although the contemporary association of "resort" with a place of recreation is only a few centuries old, there is a relationship between all these words that share a certain anxiety: *en dernier ressort,* a turn (in the last instance) to, a running back or flight, a retreat to back up and reward tedious routine, a reparation or compensation for the monotonous schedule of work that must eventually get back to business as usual. The groovy dream-space of the Caribbean becomes significant (if that) only as an accessory of the more substantial centers of capital and diaspora for which it plays this rejuvenating role. Derek Walcott satirically morphs the entire United States into a tourist who "dangles the extended foot of Florida as inflated rubber islands bob and drinks with umbrellas float towards her on a raft."[4] The languid gesture is not just culturally and economically enabled by U.S. dominance and material wealth, but geographically made possible as tropical cocktails drift, and Florida almost tramples the synthetic archipelago mapped in a servile position. Although the Caribbean was gendered female in the early modern emblems of the undressed sultry Americas lounging in wait for the masculine European voyager to discover and taste her charms, today the reverse gendering that Walcott suggests is just as possible as affluent female tourists in search of quick thrills seek the services of beach boys and possibly girls.

The ocean, however, is not simply a fabulous seascape and global gateway, but the distressing site of Columbian entry, the Middle Passage, the

Kala Pani, and other voyages not connected with leisure. For Walcott, Kamau Brathwaite, and Wilson Harris, the evolution from slave ship to cruise ship is bizarrely choreographed by the trivialization of limbo, which Brathwaite claims began aboard the slave ship to provide exercise for the cramped slaves in the holds, but in its contemporary adaptation, he adds, is a nightclub entertainment.[5] Such a trifling, inebriated romance elides the region's actual conditions, particularly its accursed relationship to exploited labor and its destitute populations. "The Caribbean is not an idyll, not to its natives," Walcott trenchantly announces.[6] Europe was in dire straits when it "discovered" the New World during the infancy of capitalist accumulation. The later phase of that history continues to interpret the Caribbean as a place of regeneration for people from elsewhere in a differently beleaguered situation, but now with the privilege of disposable income for a vacation or spiritual quest to recharge batteries.

The opening section of Earl Lovelace's *While Gods Are Falling* leads us through paradise, here presented in its secular, contemporary facade in the affluent neighborhoods of Port of Spain. The unidentified narrator, assuming the persona of a tourist guide and directing the "you," the reader-tourist, through the prosperous quarter, suddenly breaks into the much-touted vistas with an abrupt directive: "But turn your head." The hitherto predictable tour then disconcertingly shifts direction, and the reader is led into the barrack yards and slums, where "all Gods have fallen and there is nothing to look up to, no shrine to worship at, and man is left only bare flesh and naked passions."[7] It is clear even at this early stage of the melancholic novel that Lovelace does not privilege in the last phrase the sexualized frolic of skimpily clad visitors that is a standard, if discreet, temptation of travel brochures. Rather, he discloses the impoverished inner-city dweller usually absent in sightseeing schedules.

The "bare flesh" of the socially dead inhabitants scarred by the aftermath of slavery and servitude and neglected, even abused, by the neocolonial state is among the subjects I examine here, the "bare life" of limited citizenship and incomplete postcolonial promise.[8] But Lovelace's conclusion to this prefatory visit ultimately expresses the double bind in a title such as *Pathologies of Paradise,* even as it challenges the stereotype of pleasurable ease by presenting its "fallen" extremity. The Janus face gazes at bipolar conditions of possibility, reproducing a paradise-hell binary that flattens the nuances of Caribbean realities and reduces the flexible, regenerative range of the Caribbean imaginary evoked by the literary grotesque, which I discuss in more detail later. While the two poles repeat themselves, this book is more interested in what lies between these extremities and thus it takes various detours on its route through paradise and pathology. As I hope to show, neither is the paradise as idyllic as it seems nor are the region's marooned only sites of abjection. The trauma story is also a partial one, and Caribbean literature expresses joy, resilience, humor, and other qualities associated with the positive carnivalesque, along with the canny adaptations of the region's peoples.

Reverting to notions of paradise regained after the pathology of loss and conquest, however, would make a cliché of the more complex survivalist tactics of Caribbean fiction. Anglophone Caribbean narrative rarely if ever follows a triumphalist path of affirmation, but neither is it only a pathological symptom of a larger malaise. This book pursues the "trickster strategy" advised by Édouard Glissant, the detours and diversions entailed by the thickly entangled rhizomes of social history, literary narrative, and cultural identity rather than the single phallic root of what he calls the "persistent myth of the paradise islands."[9] Glissant recommends the productive maneuvers of departures from the mainstream and variations from the beaten path, but he also urges "the necessary return [not to a mythical origin or pristine state but] to the point where our problems [lie] in wait for us."[10] In a dynamic process akin to the Freudian uncanny, the strange is made familiar and the familiar is estranged such that there is no settled perspective, but rather a constant repositioning as unexpected prospects and outlooks emerge.

In his reference to detours, Glissant also engages the other etymological and more resonant meanings of circuit, turn, revolution, and journey not only for those outside the Caribbean but also for its peoples whose colonial history—and even geography—has to some extent been externally imposed and rigidly mapped. J. Michael Dash interprets Glissant's mobile tropes as "ex-stasis," which he explains as the "flight from the plantation, the defiance of confinement, the movement away from stasis[,] . . . an imaginative departure from the shipwrecked, petrified condition of the colonized mind."[11] As I argue in the final chapter, this challenge to a congealed Medusa visage of history has often been enacted through humor and laughter, not in the vacuum of mindless joy, but with a tragic awareness of pain and struggle.

The narrator in Lovelace's novel winds up the brief tour with these foreboding words to the reader-tourist who is suggestively merged by the end of it with the inhabitant, the city dweller: "And they will tell you that your city is rich, beautiful, and that the steel-band is a wonder, calypso an achievement, and carnival is the greatest live spectacle on earth. And all of this is true. But there is something else here, something dark, poisonous and stinking, something like a sore in this city."[12] This stark contrast between the celebratory and the cankerous in Port of Spain and in the territory at large is almost a commonplace in anglophone Caribbean literature. Creative fiction tries to work through the "sore" spots to a less painful space, although it does not always do so, as I emphasize in my discussions of toxic domesticity, a term I use both descriptively and critically to address the remarkable emphasis on trauma in the individual and national home. Lovelace's address to the tourist and reader he transforms into a local resident is not intended to mute their differences but is an invitation to refuse a single, antiseptic point of view, assumed in the flitting glance of the tourist or the distanced gaze of the reader. It demands an attentive "turn[ing of one's] head" rather than a fixed perspective, a fuller engagement with the region as a complex spectrum of lived experience.

Although the reductive touristification of the region has rightly come in for much critique, one must bear in mind Jonathan Culler's charge of "smugness" on the part of those who attack tourists from a supposedly uncompromised position. "Ferocious denigration of tourists is in part an attempt to convince oneself that one is not a tourist," he points out.[13] Culler dismantles the easy assumptions of travel as vigorous, experiential, engaged work and tourism as mindless commodification and passive pleasure. No matter what the length of stay or type of travel (first-class airfare; cruise package; thrifty backpacking hiker; sensitive ecotourist), neither a tourist nor a traveler is a resident; and even among residents, as Lovelace demonstrates, there is no natural harmony, essential belonging, or unified group identity. The differences and even tensions between the inhabitants of the Caribbean and the diaspora of continuing migration suggest other degrees of separation. The desire for authenticity and authorized positions is a misguided one, as Culler suggests.

For those of us who live outside the Caribbean but believe that fieldwork and serious scholarship authenticate our travel, Pauline Melville's fictional but aptly named Michael Wormaol, an anthropologist from the University of Berne who self-importantly researches comparative mythology among South American Indians, deflates such assurance.[14] Wormaol's rivalry with Rosa Mendelson, a literary scholar who is conducting research on Evelyn Waugh but is distracted by a brief affair with Chofy McKinnon (of Wapisiana Indian descent), implicates the self-aggrandizing process of digging for knowledge and "going native" with other quests and mining expeditions in the Guianas, some of them, as the dynamite explosion at the end of the novel prophesies, with disastrous consequences for the Indigenous peoples who inhabit the hinterland.

While the wilderness and its tamer rural picturesque were foundational elements in the Edenic pastoral, their manifestation in the Americas piloted and lubricated "the machine in the garden," the modern technologies of the plantation that attached the tropical pastoral and agricultural georgic to European industrial capital with the arrival of Columbus's errant caravels. His itinerary from west to east was in part dictated by his conviction that the Garden of Eden lay in the southern hemisphere, and he believed he had found it as he wandered through the prolific wildlife and foliage and the cerulean seas of the West Indies and South America. In the centuries that followed, as I will discuss in the first chapter, the task of naming and cataloguing the ample yield of the tropical islands and the massive enterprise of transplanting crops, domestic animals, and humans would exploit and transform Caribbean landscape, displace and relocate millions of people, and in the process revolutionize European, if not world, history.

The partial collapse of the biblical garden following the "discovery" of a terrestrial paradise was triggered not simply by the startled awareness of fauna and flora inconceivable in Christian geography. Exposure to the other side of the luxuriant tropics—hurricanes, heat, earthquakes, insects, and other forms of "pestilence"—that assailed the unwary European journeying from a different climate and topography also tarnished the initial radiance. This postlapsarian aspect indicated a fallen state of nature that cast doubt on Edenic pretensions. The natives of the islands were either assimilated into animal or subhuman forms or else rendered altogether invisible to facilitate a narrative of anti-conquest. They were also, in the wide range of stereotypes in the colonial imagination, perceived as otherworldly beings. The first impression was one of primal innocence, although that almost immediately deteriorated. "Such of late/Columbus found th' American so girt/With feathered cincture, naked else and wild," says John Milton, but the timing of this comparison to the mythical first parents is ominous since it is immediately after the Fall in book 9 of his epic, and Adam and Eve have cast the proverbial fig leaf not only over their nakedness but over their "guilt and dreaded shame."[15]

Observing that an exultant Columbus identified the Orinoco as one of the rivers flowing from the Garden of Eden, Michael Taussig ironically adds, "The angelic natives Columbus espied suffered dearly." It was only a matter of time, Taussig continues, before the "angels" mutated into demons in a profane reprise of the heavenly Fall, although they were useful even in this guise. "Their function in the larger scheme of descent and salvation remained, calling to mind that it is only when he meets the devil and mounts his back, that Dante is carried to the terrestrial paradise."[16] The ascent was not limited to religious rewards reaped through conversions and the manifold increase of the faithful. The "devils" who literally carried explorers and entrepreneurs up or across perilous heights and rivers unwittingly facilitated capitalist expansion that also developed on the backs, so to speak, of indigenous and imported labor. As Jill Cassid notes in her aptly titled *Sowing Empire,* the transfer and grafting of plants resulted in anxieties about cultural miscegenation and hybridity even as the picturesque attempted to conceal through regulated vegetation the "disindigenation and lethal labor" that fostered this enterprise.[17] My final chapter notes that grotesque humor exposes such anxieties and celebrates the mixtures implied by the grotesque, be they vegetal, racial, or generic.

While the untamed wilderness offered its own excitements against the decorous pleasures of the country house, the botanical gardens, and, on a larger scale, the organized plantations of the colonial georgic, the other side of paradise has always trailed in its wake, as in the biblical version. A number of texts tend to integrate the paradise-hell coupling, so that one inevitably seems accompanied by the other. The tourist fantasy is challenged along with the biblical simulacrum. Olive Senior's poem "Meditation on Yellow" goes even further to conflate the demanding tourist with the insatiable conquistador with whom she begins. She itemizes the raw products that the "lazy" Caribbean provides in a series of backbreaking, laboring activities: cane sugar, bananas, oranges, ginger, cocoa, aluminum, and so on.[18] Not just the entertaining oceanic fringe of the islands but the entire landscape and human labor are expropriated by a proprietary world engaged in "consuming the Caribbean," to borrow Mimi Sheller's eloquent phrase.[19]

Just when Senior's poetic narrator is ready to rest from "five hundred years of servitude,"[20]

> a new set of people
> arrive
> to lie bare-assed in the sun
> wanting gold on their bodies
> cane-rows in their hair
> with beads—even bells.[21]

The uncomfortable conjoining of keywords—gold, cane, and beads—associated with the lethal paraphernalia of Columbian arrival emphasizes the relapse of garden into empire, the ricochets of paradise discourse that now form the arsenal of Caribbean writers. The elusive quest for the gold of El Dorado shifts to the brazen "bare-assed" worship of heliotherapy, and the "dread" of servitude and slavery amid cane-rows is trimmed into the fashionable quirks of borrowed, exoticized hairstyles. Just as the limbo on slave ships descends to the contortions of nightclub revelry and sedates its disquieting origins, the substance of Caribbean subjectivity is emaciated in these voracious processes of consumption. But the Caribbean is never a passive landscape only acted upon nor are its residents simply inert victims: they can also exert a productive (and sometimes unproductive) ruinate force on such agents of exploitation.

In its happy tourist avatar, the Caribbean has long figured as the utopian respite from the mechanized, work-driven, capitalistic routines of the overindustrialized world. Jamaican reggae and Rastafari views that endorse an anticapitalistic stance have often been conveniently translated into a hedonistic ideology of mindless pleasure and idleness, not just in Spring Break culture but in a larger context of celebratory consumption that persistently carnivalizes the Caribbean. Bob Marley's line "everything's gonna be alright" (and variations thereof) is perhaps a necessary mantra when life seems to offer few alternatives to poverty and deprivation. It may even articulate a "non-Western" philosophy that some find quietist and others believe is a healthier alternative to the unrelieved anxiety and acquisitiveness of modern lifestyles. So mistakenly identified is Marley with this sense of being laid-back that the African American Bobby McFerrin's "Don't Worry, Be Happy" is confused in the popular domain with Marley's lyrical output, much to the annoyance of the latter's serious fans.[22]

The attractiveness of such phrases as the Swahili "Hakuna Matata" and the Rasta greeting "Irie" also indicates a degree of chilling out that has wide appeal in popular culture, offering an interesting alternative to the theory of nervous natives on the edge of breakdown. In this philosophy (or, for some, the pose) of being cool, the West is located as the hysterical site of neuroses and the so-called Third World is endowed with the magical healing potion because of the perceived difference in lifestyles and values. And yet, as my chapter on the Jonestown tragedy in Guyana will argue, even this elixir acquires the poisonous potential of the Derridean *pharmakon,* repeating the paradise-hell coupling when the idealism of the commune in the tropical bush degenerates into the terror of the camp and the dementia of the overbearing Reverend Jones who drove hundreds into mass suicide or murdered them by coercing them to drink Flavor Aid laced with cyanide.

As Gabriel García Márquez describes in *The Autumn of the Patriarch,* the sovereign barely pronounces the curse of mortality before numberless citizens vanish, not in the exceptional individuality of the *homo sacer* but in the multiple massacres where thousands are killed with impunity. Against the spectral sightings of "three caravels of the admiral of the ocean sea," new genocides are condemned to repeat the past in mass killings of the nation's citizens under dictatorship.[23] José Ignacio Saenz de la Barra, the hired mercenary, sends a sack of "seeming coconuts" to the despot who seeks retribution against the assassins of Leticia Nazareno and his child.[24] The depletion of natural resources under the reign of the dictator is metonymically—and literally—multiplied in the banal harvesting of human heads (an obscene reference to the cannibal stereotype) until even his mind boggles at the infinitude of this hydra-headed endgame: "How is it possible that there are so many of them and they still haven't got to the ones who are really guilt[y], but Sáenz de la Barra had made him note that with every six heads sixty enemies are produced and for every sixty six hundred are produced and then six thousand and then six million, the whole country, God damn it, we'll never end, and Sáenz de la Barra answered him impassively to rest easy, general, we'll finish with them when they're all finished, what a barbarian."[25] What Kumkum Sangari calls the *"fecundity"* of "the long sentence" signifies not the lush tropics materialized in the baroque of magical realism, but the overripe, interminable dictatorship and the inexhaustible multitudes available for extermination.[26] Even the tyrant is piously sickened by the reek of the violence he commissions.

The phantasmagorical power of the dictator and the disciplinary control over the landscape and human subjects are neither recent nor imaginary. Indeed, the modern Caribbean as García Márquez signifies in the specter of the caravels was natally tied to the sovereign domination of land and subjects. Nature and culture are dialogically involved with each other as the reconstruction of the Caribbean into agricultural labor regimes and plantation enclosures catastrophically transforms nature and the people engaged in this enterprise even as it opens up a new world. The word "paradise" derives from the Old Persian *pairidaeza,* meaning an enclosed park or orchard.[27] But George Lamming's resonant phrase "the empire and the garden,"[28] which inspires the first chapter, implies that the revival of paradise in the New World meant anything but an ideal enclave for the original inhabitants and for those who were enslaved or indentured to labor in its confines. The New World that was to be foisted on the Indigenous peoples meant not the benediction of Genesis or the divine grace of Resurrection, but Apocalypse, the end of their world as they knew it.

The "discovery" project of Columbus, with its imminent sense of joyous reunion with paradise (notwithstanding the dangers), centered on islands as the appropriate topos for merging the aesthetic with the utilitarian, the spiritual with the worldly, the altruistic with the lucrative. European voyagers had long visualized islands through tropes of paradise and utopia, the sixteenth century in particular—the period of great sea voyages—favoring such representations. John R. Gillis notes that islands have figured prominently in Christian cosmogony, which, in medieval times, was temporally and spatially consonant with the present. The Garden of Eden, now shattered into shards but still waiting to be (re)discovered, was both a sign of God's wrath and an emblem of future hope and redemption. As Gillis explains, "Europeans had always imagined Eden as insular, representing it as either landlocked or sea-girt. So what better place to imagine its New World location than tropical Caribbean islands, whose remote and bounded nature enhanced their claim to be lost paradise. As each newly discovered island proved to be disappointingly postlapsarian, the quest simply moved on, ultimately migrating to the Pacific. Thus the myth of Eden, like that of other legendary isles, was kept alive by the process of discovery itself, with Eden always located one step beyond the moving frontier."[29] From the so-called Age of Discovery to the end of the eighteenth century, virtually every Atlantic island, he adds, had been "found," explored and exploited until what he calls the "islomania" of the earlier centuries spent itself.

The boundedness of the island space also encouraged a perception of its restricted territory as conveniently colonizable—surplus property there for the taking—as Columbus and his followers proceeded to demonstrate ritually, to the likely mystification of any native observers, by throwing themselves on their knees when coming ashore, calling upon heaven, planting flags and crosses, and claiming various islands for the dual mandate of enriching the treasuries of royal Spain and expanding the domain of Christian salvation. The changing same of the paradise motif leads the Guyanese writer Jan Carew to identify a creationist and neo-creationist myth of ownership: the first that of a singular male deity who created the universe and granted dominion over it to humans whom he made in his image; the second of Columbus, who "discovered" the Caribbean and bequeathed it to Europe.[30]

But the Genesis version of creation obviously had some difficulty reconciling itself with radically alien people, cultures, and topography. The tales that voyagers brought back, particularly the wild possibilities of men with feet in the air and tails on their backs, the outlandish descriptions of monsters at sea and on land, must have warranted some evidence, even in a late medieval world that had not officially banished myth from fact and imagination from history. How to trust such improbable travelers' tales despite all the anxious conventions of verity and eyewitness?[31] It could well be claimed that the birth of the new sciences in Europe was impelled by the need to authenticate hearsay, while instruments such as the microscope and telescope propelled the more rigorous methods (for the time) of direct observation and detailed study.

This is not to debunk the wealth of new knowledge simply because it was Western or imperialist and argue for some nativist return to a pure or original designation. Nor do I want to suggest that these new systems became dominant universally without internal struggle, heated scholarly debates, controversy, and intense rivalry within Europe. Even to claim that a definitive mode of inquiry, investigation, and nomination was established is arguable.[32] It must also be noted that whatever the catastrophic impact of imperialism, it did not simply involve rapacious deforestation, and some of its agents, as well as its critics, were conservationists who were keen to protect the environment.[33] But it cannot be denied that "the order of things," to cite Michel Foucault, took on a decidedly Western cast that then came to be seen as commonsense or as rational, even when it was theoretical or speculative.[34] The Swedish botanist Carl Linnaeus himself frankly admitted that his "natural" classifications in the eighteenth century were often arbitrary and artificial, but they gained hegemony because of their convenience to those who preferred to use them. It bears repeating that the very term "Indians" erroneously renamed, one may say "christened," the peoples of the Americas, and tribal characteristics were simplistically assigned to the Arawak and Carib Indians, for example, based on Columbus's often-misguided expectations and assertions. Much of this became received knowledge, settled views, through what Carew dismissively calls the "echo chamber" of experts who became normative through incestuous self-referentiality.[35] Nature and culture were up for grabs literally and conceptually:

> Native peoples might live among a profusion of birds and plants—indeed, the tropics contained a greater diversity than any European country—but from Linnaeus's perspective the local inhabitants were lacking the most basic knowledge. They did not know who created the plants and animals surrounding them, what these objects should properly be called, and how they fit into

> the established order. According to Linnaeus, the local names possessed no scientific value, nor did they reflect a deeper religious recognition of God's creation, His Design, or His Will. Just as missionaries attempted to save the souls of indigenous peoples, Linnaeus's apostles sought to save the species of the world for a second naming.[36]

The process of renaming implied the dominance of European systems of knowledge as other systems were perceived as irrational, outdated, or simply poor copies.

Walcott famously countered V. S. Naipaul's assertion of Caribbean mimicry of Europe with the retort that, on the contrary, what the New World had to offer was like nothing the Old had seen before. From all accounts of the Columbian voyages and for at least a few centuries following the epochal year of 1492, traveling eyewitnesses would have been willing to take Walcott at his word.[37] The mutual scopophilia of sailors and natives would have found plenty to marvel and wonder at when they first gazed upon each other, but the Europeans were just as bemused by the fauna and flora that frequently appeared to be figments of wild imagination and were often described coterminously with the aboriginal people. It was not simply that fantastic creatures such as unicorns were said to exist in these parts. When there was no readily deployable frame of reference, no alphabetized index, no international botanical or zoological nomenclature as yet to accord with what they saw, category confusion was rampant. Thus, Claude Lévi-Strauss points out, boa constrictors, hippopotamuses, tapirs, and sharks were transcribed in muddled formations as snakelike crocodiles, ox-bodied creatures with elephantine tusks, ox-headed fish with four legs, and man-eating tiburons. In an age when people described the then unfamiliar cotton plant as a "sheep tree," even drawing it with sheep dangling from its branches and obligingly waiting to be shorn, Lévi-Strauss adds that Columbus's alleged sightings of sirens in the Caribbean would not have seemed wholly incredible.[38]

While natural historians were still grappling with the mysteries of biogeography, a massive exchange of plant and animal species would make their task more difficult before they made it simple for themselves.[39] Even before Adam's supposed descendants acceptably categorized the fauna and flora of local origin, the modern international market would launch the formal advent of Western capitalism with a breathtaking transformation of regional geographies. Columbus brought not just the revolutionary sugarcane, but horses, cattle, dogs, pigs, chickens, and goats, which, like some of their owners, proceeded to thrive in their new habitat in inverse proportion to the autochthonous inhabitants and pasturage, probably accelerating "the extinction of certain plants, animals, and even the Indians themselves, whose gardens they encroached upon."[40]

The abode of the various natives turned into killing fields, according to Alfred Crosby, as their insulated constitutions, unused to the pathogens that had a long life in the Old World, fell easy prey to the various diseases (measles, pneumonia, typhus, chickenpox, and the fatal clincher—smallpox) the Europeans brought with them. While David Arnold agrees generally with Crosby's epidemiological conclusions, he is critical of what he believes is the latter's tendency to mitigate the active violence of the conquistadores and other invaders by attributing primary cause to the "invisible killers" of invasive biota rather than to the historical consequences of colonization represented by "Indian killers" such as Cortez and Córdoba who mercilessly slaughtered their perceived foe. Individual human culpability and economic greed therefore pale before the malevolent but uncontrollable forces of human biology, implicating Crosby, in Arnold's view, in racist ideologies of social Darwinism and the inevitable conquest of the weaker by the stronger.[41]

But to be fair to Crosby, even if he does seem to be rather impressed by the remarkable success of European expansionism, the title under which he presents it—"Conquistador y Pestilencia"—is hardly flattering. However unbiased such terms may be to zoologists and apiculturalists, to speak of Europeans leapfrogging across the globe or swarming "again and again" despite initial repulsions is loaded language in a contemporary scenario that rarely applies such expressions to white incursions but is all too ready to complain about aggressive hordes—people and pests—from the Third World.[42] Likewise, while current hysteria in the industrialized world is easily triggered by images of "African" and "Haitian" AIDS, "Asian" flu, and so on, to refer to the English as "efficient disease carriers,"[43] who annihilated the hapless Amerindians simply by breathing on them, or to declare bluntly that "Every Eden has its snake, and that is the role Europeans played in the Canaries"[44] is to remind one of a period that many have forgotten in its unpalatable details, particularly in romanticized idealizations of paradise regained.

The gardens of eighteenth-century Europe, undeniably enriched by the foraging activities in the earlier period catalogued by Crosby and others, secularized the Eden myth, allowing the new sciences to study nature in and of itself rather than as an exclusively divine manifestation. Botanical gardens at Uppsala under Linnaeus, at the Jardin du Roi in Paris under Georges Buffon, at London's Kew Gardens under Sir Joseph

Banks, and the official directorships of the Hookers encouraged the development of botany (compatibly with abstract learning, hard-headed business, personal pleasure, individual knowledge, and public interest) through three centuries. While the botanic gardens of the Caribbean in Trinidad, British Guiana, Grenada, and Jamaica would be instituted a century later, the eighteenth century foresaw the Victorian plant craze that, along with the consumption of commodities such as sugar, tea, coffee, and chocolate, would make the accumulation of *tropical* ornamentals an *English* pastime. Plant collections of private collectors blossomed even as colonial metropolises vied for the control of booming plant industries, occasionally smuggling crops and seeds and stealing from each other.[45] Fads for tropical and exotic plants such as orchids in the British empire—both in England and in the colonies—ironically flourished as English landscape became identified with national character. Jamaica Kincaid finds this trend not at all perplexing. "Almost as if ashamed of the revulsion and hostility they have for foreign people, the English make up for it by loving and embracing foreign plants wholesale," she says caustically.[46]

The pleasing prospect of landscaped gardens directs the vision of the observer whose disciplined enjoyment of the beauties and bounties of nature is channeled by human organization and unobtrusive labor. However, order and regularity were particularly vital not simply to the domestic enclosure of the garden but to the commercial enterprise of the plantation.[47] This "vision of empire" structured and reconstituted the geography of the Caribbean and shadowed the literature of the region, as I will trace in the anglophone Caribbean texts to which I will turn. If I dwell here on the European context, it is to frame Caribbean perspectives more concretely, not to limit their production singularly to a "writing-back" perspective, but to note that they necessarily operated through and against the epistemologies and practices of empire. I frame the analysis that follows through Raymond Williams's discussion of "culture," which traces its etymology in multiple senses, including colonization and cultivation, co-conspirators, one might say, in the modern formation of the Caribbean.[48] Chapter 1 expands the discussion of the colonization of nature through the nature of colonization, which entailed the writing over of Indigenous and nonwhite cultures along with the construction of new genealogies. But this erasure did not stop with the end of colonial rule, and writers following the anticolonial generation brought visibility to the overlooked or underwritten aspects of gender and sexual politics in national genealogies.

Anglophone Caribbean literature with few exceptions is yet to integrate in any meaningful way the precolonial cultures of the region, but the better-known colonial narratives of slavery or indentured servitude and their postcolonial descendants are unable to assimilate the myths of paradise and the garden. Instead, nature and agricultural activity are disfigured by colonial domination, which left deep psychic scars on the inhabitants as well, a condition Michelle Cliff identifies as "contagious melancholia." In a short story of the same title, the first-person narrator dwells briefly on the contentment of paradise, only to chart a very different genealogy of being. "Girlhood chums of my great-grandmother, they cluster together in my mind with all the other mad, crazy, eccentric, disappointed, demented, neurasthenic women of my childhood, where Bertha Mason grew on trees. Every family of our ilk, every single one, had such a member."[49] To what extent Cliff is satirizing the crazy Creole legend circulated by the English canon remains unclear here, but the depiction of Bertha Mason as a kind of "strange fruit"—an emphasis on mental instability and also an evocation of lynching—constructs her as yet another produce of colonial (agri)culture.

The garden in Caribbean literature is never simply the site of pleasure or lost innocence, since, as Naipaul asserts in *The Enigma of Arrival,* it has an evil twin in the plantation. Jamaica Kincaid, who agrees with this pairing, describes the ravages of AIDS on her brother's body in horticultural metaphors. "The plantsman in my brother will never be, and all the other things that he might have been in his life have died; but inside his body a death lives, flowering upon flowering with a voraciousness that nothing seems able to satisfy and stop."[50] From the hapless casualties of contagion following the arrival of Columbus to the self-destructive choices made by Devon Drew who died of AIDS in 1996, we have come a long but not always healthier way. However sympathetic Kincaid is to her brother's dread of social stigma and the subsequent secrecy of his desire for men, ultimately she is unable to exonerate him not for his sexual preferences but for his reckless behavior, expressed in a homophobic society as the overcompensatory performance of the village ram, the strutting hypermasculine cock who takes drugs and has unprotected sex with women and secretly with men.

Drew's face becomes waxy and masklike as the disease advances, warping the promise he never cultivates: "His face was sharp like a carving, like an image embossed on an emblem, a face full of deep suffering, beyond regrets or pleadings for a second chance. It was the face of someone who had lived in extremes, sometimes a saint, sometimes a sinner."[51]

The oppositions of heaven and hell are emblematized in her brother's stereotyped Medusa visage, not the scrupulous Levinasian face that averts butchery, but a face that terminates all hope of life. Even gardening, the only occupation he seems to show affinity for, assumes a virulent aspect as it takes on the doggedness of mortality—"inside his body a death lives, flowering upon flowering"—and nurtures, like his mother, only his disease. Kincaid implicates her family and eventually Antigua itself as the fetid source of disorder and disease, and her candid admissions of being sick of her dying brother carry over into a corresponding weariness with her place of birth.

The risks of anti-paradise discourse and contagious melancholia, even in a critical vein, bristle in such pathologies of the Caribbean mutated from verdant paradise to nightmarish inferno and capable of little beyond killing its subjects or driving them into exile. What is striking about such discourse is that it is no longer the prerogative of colonialist and modernist travelogues, even if it has the same DNA. The obsession with morbidity, violence, and death that Kirkpatrick Sale identifies in early modern Europe and which, according to him, preceded its great age of exploration and migration, its frantic compulsion to flee its borders, can also be recorded in the postcolonial anglophone Caribbean as author after author dictates chronic imperatives of flight and expulsion.[52] Unlike the Europeans, they do not come to conquer but to experience fresh crises in new homelands. In chapter 2, I focus on "toxic domesticity," the condensation of trauma in the individual home and the nation at large, including its continuing diasporas, and draw both men and women within its confines. Despite the repeated exposure of wounds, the very act of writing also lances this suppurating discourse and rearticulates the Caribbean as a productive space. In chapter 3, I continue to examine toxicity and flight, and move between literary and performative cultures. Following Harris, I argue that the depictions of the Jonestown tragedy in Guyana and the Michael X killings in Trinidad combat social trauma through a carnivalesque frame.

Many of the texts I discuss dwell necessarily on adversity, but occasionally they do so at the risk of confirming another stereotype: that imperialist declarations of blighted cultures were correct after all. Continuing, then, to pursue the detours recommended by Glissant, I turn in chapter 4 to the benefits of magical thinking. Against the tendency to disperse magic, science, and religion into oppositional streams, I read them together in a relational triad. Early modern Europe at the dawn of colonization was just beginning to separate these categories, but their intersections often present intriguing points of comparison. The quest for order and method was based not simply on the scientific mind but on the religious belief that God's garden was thus regulated. What Richard Drayton calls "Nature's Government" (by which he means how nature was governed and what Foucault in a wider perspective would call governmentality) oversaw a world-changing order of biopolitics even as it vanquished those excluded from its profits. In an echo of Lamming (to whom Drayton dedicates his book), the latter notes the gargantuan strides through centuries that Europe would make from medieval natural history and philosophy to modern medicine and pharmacology, social and life sciences, agriculture and technology while founding an enormously lucrative empire. "A king, a statesman, or a colonial governor could also come to be construed as a divinely appointed gardener," Drayton points out, noting how the science of agriculture was often patronized by the aristocracy who were at the time believed to be divinely anointed to power.[53]

However, the undoubted "improvement" of the rest of the world came also at a great cost to much of it, particularly the people whose land and living were usurped in the juggernaut advancement of science and technology. Their contributions were rarely acknowledged, since they were relegated to the time lag of the premodern and dismissed as ignorant savages who were assigned a tutelary, infantilized relationship to their "mother" countries. As Sheller confirms in her discussion of Sir Hans Sloane and his work with the Chelsea Physic Garden founded in 1673, the development of European botany, medicine, and pharmacology in the eighteenth century depended on plants from other parts of the world. Yet the colonies that cultivated them were always regarded as marginal to Western modernity.[54] While the Maroon Nannies, Titubas, Christophines, and Makandals were demonized as obeah practitioners and dealers in the dark arts of witchcraft, their knowledge of botanical lore provided self-determination and leadership, even if they were punished for it. Michelle Cliff hails Maroon Nanny as "the Jamaican Sycorax" and as a "Science-woman," deliberately uniting magic and science in the colonized female.[55]

I use the generically hybrid work of Nalo Hopkinson to relocate the Caribbean in discourses of science and technology, although here too the toxic elements infuse the therapeutic. Hopkinson expresses the aftershocks of scientific progress achieved in great part through colonial conquest in the language of dystopian science fiction and fantasy with hints of a feminist utopia. In the Caribbean context, fantasy and magical realism, the literary expression of a certain kind of magical thinking, do not repudiate history or reality as critics of magical realism claim, but tend to distort and distend them in order to provide more perceptive insights. The weapon magical realism constructs may just as well "blast open the continuum of history," rather than escaping or evading it altogether.[56] The post-apocalyptic wreckage of empire is reconstituted into new, even alien, life forms stubbornly combating the curse of mortality pronounced by various Dark Lords, mutated from the conquistadores to native spawn of the postcolonies. Magic and science fiction are summoned not so much to sugarcoat reality with fairy-tale happy endings or to ward off disenchantment, but as a desperate measure to engage desperate times.

"Of what import are brief, nameless lives . . . to *Galactus??*" demands the first epigraph to Junot Díaz's *The Brief Wondrous Life of Oscar Wao*. The invocation of a Marvel comic-book character sets the tone for the fantastic, magical realist, and science-fictional mélange that I will discuss at more length in chapter 5. Inspired by Emmanuel Levinas's philosophical concept of the face, Judith Butler locates our vulnerable "injurability" as well as the ethical imperative prohibiting murder, and thus the divine interdiction against killing, in what one might call the countenance of humanity. "To respond to the face, to understand its meaning, means to be awake to what is precarious in another life or, rather, the precariousness of life itself," says Butler.[57] But this face that signals the human plea and the divine ban against killing unconscionably disappears in the effacement of human rights enforced by the murderous regimes of dictatorship, poverty, inherited racism, ethnic conflict, and gendered or homophobic violence. Against such disappearances, however, Caribbean fiction insists on reinscribing its genealogy of faces and names, a historiography that battles *"en página blanco"* even if it fails to fill in every gap. Life, brief as it may be in such conditions, is also wondrous in the Caribbean, perhaps all the more so for its precarity. From Naipaul to Díaz, laughter, comedy, and humor make their irrepressible presence felt and imaginatively repopulate and rehumanize Caribbean history.

While I do not want to dismiss the anti-affirmative character of anglophone Caribbean fiction, it need not have the last word. Against the overdone presentations of the Caribbean as irrevocably carnivalesque and fluidly errant, the memory of lived trauma that one finds in the literature is a necessary negation. I often read the "pathologies" exposed in the literary texts in the productive sense of negation, as troubling thoughtlessly paradisiacal affirmations. But to end there would repeat the risks that I believe lie in the paradise-hell coupling and congeal a history of suffering. So I take yet another detour. Hélène Cixous famously reread Freud's essay on Medusa through the laughter, the defiant *jouissance,* of the demonized Gorgon.[58] My final chapter explores how Louise Bennett, Naipaul, Andrea Levy, and Zadie Smith, among others, sharpen their exposures of social dysfunction and leaven their critiques through humor. Comedy implies the essence of life (even the refusal to die) and the persistence of soul, while humor preserves the vitality of Caribbean literature. If, according to Walcott, history was "that Medusa of the New World," then the writers I present in this chapter will demonstrate how Medusa laughs despite, or perhaps because of, the petrifying weight of the past.[59] Because laughter under such conditions is never simply about uncomplicated enjoyment, I read humor through the frame of the grotesque, as an indeterminate intermingling of laughter and tears, comedy and tragedy.

Harris's faith in "infinite rehearsal" and "unfinished genesis," Walcott's poetic surveys of the oceanic bed wherein lie interred the bones of slaves framed in exquisite gothic cathedrals of coral or mausoleums of sea-fans, and Glissant's astonishing image of the "balls and chains gone green"[60] all suggest the potential of a reparative aesthetics in the aftermath of calamitous events. For some writers the exercise of memory and imagination is not so much about recovering Adamic wonder as about sheer survival. "I became a writer out of desperation," says Kincaid, and calls her writing "the act of saving [her]self." She continues, "When I heard about my brother's illness and his dying, I knew, instinctively, that to understand it, or to make an attempt at understanding his dying, and not to die with him, I would write about it."[61] For many of us, the act of reading is likewise "an attempt at understanding," and an act of saving ourselves.

Despite all the current focus on science and technology as the primary gateways to a new future and our corresponding anxieties about the underfunded humanities, Caribbean literature demonstrates the continuing restorative power of its Scheherazades, even when the stories are not easy to pass on, as Toni Morrison warns.[62] I situate the Caribbean as a global space in textual, historical, and theoretical conversations with hemispheric, (Black) Atlantic, feminist, diasporic, and postcolonial discourses. Alison Donnell critiques the erasure of local and literary specificities in the prevalent currency of diaspora and popular culture, where normative Black Atlantic paradigms mean little more than the imposition of African American realities over a diverse range of populations and histories.[63] But as Elizabeth M. DeLoughrey claims, an overemphasis on "landfall" and the postcolonial nation space ignores Atlantic and other oceanic routes that are both formative and continuing in the constitution of diaspora.[64] The terrestrial and the "tidalectic," the national and the diasporic, can have a productive dialogue, and a more flexible approach would not use one paradigm to exclude another. The regional and national particularities are not ignored, but the Caribbean has cross-cultural convergences with the above categories, predominantly in their focus on bare life, the cultural debris overlooked by colonial and other deceptive progress narratives.

Thus, even as I focus on the anglophone Caribbean, just what can be included in this category is broadly conceived. As the epilogue to this book concludes, Caribbean genealogies involve large and rambling family trees, and one can trace connections between writers in translation from francophone islands (Glissant and Maryse Condé) to those who write in English but whose nativity would limit them to non-anglophone islands (Julia Alvarez, Danticat, and Díaz). One of the realities of Caribbean literature, disagreeable to some and unavoidable to others, is the predominance of writers who have lived mainly outside the region and whose concerns necessarily span a large and mobile cultural geography. Paule Marshall is just as likely to be taught in African American and black Atlantic or diaspora courses as in Caribbean ones. Caryl Phillips can claim, like many Caribbean writers, different homes from St. Kitts, to England, and now the United States. Naipaul appears in modernist, Black British, and South Asian diaspora studies. Those who take his disavowals seriously may disown or celebrate him as a rootless cosmopolitan. Given that he is most associated with a complex narrative of pathology, he appears frequently enough here to emphasize his specifically Trinidadian origins as a writer even as his global reach demonstrates that of the Caribbean.

My focus is literary, although here, too, the region refuses to fence itself in, and the literature is a fertile ground for other disciplinary vegetation to flourish. Nevertheless, thick descriptions of primarily fictional works are braided together (borrowing Danticat's trope[65]) to provide a coherent frame for each chapter, proving that the literature, however varied, runs from the same streams into the same sea of stories. The many writers I examine here are by no means a comprehensive list, but they exemplify the extraordinary productivity of the Caribbean literary corpus. I make no claims that the texts I select here are the only or even the most appropriate representatives of the major cultural memes of this book. Indeed, along the route, many writers and texts dropped out as companions due to limits of space rather than relevance. I would hope, though, that the range of writers included here and the many more that can be added give substantive cohesion to the topics in each chapter. The strategy this book follows emphasizes selected themes in a broad array of texts rather than pursuing long close readings of a few texts and authors. In doing so, it suggests that the particular themes that the chapters focus on are pertinent to a broad swath of anglophone Caribbean fiction and can perhaps be just as relevant to other linguistic areas as well.

According to Díaz, the "fukús" or curses following colonialism—the neocolonial, neoliberal, neoconservative—require the miraculous force of writing to expose their pernicious, often hidden, presence. Colonial discourse may have poisoned its well, but while the Caribbean cannot yet escape that toxicity, it also provides the antidote in its rich cultural contributions, particularly its literature. The "zafa," the magical ruse of the word, can arrest the blight of the fukús, as the youthful, aspiring writers in Díaz's novel believe.[66] Caribbean literature wields an enlivening if not death-defying magic. In providing reconstituting narrative counterspells even as it reveals the harrowing events of its history, it offers a vision of a far more interesting world than either the bland utopia glimpsed in the myth of paradise or the equally one-dimensional dystopia of its pathologies.

1 The Empire and the Garden

Exhuming Bones, Inscribing Genealogies

Gardening in the Tropics, you never know
what you'll turn up. Quite often, bones.

—Olive Senior, *Gardening in the Tropics*

Might it be that flowers are in effect human bones. . . . Like life, only more so, flowers are beautiful and fragile, and this may be why many people consider them appropriate for death and even more so for disaster.

—Michael Taussig, "The Language of Flowers"

THE SEEDS of European modernity and its countercultures were sown and reaped not only in Europe and the Old World tropical colonies, but also in the Americas.[1] A new world of Western genesis and a global phase of modernity instituted through European migration to the Caribbean resulted in native genocide or dispossession, transatlantic slavery, and indentured servitude for other populations, leading writers from the region to challenge Edenic narratives of colonialism and settlement in the Americas with counter-narratives of "Caribbean geneses." In their accounts, an anti-Adamic impulse rejecting certain acts of naming coexists with Derek Walcott's project of calling upon new "adams" to rename and repopulate landscape with local significance and not just view it as a colonial appendage.[2]

This chapter explores how Caribbean writers remap the landscapes their ancestors labored over and perished in, excavating repressed memories and unearthing forgotten bodies in their narratives of recovery and re-creation. The authors I discuss here, including Jamaica Kincaid, Harold Sonny Ladoo, George Lamming, Shani Mootoo, V. S. Naipaul, and Derek Walcott, reject an easy extension of the pastoral myth into the tropical garden. Even writers like Yseult Bridges and Lakshmi Persaud, who are influenced by the pastoral mode, cannot avoid heavy turbulence.

Although postcolonial studies has seen an increase in ecological and ecocritical approaches, my discussion of gardens and landscapes skirts the rather different issues a strictly ecocritical perspective would raise. My analysis is more along the lines of Wilfred Cartey's *Whispers from the Caribbean,* which explores the relationship of literature to the landscape. The sustained attention by Lawrence Buell, for example, and, more specifically, postcolonial interventions by Graham Huggan, Helen Tiffin, Elizabeth DeLoughrey, and George B. Handley have expanded ecocritical discourses, but the writers I consider here are not precisely environmental activists, however much their work may describe landscape, wilderness, pastoral, environment, and ecology. As Huggan and Tiffin note, postcolonial ecocriticism hinges on two already debatable categories with a heterogeneous variety of concerns across vast geographical territory, although this is not to deny their coherence as terms or the relationship between them. While the diversity of agendas that postcolonial ecocriticism encompasses is important, here I am considering the particular resonance of gardens in Caribbean literature. One can extract an ecocritical consciousness from the writers I explore here, but their primary concern does not seem to be environmental protection, even if it is not abandoned altogether. Instead, they use the garden as a literary trope to uproot the potted histories of colonialism and reveal the multiple entanglements of race, class, gender, sexuality, and ethnicity that developed in the specific transformation of the Caribbean from a supposedly Edenic garden into a plantation machine.

Caribbean Gardens from a Plantation Perspective: Pastoral and Anti-pastoral

I borrow the title of this chapter, "The Empire and the Garden," from George Lamming's first novel, *In the Castle of My Skin,* now a classic of anglophone Caribbean, postwar literature. The unnamed narrator describes Empire Day (in honor of Queen Victoria's birthday on May 24) celebrated in a tiny Barbadian village through a series of school events, including parades and marches. An interrupted sequence of whispered conversations between a few schoolboys tries to unravel the mystery of remote overseas monarchs and comprehend why black children in Barbados would commemorate them on such occasions. One of them finally offers a postlapsarian account in which Heaven, the garden, is forsaken by the rebellious angels who refuse to be God's slaves, leading to their descent to earth where they, wracked by guilt, repentance, and nostalgia for the lost garden, eventually introduce slavery among humans. We are told in a sweeping continuum of biblical lore and British colonial ideology, "The queen freed some of us because she made us feel that the empire was bigger than the garden." But they're now as one, the boy believes. "The empire and the garden. We are to speak of them the same way. They belong to the same person. They both belong to God. The garden is God's own garden and the empire is God's only empire. They work together for us."[3]

In this rather cryptic parable, however imaginative the schoolboy's invention of history, he certainly has his essentials correct in revealing the contradictions of English liberalism and democracy that cohabited with colonialism and slavery for centuries. The pious but dubious benevolence of the slave pastoral—slaves as chosen beneficiaries of providential empire and voluntary caretakers of God's fertile land because "they work together for us"—is internalized by both master and slave.[4] The sheer spectacle of colonial pageantry at G.'s school (ornamentally disguising the quasi-military formations and corporal punishment of its disciplinary regimes) and the accumulative hegemonic force of colonial education repress the not too distant past of slavery. The whitewashed collective memory and the sanctified bondage of religion instigate the loyal obedience to British monarchs, the "shadow kings" and queens, as abstract and distant yet as venerated as divinity.

Thwarting this ideological wand that waves away the terrors of slavery and servitude, Caribbean literature records not just a "slave sublime," but a broader social memory, a carefully preserved narrative of genocide, trauma, and suffering that resuscitates in the text the buried remains of the individual and historical body.[5] Death in different forms, from murder to massacre, is a major motif. History does not just "echo in the bone," as in Dennis Scott's play; it gleams stubbornly and startlingly white and sepulchral years after biodegradable flesh turns to soil, as in Senior's volume *Gardening in the Tropics,* or Edwidge Danticat's *The Farming of Bones,* a heartbreaking account of the 1937 massacre of Haitians in the Dominican Republic. The very title of Danticat's novel implies that the Caribbean agricultural landscape is lushly fertile due to the profusion of human beings—the Indigenous peoples, the slaves and indentured servants, the warring Europeans—who once labored and fought over it and whose corpses now fertilize the soil. Against the anxiety that the beauty of the environment, vacuously exploited in its contemporary tourist versions, glosses over the horrors of history, these writers tend to translate and incorporate the natural script of the land into the cultural script of archival and historical record. History is itself the corpus delicti in Caribbean literature, the ghastly evidence that crimes have been committed revealed in what the soil and sea turn up. As Walcott succinctly puts it in his Nobel lecture, "It is not that History is obliterated by this sunrise. It is there in Antillean geography, in the vegetation itself. The sea sighs with the drowned from the Middle Passage, the butchery of its aborigines, Carib and Aruac and Taino, bleeds in the scarlet of the immortelle, and even the actions of surf on sand cannot erase African memory, or the lances of cane as a green prison where indentured Asians, the ancestors of Felicity, are still serving time."[6]

I would be distorting the depiction of Caribbean geography if I focused only on the traumatic aspects. Caribbean texts have their own version of pastoral, and even European voyagers and some of their descendants found in the striking beauty and fertility of the landscape a ravishing cornucopia, not merely miasma or the plantation misery of a later history. Both *Child of the Tropics: Victorian Memoirs* by Yseult Bridges and *Butterfly in the Wind* by Lakshmi Persaud, published only a few years apart, have in common an afterglow that alleviates the trials faced by the individual protagonists in Trinidad despite the distance in chronology and difference in ethnic background. The nostalgic tone of the "Victorian memoirs" is revealed in the first line of the blurb on the back cover: "This is the story of a girl who grew up in Trinidad in its Victorian heyday, and it gives a loving picture of that now-vanished world." Yseult Bridges belonged to a distinguished line of ancestors from England, France, and Trinidad, with several inventors in her family. Her English father, Robert John Lechmere Guppy, served in an official capacity in Trinidad, and was famous for his contributions to the study of local geology and marine life, ultimately having the honor of seeing his name bestowed on a fish he had "discovered," and which is now a common exhibit in home aquariums.

After her first marriage ended, Yseult married Michael Bridges, who was in the Nigerian Civil Service; wrote about Yoruba customs while she lived in Nigeria; published crime fiction in England where she retired; and eventually died at a ripe old age, her nephew and editor Nicholas Guppy tells us in the foreword, after a fall in her garden. That either Bridges or her nephew (himself an ecologist and ethnographer) is scrupulously mindful of her lineage is obvious in the inclusion of a diagram of their family tree with both the English and French roots traced back to medieval times and neatly tabulated until the nineteenth century. In the autobiographical narrative that follows, Bridges provides vignettes of her immediate family in Trinidad including, it must be noted, the servants who remain loyal to them.

The text introduces predictable types, different species of faithful black domestics such as the enigmatic and intimidating 'Zabette, who was once a slave on the estate of young Yseult's French great-grandparents, and who describes to the enthralled girl the balls they held, the slaves with flambeaux who greeted the guests, stomping in tune with their songs, after which they drank rum, feasted on goats roasted over open fires, and made merry while "'de whitefolk' up at 'de House' [trod] more stately measures to the music of the orchestra." Shaken by these memories, a now manumitted and aged 'Zabette cries out nostalgically, "E-e-e! dem was de days fo' true!" and overcome, it seems, by the paltriness of post-Emancipation lifestyles, she mutters, "Dese-here folk dese days aint knowin' what livin' is—dey be poo' trash!"[7] There is Thompson, another pensioner who, like Uncle Tom, his fictional American counterpart, is "the embodiment of all that was best in mankind: gentle, patient, faithful, with the most perfect manners and the essential sweetness of the pure in heart."[8] The mulatto maid, on the other hand, is bitterly resentful of her place in the "back verandah," refusing, unlike the others, to enter by the back gate in the rigid hierarchy of space and movement still preserved in late Victorian Trinidad.

Despite her attention to this mute disobedience against the race and class system, her later account of a tense encounter with the poor black people who live outside the Savannah, and descriptions of abject East Indians exploited by white and black subjects, Bridges concludes that "slavery was never severe in Trinidad," and that as a result, "inter-racial tension" was mild.[9] While Trinidad is an example of a fairly brief and less brutal history of slavery, as Lamming would note, the empire beatifically resides in the garden. The memoir is replete with the sounds, sights, and smells of the natural beauty of the island, but one visit to England and a thrilling train ride are enough to convince Bridges that this is the "Land of [her] Fathers," where she will one day return to be reunited with her roots. Like many fictional narratives of Caribbean childhood, Bridges's memoir also ends with her departure, even before which her milieu grows "unreal." For all the pathetic fallacies that inform stories of life in the tropics, Bridges is acutely aware of the ultimate indifference of the surroundings to the individual human story that appropriates them for its economic and expressive use. As she prepares to sail for England, she notes of the foliage, "I felt less that I was leaving them than that they were shedding me."[10]

The placidity of seasonal change, the predictable and therefore consoling cycle of death followed by budding new life, permeates Lakshmi

Persaud's novel, which is part ethnography, part memoir, part fiction. The choice of a title like *Butterfly in the Wind* conjures up airy perambulations, literal and discursive, that flit over severe hardship and poverty, or prefers to avert its gaze after briefly acknowledging their existence. Quite possibly Persaud wishes to oppose the dominant narrative of early Indo-Caribbean hardship and fragmentation with her admittedly uneven pastoral narrative here. The first chapter, titled "Simple Joys," begins like Bridges's memoir with early childhood, and focuses on the happy innocence of the main Indo-Trinidadian character, Kamla, meaning lotus.

Similar to the rhythmic, soothing episodes of labor in the Victorian memoir, Persaud's later account presents the working lives of the villagers in gently pastoral terms. Her class difference from the other less-privileged members of her community allows her a Wordsworthian appreciation of the honest labor of the sons and daughters of the soil, as she reflects on the "tired faces and rested thoughts" of returning field workers.[11] Yet Persaud is not blind to the possibility of another interpretation that is grimmer and less bucolic. Kamla's grandmother, unlike 'Zabette, remembers not the gay social scene of the landowning gentry, but her own pain in the sugarcane fields, which she candidly reveals to her grandchildren. "There were nettles and prickles and sharp cutting leaves everywhere and my hands became sore and red with the grass knife and the sun was without mercy," she intones, deflating the earlier image of calm and contented meditation at the end of the arduous working day.[12] Instead, she literally bears the scars of her labor on her body upon which the land forcefully inscribes itself, suggesting why earning one's living by the sweat of one's brow could be perceived as a divine curse in the biblical genesis.

On other occasions, Kamla traces her own ideological transformation as she challenges the colonial accounts of the unvarying heroism of adventurers, the "Red Indian and Cowboy" films from Hollywood, and the folktales and myths of her Hindu culture that legitimize male dominance. But unlike the fiery Clare Savage in *No Telephone to Heaven*, it is significant that Kamla "quietly wept" as she became aware of the genocide of the Native Americans. The sentimental tears aptly convey the decorum that governs her character throughout. The tranquil surface of the pastoral is disturbed by Kamla's naive curiosity, occasionally generating discomfort. For instance, the "Madrassis," a community of South Indian origin, seem alien to Kamla not only because of "their dark skin and deep red mouths," stained by their incessant chewing of *pan*, but because they dance on their way to a funeral and weep when a child is born. Her innocent inquiry into these customs and the habit of *pan* chewing in particular leads her mother to explain that some of the ingredients in the betel leaf and nut concoction have a narcotic effect. Why would they chew *pan* all day, wonders Kamla, perhaps a little disingenuously, considering that her father sells rum and she is well aware of the effects of alcohol on her community, also a common stereotype of Indo-Caribbean plantation culture. Her mother responds simply, "When life is painful."[13]

While Persaud's novel hints at anti-pastoral elements, Harold Sonny Ladoo's *No Pain Like This Body* presents them front and center. Like the "Madrassis" who greet newborns with tearful empathy for what awaits them, Ladoo's novel elaborates a Hindu nihilist notion of life as a cycle of fated wretchedness from which madness and death are a blessed release. The history of indentured servitude, the "prison [of] cane" as Walcott puts it, is encapsulated at the beginning of the novel in a radically different genealogy from that of Bridges and her European and Creole antecedents. A brief history of fictional "Carib Island," dating it from Columbus's entry there in 1498, and an equally bald list of its imports, "Sugar, petroleum, rum, cocoa, coffee, citrus fruits, and asphalt," adjoin a map of Tola District before the text opens. In contrast to the Guppy family tree, individual names of ancestors in neat rows are eliminated and, instead, ragged black areas on the map are tagged thus: "House of Ma and Pa," "House of Nanna and Nanny," "Bound Coolie Estate." Other shaded markers include Riceland and Sugarcane, the entire spatial graph and the preponderance of generic rather than specific names embodying the subordinate status of the "lower orders" in the ranking of human significance and the symbols by which their historical existence is sparsely documented.

While Ladoo does not make explicit the racialized subtext of degeneracy as it was applied to the Indo-Trinidadian community, the tropicalized conflation of land and body and the effects on the psyche were not restricted to Indian and African populations. The associations between the indolence of the white Creole, the easy lapse of morals, the deranged mind, and the sulfurous landscape have been immortalized in notorious passages in *Jane Eyre,* following which Rochester turns in relief to the cool, invigorating breeze from across the Atlantic.[14] However, the onus of redemption ultimately falls upon swarthy races in the Caribbean. Miss Natalie in Phyllis Shand Allfrey's *The Orchid House* wryly points out that according to Father Toussaint "nearly all the people in this island were born in sin."[15] It is hard to tell if the odium relates to children born out of wedlock, mixed-race children, or, given the times, both.

As in *Wide Sargasso Sea,* the doubly bastardized (racially mixed and illegitimate) mulatto is a hysterical subject, but this is a relative condition

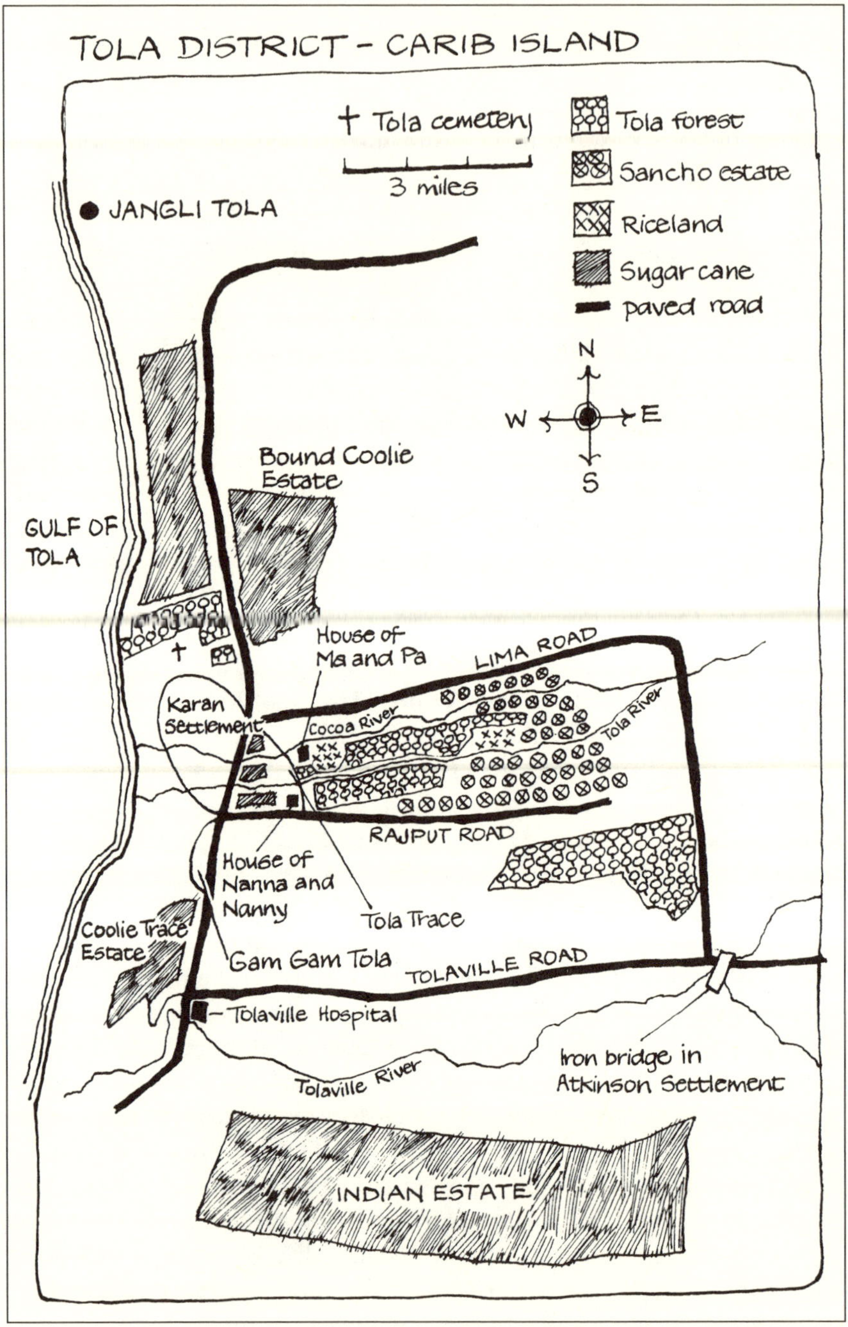

From Harold Sonny Ladoo, *No Pain Like This Body.* (© 1972 Harold Sonny Ladoo. Reprinted with permission from House of Anansi Press, Toronto.)

in representations of Creoles of any racial descent. A white drug addict father, a black nurse with a tumor, and three passionate and headstrong sisters only compound the overall aura of ill health and despondency in *The Orchid House.* "Beauty and disease, beauty and sickness, beauty and horror: that was the island. A quartering breeze hurried eastward, over cotton tufts of clouds; the air was soft and hot; colour drenched everything, liquid turquoise melted into sapphire and then into emerald," observes the narrator.[16] As I will discuss in a subsequent chapter, "infected" prose expresses the toxicity embedded in an undeniably beautiful environment, such that the natural beauty of the landscape is intimately bound with human suffering and even disease, as in Kincaid's brother, Devon Drew, whose AIDS-ravaged body is described in *My Brother* as a plant harboring parasites and devoured from within. In the many parallels between Allfrey's novel and Rhys's later work, the excess of beauty in the Caribbean paradoxically infects it, wearies the spirit and soul, and sickens the body. In *The Orchid House,* Stella reflects, "Beauty grows like a weed here . . . and so does disease."[17]

Antoinette's husband echoes this sentiment in *Wide Sargasso Sea:* "Too much blue, too much purple, too much green. The flowers too red, the mountains too high, the hills too near."[18] What, one may ask, is the implied point of comparison here? Where is the presumably moderate site, the more temperate zone against which the flamboyantly repetitive Caribbean islands, represented in this case by Dominica, are "too much"? The answer is obvious before the Rochester figure unveils his plans to incarcerate "the maniac" in England. Even as his perspective of the natural environment distorts it through an imagined surfeit, the attenuation of Antoinette into the stick figure he idly doodles while weaving his plans for her future attempts to diminish that surplus, to control it, and to dominate her. Antoinette, for all her growing agitation, is astutely aware of the double jeopardy of her plight. "Bertha is not my name. You are trying to make me into someone else, calling me by another name. I know that's obeah too."[19] The transformation of the Caribbean Antoinette into an English Bertha, in Rhys's brilliant evocation, is an act of wizardry that changes more than just the name. It alters Antoinette from a complex human with a story to tell into a (literally) profitable Caribbean stereotype—and then it contains and transports her, like the biological specimens that were shipped in Wardian cases, to England. Only, her destination is not a tasteful botanical garden but an ignominious attic.

None of this is to imply that England, or any of the regions that could be grouped together as the "Shivering Northern Wetlands"—an allegorical region in Mootoo's novel *Cereus Blooms at Night* to which I will return—remain unchallenged as the rational destination, or, as in Rochester's romance, the destination of rationality. Climatological stereotypes are hardly the sole purview of any one culture or region. People in warmer lands are just as apt to conflate the cold weather of some areas with the pale hues and frigid, uncongenial temperaments of some of their inhabitants.

In contrast to the images of chaos, incompetence, sickness, and poor hygiene of the tropics, industrialized countries, particularly those with dominant white populations, are stereotyped as soullessly rigid, hyperconscious about germs, and inhospitable because discipline and propriety are valued over human intimacy. The English have certainly been on the receiving end of such perceptions, most people outside of (and sometimes within) the country rarely detecting traces of a "merrie old England." As one of the characters puns in a Walcott play, "We aren't a very frivolous race, the Brrr . . . itish."[20] However anticipated the eventual return or departure to England, the story doesn't always end there, even if the plot does. Reports about the shock of arrival, the chilly reception, the miseries of a cold climate, and strange Western customs are now legion in literature and popular culture from other parts of the world. "There is always the other side," Antoinette insists to her husband.[21] Her own perception of England as an unreal, gray, paper world counters the romantic aura surrounding Caribbean portrayals of the country before the writers migrate there. Not just London but also the rural pastoral turns out to be far more complex in reality than the writer's longed-for ideal. Naipaul's novel *The Enigma of Arrival* and Kincaid's gardening memoirs in *My Garden (Book)* explore the authors' experiences in Salisbury and Vermont, respectively, and reflect on colonial history from an ironic perspective that illuminates how the empire fused the garden with the plantation.

Those who read Naipaul's novel uniformly as a tribute to England and his final sense of homecoming may be ignoring the ambivalence underlined by "enigma." Although noted for the clarity of its chiseled prose, the text is rife with misgivings. The usual Naipaul keywords, "anxiety," "nerves," "rawness," exacerbate his sense of being out of place and not quite knowing where he fits in a hoary tradition. Like most colonial children, the first-person narrator, who is not always distinguished from the author, was initially acquainted with England through books and pictures, as with the glimpse of Salisbury from a "four-colour reproduction" in his third-standard reader. His bookish, secondhand, and therefore slightly off-key familiarity with the land of his dreams is mediated through landscape and language. "Apart from the romance of the Constable reproduction, the knowledge I brought to my setting was linguistic. I knew that 'avon' originally meant only river, just as 'hound' originally just meant a dog, any kind of dog . . . I knew that both 'walden' and 'shaw' meant wood," he painstakingly elucidates, and it soon becomes clear that there is just a touch of insecurity in his need to prove that he is an outsider become insider.[22] He admits later in a moving passage that the elegant but crumbling Edwardian manor grounds where he rents a cottage and the "perfection" of its gardens had first been designed with "no room for [him]."[23] Land and dwelling are mapped on an unstable space and questions of place and memory, history and identity, belonging and exile circulate restlessly from island tropics to "mother country" with no quick or easy resolution.

The narrator's gradual sense of nativization, as the dairyman and the gardener's wife conveniently demonstrate, is enabled through class difference. His finicky, cultured sense of language through which landscape is learned and verified and named (unlike the unlettered, experiential familiarity of a peasant, one assumes), would not be possible without his educational background or his vocation as a writer, and it follows that he will ultimately claim diasporic belonging through his writing. He credits the English environment with nurturing his talent, implicitly associating the other countries he has ties to with an impoverished literary creativity:

> I had no means of knowing that the landscape by which I was surrounded was in fact benign, the first landscape to have that quality for me. That I was to heal here. . . . that at last (as for a time as a child in Trinidad) I would learn to link certain natural events, leaves on trees, flowers, the clarity of the river, to certain months. That in the most unlikely way, at an advanced age, in a foreign country, I was to find myself in tune with a landscape in a way that I had never been in Trinidad or India (both sources of different kinds of pain).[24]

Even as he sees echoes of his anguish in the people around him and undergoes his own tortures of acclimatization in England, the particular pain of India, from where his ancestors migrated as indentured laborers, and Trinidad, where they worked on plantations, creates an almost irreversible rupture. He is constantly disappointed by his misreadings of various English characters, when he assumes they have a rootedness they turn out not to have, being as new to the neighborhood as he is. At the same time, he finds it difficult despite all these setbacks to give up his idealized, bookish vision of England. Pitton, for instance, is not his "idea of the P. G. Wodehouse gardener" or the "gardener in *Richard II,* poetically conversing with a weeping queen."[25] Pitton is mistaken for the landlord by one of the guests because he refuses to play or look the part of the traditional English gardener who is, according to Naipaul, "antique or forlorn or elegiac."[26]

While the narrator's confusion about what is authentically English or what can no longer be considered so is aggravated by his textual subjects (the English who seem disinterested in the behavior that was typified in the literature he has consumed), it still does not reconcile him to the radical difference of "Asiatic-Indian" gardeners. And that may be because in his view there were no gardeners as such in Trinidad. Thus, for Naipaul as for Rochester in *Jane Eyre,* the original garden, the authentic pastoral, could only be found in England. For Naipaul, the history of African slavery and Indian indenture in the Caribbean—empire, as Lamming would say—ultimately explains the gulf between English and Caribbean dissonances in gardening histories. The English past, at least in Naipaul's opinion, had some idyllic pastoral model to fall back on: "seeing around me the remnants of agricultural life (the remote, distorted original of the Trinidad estates), that earlier knowledge revived in me," clarifies the narrator.[27] The magnificence of rolling parklands that demanded sixteen gardeners (albeit now reduced to a single Pitton who is himself about to be fired) may survive only in "remnants" in England, but the geography and culture of Trinidad have been dominated by plantations, not gardens.

Gardening, Naipaul believes in contrast to Senior, is the ultimate privilege of the manor-born: the leisurely, luxurious hobby of the landed gentry with their avid horticultural pursuits and their extensive staff to do the real work for them, the latter striking picturesque-enough poses to earn them acclaim in literature. Slaves and workers were just as likely to be inscribed in scenic frames, but Naipaul emphasizes the unavoidable (and unpaid or low-paid) drudgery of plantation labor, and one sees his point even if one does not want to devalue the labor involved in gardening. The "childhood delight," the "magic" of germination, the pleasure, even the human "instinct," Naipaul calls it, "to plant, to see crops grow," has a bitter legacy in the Caribbean to the point where the instinct itself has been "eradicated."[28] The charismatic image of the crusty but loyal English gardener clashes with the threatening black and brown "yard boys," the "mud and sun and bare feet, damp huts, and oily or sweated felt hats" of their labor-intensive, harsh Caribbean setting.[29] This vision constrains any romantic portrayals of the sweetness of sugar's history, but it is so extreme that any potential agency and pleasure seems to be removed from Caribbean cultivation, including the relative autonomy and fulfillment of provision grounds and gardens. For Naipaul, the garden in England is a nostalgic trace and the landscape of the Caribbean is a disorienting simulacrum, since much in there, the "travel-poster beauty—coconut, sugarcane, bamboo, mango, bougainvillea, poinsettia," is not native to the Caribbean, but transplants of a post-Columbian makeover.[30]

But although Naipaul seems content to don the garb of an English country gentleman after judging the tropics uninhabitable, his novel, set centuries after that "first" arrival to the Caribbean and based in England, is not as placid a pastoral as one may expect. It is beset with deaths, the high body count of characters augmented by events such as the loss of the traditional retinue of staff that kept the estate running. In the novel, the decay of the manor and its reclusive, invalid English landlord (suffering ironically from acedia, the lassitude associated with the tropics) is symbolized by the destruction of the elms. An interesting parallel of torpor is raised across the Atlantic and in a different time frame from Naipaul's residence in the country estate. In *Wide Sargasso Sea,* Antoinette morbidly broods not over diseased elms but over "snaky looking" orchids in the garden-turned-wilderness when the slaves walk off Coulibri estate. In white Creole circles, the mass exodus of exploited slaves is euphemized as "Emancipation troubles."[31] The narrator, focalized through Antoinette's perspective, wonders, "Why should *anybody* work" after slavery?[32] As Ileana Rodríguez notes in her analysis of this novel, whatever the pathos of Antoinette's marronage, her moping conversely indicates "liberation, self-determination, and national formation" for the slaves who refused to work on plantations.[33]

While the ruin of Coulibri signifies the end of plantation economies (although Christophine is rightly skeptical of how free the slaves really are at this point), in Naipaul's case the decay and lethargy signal the end of empire, also not a cause for universal sorrow whatever it might mean for England and the narrator of the novel. The elegiac tone, the pleasurable melancholy of the ruined prospect (both of the pastoral landscape and of the narrator's artistic power), shifts finally to a sharp but restrained grief, a mourning that is expressed most directly in the untimely death of his sister, who dies in Trinidad of a brain hemorrhage. Characteristically, the narrator is at first cold and unresponsive, but his touching account of her funeral at the very end of the novel shapes the final reconciliation with his personal and national history and completes his "second arrival" in England.[34] The narrator accepts that neither the wounding consequences of the Columbian entry nor the untimely death of his kin can be mourned interminably. As he grieves, he recovers from the blow to his creativity, and he begins to write speedily, looping back in the conclusion to the opening section, titled "Jack's Garden."

Before we sign off with a sense of affirmation, however, one significant silence must be recorded. For at least part of the period in which the novel was written, Naipaul must have been reeling from the death of his brother, Shiva, who also died relatively young. There is no explicit reference to this tragedy in the novel, although it is dedicated "in loving memory" of his brother. We are left to wonder if the final outburst of literary endeavor evades a sorrow so deep it cannot be named except outside the frame of the personal narrative. Given biographical revelations of Naipaul's superior attitude toward his younger brother and the latter's resentment of his older brother's hypercritical stance, perhaps there is some guilt as well.

Kincaid's autobiographical account in *My Garden (Book)* comes to the same conclusion as Naipaul's narrative, but is more tart than a surprisingly mellow Naipaul in *Enigma,* the acerbic tenor of his other works generally unrivalled in the anglophone Caribbean. Unlike his compromise with Columbian conquest, at least in the conclusion to *Enigma,* Kincaid poses her insight as a profession of defeat: "I cannot do anything about it anyway. I only mind the absence of this admission, this contradiction: perhaps every good thing that stands before us comes at a great cost to someone else."[35] Here, too, the frame of the narrative is striking, not as Naipaul's tight-lipped memoriam, but in the charming illustrations of flowers, animals, vistas, and patterned leaves interspersed with or bordering the text throughout. In keeping with the appealing illustrations (by Jill Fox), reminiscent of children's books and characteristic of Kincaid's style and tone, the narrative pitch often takes on the simple, repetitive quality of a story for the young. The deceptively mild tone almost slips by until its acidic flavor seeps in. Confessing her desire for her neighbor's larger residence in Vermont, for instance, Kincaid reveals that she had once lived "in a poor country with a tropical climate" (Antigua) in a shack smaller than any room in this house. She adds, "But I had lived in America for a long time and had adjusted to the American habit of taking up at least twenty times as much of the available resources each person needs. This is a trait that is beyond greed. A greedy person is often cross, unpleasant. Americans, at least the ones I am personally familiar with, are not at all cross. They are quite happy and reasonable, as they take up at least twenty times as much of everything as they need."[36]

The others suffer more with this strategy of polite indirection, the thorns buried in seemingly innocuous statements and then suddenly piercing:

> To us, it was an unusual idea: a [botanical] garden in which were gathered specimens of plants from various parts of the British empire; but we soon absorbed it, got used to it, took it for granted, the way we did with another European idea, that of leaving your own native (European) climate and living in places native to other people whom you cannot stand. Again, it was an unusual idea and we associated it with our dominators, the English people, their love, their need to isolate, name, objectify, possess various parts, people, and things in the world.[37]

The literally expansive, dangerously affable American personality comes off only slightly better than the English who swallow their loathing of the natives because they love the land of settlement, and, like Senior, Kincaid is having none of the ideology of reason, entitlement, benevolence, or superiority.

As in Senior's poems, the dullness of a cold climate is tied to racial prejudice, reflected in the "nigger colors" of flowers.[38] Kincaid envisions in tufts of raw cotton the polarized but entangled history of race in the Americas, the white fluff clinging tenaciously to the black seeds and vice versa.[39] She reserves her most pungent attacks for the possessive act of nomination, arguing that the Latin names are a mere affectation, and insisting on using the "common" names of plants. She resents the identification of flowers with their European "discoverers," as in dahlia, bougainvillea, poinsettia; to her, one more instance of the emptying of native signifiers and the inscription of European dominance. Names and titles often carry certain privileges: identity, rank and status, first rights, copyright, and legal ownership.

The "naming of things is so crucial to possession," Kincaid observes.[40] But possession is not the only catalyst here. Foucault views this impulse to name as central to natural history, associated with the complementary ambitions to order and to classify. Hence language, he claims, is fundamental to this arrangement of knowledge. Kincaid's relationship to European gardens is ambivalent, but in her critical mode the natural history book is a charnel house of bones, or a space in which the rich complexity and diversity of life is reduced to rigor mortis. In Foucault's analysis it has a more productive function: "The book becomes the herbarium of living structures."[41]

I will return to the productive function of naming, but at the moment I want to stay with Kincaid's negative assessment. Foucault himself would agree that naming and classifying were hardly innocent tasks, since part of their purpose was also to discriminate between species and normativize ontological and epistemological hierarchies. In the racial, cultural, and geographical ordering that was the business of Europe in the eighteenth and nineteenth centuries, Kincaid would argue, the colonies and their inhabitants were discriminated against and reduced to inferiority, even invisibility, as in the enforced doctrine of terra nullius over original inhabitants. While nature exerts power over cultural histories when used in a deceptively transparent manner to police social behavior, the reverse power of cultural script over natural landscape is obvious in the mapping of the land as terra nullius. Such a territorial baptism, Kincaid might add, is another approach to the natives one "cannot stand": it conveniently makes them vanish off the face of the earth. Both Naipaul and Kincaid write about the twisted relationship between the empire and the garden, but the decline of empire does not imply the end of discriminatory practices. I move now to an Indo-Caribbean novel that restages, through the trope of the garden, conflicts of naming and identities, of natural and unnatural social codes that continue to bind the heirs of plantation regimes in postcolonial contexts.

Undoing the Order of Things: Liminal Spaces and Identities

Shani Mootoo's *Cereus Blooms at Night* attempts to revalue, if not overturn, the established principles of the (post)colonial axiomatic on many levels, but significantly complicates the models I have so far been discussing through her focus on gender and sexual discrimination. I use "axiomatic" in the sense that Eve Sedgwick does, when she challenges us to think of sex and sexuality as not constituted just by gendered assumptions alone, but also by other determinants such as class or race. Sedgwick's suggestive invitation also raises possibilities for reconfiguring the axiomatic of sexual practices in order to allow us "a more richly pluralized range of imaginings of lines of gender and sexual identification."[42] Mootoo's novel unsettles the dominant colonial discourses of nature, culture, gender, and sexuality by providing some such imagining. Gendered discourses of nature have varied from the organic model of earth as mother (and humans as both "her" children and stewards) to the mechanistic notion of earth as inert feminized mass open to manipulation; from benevolent images of alluring femininity inviting penetration to negative personifications as malign force demanding masculine control. Karen Warren argues that we eventually need to "overcome metaphors and models which feminize nature *and* naturalize women to the mutual detriment of both nature and women,"[43] but one cannot ignore the frequent conflations between women and land, women and nature in Caribbean literature.

As G. R. Coulthard notes, there has been a long poetic convention of using tropical fruit—sapodillas, star-apples, avocados, tangerines—in conjunction with Afro-Caribbean women. He provocatively suggests that the choice of fruits over the English preference for equating flowers with women emphasizes the black woman's "frank sensuality" and fertility unavailable to English women.[44] Naipaul, however, parodies the fruity trend. Commenting on a fellow Trinidadian's writing, he says, "The nationalism was aggressive. Women swayed like coconut trees; their skins were the colour of the sapodilla, the inside of their mouths the colour of a cut star-apple; their teeth were as white as coconut kernels; and when they made love they groaned like bamboos in high wind."[45]

Cereus seems occasionally seduced by the woman-nature conflation, although Mala's garden, the location of much of the action and description, fits no singular configuration of the nature/culture binary, but occupies a liminal position. Mootoo sets the novel in the fictional small town of Paradise on the imaginary island of Lantanacamara, both names obviously invoking the familiar stereotypes of the Caribbean. Mala's story, starting with her childhood, is retold in fragments in a first-person account by the "effeminate" male nurse Tyler, a self-confessed outsider to the town, supplemented by other characters, and a third-person narrator. Tyler certainly needs all the help he can get, since by the time he meets Mala, she is a prematurely aged, deranged woman who is accused of murder and consigned to—or, more bluntly, dumped in—the asylum where he works. Despite the polyphony of voices that tell her story, she has at this point virtually stopped speaking, using insect and bird cries and refusing to communicate with people.

In a discontinuous time frame spanning several decades, the narrative chronologically begins with Chandin Ramchandin, the son of a poor East Indian laborer, who is converted and then adopted by white missionaries from the Shivering Northern Wetlands. He loses no time in renouncing his degraded agricultural connections, pathetically imitating his adoptive father, and falling in love with his adoptive sister, Lavinia Thoroughly. The theoretical incest of this prohibited desire for his sister—forbidden more, the author makes clear, for the interracial taboo even as Reverend Thoroughly uses nonexistent kinship as a flimsy alibi—explodes into the profanity of actual incest with his daughters Mala, nicknamed Pohpoh, and Asha. The incest follows the typical scenario of the absent mother but not, in this case, the colluding wife, when the East Indian Sarah, whom Chandin marries in a fit of pique after being rejected by Lavinia, elopes with the latter to the Shivering Northern Wetlands.

The complicated spirals of desire and betrayal trap Mala, who becomes surrogate mother and wife, protecting Asha as much as she can from her alcoholic father's demands and sustaining the house and garden. Initially, Mala embodies the domestic, passively suffering Indian female whose very nature is to nurture, although as a child she gamely fights against the school bullies and shows flashes of fire even later as a restrained mental patient. Asha escapes but Mala stays on, bound by the coils of guilt and compassion for her "wounded father," until her own introduction to consensual sex with her young admirer, Ambrose Mohanty, seals her doom. Discovered by her jealous, enraged father, she endures a series of brutal rapes and sodomy and finally kills him, a plot twist that is revealed only at the very end of the novel.

The incest taboo as explained by Claude Lévi-Strauss is the necessary prohibition that marks the evolution of culture (from an original state of nature) and the institution of kinship through the patriarchal gift exchange of women between men. In Western feminist readings, the necessity of the gift exchange is more fraught and Freudian, since the presence of the daughter in the family is a sexual threat and the object of desire must be safely "given away" by the father to avoid the temptation of incest.[46] Chandin's mumbled threats, when an inexplicable pain in his chest leads him to discover Mala and Ambrose, predicates the girl-child similarly into a patriarchal system of ownership following this disturbance in blood circulation. But the refusal to circulate blood signals Chandin's rejection of the incest taboo. He makes a suicidal endogamous choice to an exogamous one, his volatile reaction to his implied castration ultimately leading to extreme violence against Mala and then to parricide. "A man tiefing my baby? . . . I ent go let nobody tief my woman again. No man, no woman, no damn body go tief my property again."[47]

One of the consequences of colonial disruptions of patriarchal property and bloodlines, leading to obscure yet telling family charts as in Ladoo's novel, was the renewed aggression against native women's bodies that had been "tiefed" from the colonized male subject. His conventional dominance over "my woman" had to be reasserted to compensate for the manhood imperiled by white control. The series of appellative slippages from baby to woman to property ties both wife, whose specter appears here as "tiefed" by Lavinia, and daughter, whose desire for Ambrose threatens Chandin, to an insecure male possessiveness. Here the family romance is encoded through gendered and not just colonial history, with Chandin's house and not simply the plantation as the carceral, and the garden, inherited from her mother by Mala, as a temporary refuge. The townspeople, while disapproving, do not intervene, conveniently scapegoating the "insanity of his [Chandin's] own wife," who, "with a devilish mind of her own, left her husband and children."[48] The sins of the mother, in other words, are visited upon her daughters. An oblivious Ambrose, who has returned after advanced study in the Shivering Northern Wetlands, and for reasons the novel does not explain, the only one who remains clueless about Mala's situation, woos her, perplexing the public, which marvels at his infatuation for "a woman whose father had obviously mistaken her for his wife, and whose mother had obviously mistaken another woman for her husband."[49]

The novel boldly challenges cultural arrangements justified through conventions about the natural and the unnatural, at one point suggesting that Chandin's refusal to follow the universal taboo unnervingly raises questions about what is natural and what is perverse and why. Who, Tyler wonders, determines correct or "mistaken" lines of kinship and permissible familial, gender, and sexual roles? Could a mother be a father to her child, could a sister be a brother, a brother a father, a father a grandfather as well? Tyler excuses the series of tangled or multiple relationships as the naïve curiosity of a child, but the fact that children do ask these questions suggests that genealogies and kinship roles do not unfold instinctively or naturally or even keep to their place in neatly tabulated boxes. They crisscross in complicated ways and need to be rigorously pruned through social injunction and interdiction. As I will argue in a subsequent chapter, non-normative kinship roles are not necessarily more pathological than normative patriarchy. "Over the years I pondered the gender and sex roles that seemed available to people, and the rules that went with them," says Tyler.[50] Ultimately, he condemns the violent and forcible "perversity" of the nonconsensual incest but refuses to let that include "his shared queerness" with Mala.[51]

The lack of clarity and the incoherence of acts and identities, of orientations, roles, and desires, in Mootoo's novel unsettle stable moral and cultural norms without, however, renouncing ethical choices. In the novel's conclusion, a female-figured Tyler who is attracted to men pursues a male-figured Otoh who has so far sought sexual relations with women, although never to the point of full-frontal disclosure. The fact that a cross-dressing male is matched with a cross-dressing female might imply that a heterosexual companionate plot is the ultimate recourse of what is a superficial challenge to compulsory heterosexuality. But I want to argue instead that Mootoo is simply not interested in plotting a rigid hetero-homo binary any more than she wants to portray a clear-cut male-female distinction. While she does not present in any detail the mating habits of other species in the novel, her elaborate attention to several varieties of flora and fauna suggests that she would probably agree with Sedgwick's observation that nature is not the ideal space to seek strictly male-female or intra-species sexual prohibitions as the sea horse (the male carries the eggs to term) and the mule (offspring of horse and donkey) demonstrate.

Mootoo's novel refuses to name a sexual identity in fixed modern terminology: there is no reference to gay or lesbian, homosexual or heterosexual. Nor does it mention cross-dresser, androgyne, or hermaphrodite, although it does include "pansy," "funny," and "perversity."[52] Like Mala, who "was not one to manacle nature"[53] and who "did not intervene in nature's business,"[54] allowing insects and plants to live and mate and die at will, Mootoo challenges the reader "to accept and love the adult Tyler, who was neither properly man nor woman but some in-between, *unnamed* thing."[55] The narrator notes also that among the hundreds of insects Mala nurtures, there are several "that in the world of naming remain untitled."[56]

Sedgwick calls the refusal to allow people "the authority to describe and name their own sexual desire . . . a terribly consequential seizure."[57] Particularly in the prevailing atmosphere of virulently homophobic panics, in the now defunct "don't ask, don't tell" wink-nod collusion of silence, American federal agencies and lawmakers, citizens and subjects, were only too happy *not* to hear the name gay or lesbian or anything related to it. In the Caribbean, such silence is even more mandatory, as made clear in Kincaid's brother's clandestine transgressions of social taboos.[58] Similarly, one of the most damaging aspects of surviving incest is not the taboo itself but the taboo against naming it, against acknowledging that it even exists.[59] A return to the untrammeled mysteries of nature and its unnamed subjects obviously does not check the discriminatory impulses of culture and may even romanticize the former. But to qualify my argument, I would say that Mootoo's intransigence here is not against naming practices as such but against the way in which certain taxonomies and axiologies, ways of living and ways of understanding what is permissible, are taken for granted as natural and therefore universal in application.

"A name change for Chandin was briefly discussed by the Reverend and his wife. Mrs. Thoroughly thought that a Christian, if not Wetlandish name was more suitable for a son of theirs. Chandin was eager to have his Indian name replaced. Mrs. Thoroughly suggested Matthew, Mark, Luke or John. Even Ovid, Errol, Oscar and Atticus were considered."[60]

The parody of the colonial intertext becomes increasingly apparent by the end of the list, but the Reverend finally does not endorse a name change, because he thinks the retention of the Indian name is more strategic in that it will win more East Indian converts: "people were most likely to be swayed by one of their own kind." Even as Chandin is interpellated into the role of the apostle, the acknowledgment by the Thoroughlys that he is not "one of their own kind" marks the religious limit of conversion and the genetic limit of adoption. As if in response to this patronizing gesture, Mootoo offers her own inventory. Some of the fauna and flora listed—battimamselles, peekoplats, bachacs, jenghie, shandolay, baby bonnet, shado-beni—are specific local names with no glossary provided.

Naming has weighty consequences and comes with often unbearable cultural baggage, as when Mala, like Antionette in *Wide Sargasso Sea*, rejects the name most tied to her trauma, in this case, incest: "*Pohpoh*. That is not my name."[61] Otoh Boto gains the nickname as an acronym for "on the one hand but on the other hand" weighing of things. And Otoh's in-between position of gender suggests that names do matter not just in themselves but also as a reflection of individual character, historical identity, familial roles, and national belonging. "In the Neo-Positivistic order, then, land, cattle, rubber, and also women and the labor force, are enclosed, fenced in, and bound, tied by the new law. Placing women and laborers on the same semantic plane as land, cattle, and rubber—making them chattel, items on the agenda for the new ruling group, serving as means for the primitive accumulation of capital—de facto denationalizes them, for they are not written into the Constitution as subjects of law," argues Rodríguez.[62] In exploding the privatized space of the home and garden, Mootoo locates the conflicts they stage squarely in nationalist struggles of citizenship, addressing not just European racism, but Caribbean sexism and homophobia.

Naming is an assertive act of identity but it can also be a form of epistemic violence. The practice of naming, idealized in the Adamic imagination, sometimes renders ahistorical and commonsensical what are ideological and exclusionary practices. "The Bible says Adam and Eve, not Adam and Steve" is the banal chant of opponents of same-sex relationships (and, by extension, supporters of conventional gender divides for whom Eve is culpable in Original Sin). In this particular case, the names encode rigid gender dichotomies that then condemn same-sex relationships as "unnatural" or "ungodly." Mootoo follows a calling that is different from the Adamic imperative, and we are invited to consider the possibility of adams, eves, steves, and multiple others in more flexible gender formations and sexual relationships such that no singular One (or Two) attains normative authority. Vera M. Kutzinski cautions against the uncritical use of identity labels and their subsequent policing. Her claim that "everyone is potentially an *other,* Tyler no less so than Mala"[63] is endorsed at the end of the novel, when Elsie queers the entire community. "You grow up here and you don't realize almost everybody in this place wish they could be somebody or something else?" Elsie asks Otoh.[64]

Colonial practices of naming the landscape overrode specific differences to the point of absurdity. "When our landscape is so tampered with, how do we locate ourselves?" demands Cliff. "When the rainy season becomes an unnaturally tempestuous spring; mango season the dog days of summer; hurricane season an untamable autumn?"[65] When, in other words, the colonial "reality" is the paradigm against which all else is measured and inevitably fails, Chandin will make an inadequate Matthew, seasonal weather is reduced to "tempestuous" crisis, and Rochester's parallel will find bright colors on the islands intolerable after the pastel shades of his country. Cliff does not, however, assume that every colonial situation leads to inauthentic mimicry. In her rendering, the landscape and the climate are never passive, malleable blank slates open to endless manipulation and inappropriate categories. Her sense of "ruination" is similar to Senior's portrayal of the patient, inexorable triumph of "the immovable tenant," in a poem with the same title, who will not be uprooted:

> I always repossess it, inch by inch.
> With the help of the steadfast tropical
>
> sun, wind, rain, with the help of the
> termites, the ants, the wood lice, and
> the worms, I always reclaim. I can wait,
> unforgiving.[66]

Both ruinate and ruination are Jamaican neologisms, Cliff points out, signifying the "reclamation of land, the disruption of cultivation, civilization, by the uncontrolled, uncontrollable forest. When a landscape becomes ruinate, carefully designed aisles of cane are envined, strangled, the order of empire is replaced by the chaotic forest."[67] There must have been considerable anxiety over such repossession to warrant a name for it.

Historically, botanical gardens, herbariums, even libraries were constantly threatened by the wilderness or consumed by the insects. Expensive conservatories could be demolished by rot or eaten by termites.

Agents of disorder lurked close at hand, always ready to lay waste to human effort in controlling the environment. "White ants regularly attacked wooden labels, as indeed did human vandals who stole, destroyed or merely moved them from plant to plant as a practical joke. Labels were also inadvertently moved by workmen, who put the labels back in front of the wrong plants after weeding. With all these hazards, it is little wonder that the curators became exasperated with the physical and mental effort which surrounded the labeling of plants," admits one writer.[68] Human forces can also be ruinate, Cliff suggests, as specified in her naming of Clare Savage. Clare indicates light (skin), which stands for civilization, domesticity, soft speech, and knowing one's place. Savage menaces each of the above and also implies the willful memory, the "knowledge of history, the past which has been bleached from her mind, just as the rapes of her grandmothers bleached her skin."[69]

Ruination in Mootoo's novel has a similar function, engaged as it is in a radical challenge of inexorable cultural mores and in rendering nature as the dangerous supplement. In a striking reversal of hostile tropical topography, the home, supposedly an inviolate space presided over by the chaste domestic woman, is rejected for the security of the external wilderness. Mootoo draws in luxurious detail an ecological utopia, a teeming world of fauna and flora, including creatures normally considered repulsive or insignificant, that offer a secretive harbor for the increasingly estranged Mala, who is expelled from the social world and apparently going wild. The decomposed, rotting corpse of the father lies undiscovered for years in the house that Chandin made, now annexed to its vegetation such that we cannot tell where one ends and the other begins.

Mala's strategy of encouraging the natural environment literally to grow over, infest, and feed off her father's body accelerates the process of decomposition and allows the surrounding garden and its insect and plant life to screen the violent evidence of murder. She nurtures but is also nurtured in turn, everything but the human world refraining from taunting and abusing her. The novel creatively embodies nature as "undomesticated ground," ultimately rejecting flattened versions of feminized nature and using it as a tool for "feminist cultural critique."[70] Significantly, given Naipaul's rueful observation about the lack of gardens in Trinidad and the causes thereof, the mother's garden in *Cereus,* with its fecund vegetation and its creatures, is neither a scene of forced labor nor one of slothful ease.

Mala's rejection of bodily decorum and social etiquette could be simplified as an idyllic return to nature, but the fact that it is initiated by extreme stress makes it hard for us to thus romanticize it. Before she starts using bird and insect sounds, Mala makes forbidden human ones, spitting, grunting, and farting at will, "with no care for social graces."[71] But her period of aphasia is also significant. Unlike utopias, which represent an orderly space of ease and comfort (obviously "chimerical"), heterotopias "are disturbing, probably because they secretly undermine language, because they make it impossible to name this *and* that, because they shatter or tangle common names, because they destroy 'syntax' in advance . . . ; heterotopias . . . desiccate speech, stop words in their tracks, contest the very possibility of grammar at its source; they dissolve our myths and sterilize the lyricism of our sentences," says Foucault.[72] If language, specifically the act of naming or being fixed "in a formulated phrase" (to quote J. Alfred Prufrock), is a means of capture and enclosure, the heterotypic moment splits it wide open.

Mala's surrender of conventional speech "contest[s] the very possibility of grammar at its source" and rejects the mechanics, not just the linguistics, of unbending gender and sexual dogmas. As if in tandem with the insects drawn over several pages in the novel, sprawled over the words, piercing them, literally dividing the text and marking off sections, Mala herself, the novel's narrator comments, "stopped using words, lexically shaped thoughts would sprawl across her mind, fractured here and there. The cracks would be filled with images. Soon the inverse happened. A sentence would be constructed primarily of images punctuated by only one or two verbalizations."[73] Here the kinship with insects suggests not modernist alienation but a rebellion against human enclosure. It might also embody the different language that trauma often dictates, another form of perception, a kind of subaltern "speech" in which images and snapshots, rather than conventionally articulate discourse, mediate expression.

But if we must insist on keeping a cautionary and not just celebratory eye on the thrills of nature run wild, on the ruins of colonial projects in the postcolonies, then the cessation of conventional speech offers an equally salutary warning about just how much one can read into resistance. Gayatri Spivak's suspicion of the sovereign subject or "self-knowing, politically canny subalterns" reins in too uncomplicated and rushed a tribute to women's healing powers and resistance to patriarchal speech in their silence, the secrets they refuse to give up.[74] Spivak challenges the ascribed agency and triumph of the subaltern—the "arrogance of the cure"—on many theoretical fronts: poststructuralist, Marxist, feminist, and psychoanalytic. She nuances more explicitly the category of the subaltern beyond relatively privileged middle-class women to the "wretched of the earth." But even after her qualifications in the later version of her essay, Spivak maintains her reluctance to affix singularly to subaltern history "the hegemonic account of the blazing, fighting, familial Durga," the demon-slayer, the multiply armed Hindu goddess of ferocious aspect and bloody protruding tongue appropriated by feminists in search of enabling allegories.[75]

Mala's mutilation of her tongue by consuming fiery spices until it swells in a parody of a turgid phallus precedes, maybe triggers, her period of silence, but just what kind of agency is dramatized here remains ambivalent if not downright harrowing.[76] It recalls not the aggressive, apotropaic protrusion of the Hindu goddess but the ripped tongue of Philomela in the Greek archetype of rape and its silencing. Although the story ultimately is told and Philomela metamorphoses into a bird, as Christine Froula notes, the warbling notes could just as well be the unintelligible song of the hysteric. However, the fact that texts such as Maya Angelou's *I Know Why the Caged Bird Sings* breaks the formidable silence of incest, Froula argues, suggests the possibility of a "talking cure," although she is rightly cautious about just how much speech alone can accomplish.[77]

Mootoo's intertextual work replicates scenes in other texts, with Mala's condition after killing her father, for instance, resembling Bertha and Antoinette's frenzy in other novels. The discovery of a sister's letters that do not reach their destination recalls Alice Walker's *The Color Purple*,[78] and the entire novel is in fact framed as a supposed revelation to Asha—the intended reader who escaped her sister's fate and who is urged to return and reclaim her sister. Despite her challenge to gender binaries in the novel, Mootoo is also invoking a specific tradition of women's literature, although, as I discuss further in the following chapter, it is not always as nurturing as Walker's concept of "mothers' gardens" expressed in this line: "And so our mothers and grandmothers have, more often than not anonymously, handed on the creative spark, the seed of the flower they themselves never hoped to see: or like a sealed letter they could not plainly read."[79] The interplay of speaking silences and warning bird cries evokes the conclusion of Cliff's *No Telephone to Heaven*, and the transgendered figure of this novel—Harry who becomes Harriet and is also a nurse—is yet another echo.

Mootoo is clearly invested in locating her work within a different genealogy of women's literary texts, those that share the painful legacy of labor in the New World, but are also marked by other wounds and survivals of history. Like the works the novel intertextually references, it refuses a completely happy ending, reflected in Mala herself who is linked to the cereus: bedraggled and inconspicuous most of the time, but on rare, usually unseen occasions, bursting into quiet, enchanting bloom. And almost as an afterthought, Tyler reveals, Mala is beginning to speak again.

While nationalist struggles in different colonies emphasized the importance of land and home ownership as a means to sovereignty, the works I have discussed so far are not all necessarily concerned with claiming land for political and economic control or battling environmental degradation. But nor do they randomly approximate nature writing, ecological, and environmental perspectives. The literary imagination uses land to reconstruct history and reconceive Caribbean subjectivity. When the foundational fiction of the garden in the Caribbean is placed in intimate and unsettling proximity to the plantation rather than posed as a charming hobby of individual homeowners, it becomes, as Sidney Mintz has shown with the circulation of sugar in food pathways, not simply a private seat of nature, but a cultural and economic site with global impact.[80]

It must be noted that neither the beauty of the natural environment of the Caribbean nor the very real pleasure in gardening is ever lost—not even for Naipaul. He reflects on the bitter history of cultivation in the Caribbean, but ultimately returns to "Jack's Garden" to continue healing and complete his novel, which has stalled. While his ongoing rehabilitation is indirectly enabled by nature, Kincaid now pursues gardening avidly, and has developed its symbiotic relationship with her writing. Naipaul finds inspiration in Wiltshire, Kincaid develops her passion in Vermont, but this does not preclude the garden in the Caribbean from playing a therapeutic role as well, as we see in Mootoo's novel. However, as Kincaid reminds us, we can "write a history of empire through plants." Even as she allows for the joy of gardening, she insists, "It's surprisingly shocking how human beings have changed the face of the earth, the way it looks, the arrangement of the landscape. It's always an expression of power, though it looks so benign. It looks wonderfully unthreatening, but it's an exercise in power."[81]

As the works discussed in this chapter demonstrate, the supposedly benign domestic garden reveals how the reconstitution of nature and imperialist normative practices has had material effects on human subjects. Similar to Foucault's invocation of genealogy, the fictional genealogies here do not tabulate records of legitimacy and pure descent nor do they invite us down a linear path of inquiry.[82] In their detours, they expose multiple, intertwined knots of conflict that bind together nature and culture. The Caribbean orientation of the supposed site without history explodes the transcendence of the garden in myths of paradise, and embeds it in complex colonial and postcolonial regimes of knowledge/power.

2 Toxic Domesticity, Curative Kinship

Individual and National Trauma in Domestic Fiction

But the big decisions I made—leaving my family, not seeing them, not being the sort of dutiful daughter that was expected of me—I would do it again in ten seconds.

—Jamaica Kincaid, "A Lot of Memory"

They wrapped me in a family history and swaddled me tight in its stories.

—Andrea Levy, *Fruit of the Lemon*

EMERGING FROM historical and, in many cases, continuing contexts of migration, diaspora, and exile, anglophone Caribbean literature depicts a longing for the nostalgic ambiance of home and its material manifestation, a house, but generates an equally intense dystopia in its visions of domesticity. Home (and by inference the house) is a byzantine term, conjuring up a range of potent, if contradictory, meanings. In the middle-class, separate-spheres ideology of Victorian England, it represented the hallowed hearth of ladylike influence, as opposed to the power of the public sphere, properly the male/main domain. The patriarchal Indian edifice of the inner-outer worlds, "*ghar bahir,*" was similarly gendered. With the legacy of slavery and indentured servitude in the Caribbean, by contrast, many homes in the literature do not function as cozy settings of bourgeois domesticity.

In Caribbean fiction of any ethnic background, the private space of the home is never too disconnected from the history of slavery, servitude, violence, and exile. In some cases, as in Edgar Mittelholzer's sensationalized Kaywana trilogy, the literal breaches of plantation homes by Indigenous attacks or slave revolts are attended by persistent domestic discord and dysfunction, as if the social turmoil outside assails the individual home, no matter how barricaded, and refuses any internal sanctuary. Conventionally, home conveys notions of shelter, stability, nurture, and protection, the locus of the stable family unit. But in several novels, particularly in the case of abused women, it is the site of childhood trauma and marital conflict, where patriarchal authority, secrecy, violence, incest, and rape scar them.

In the most literal interpretation, home is the primary site of one's childhood, the symbol of upward mobility, the idealized private, safe, secluded space of individuation and achievement: it is both origin and aspiration. But home in a broader sense also signifies the nation, generally the country of one's birth, the nostalgic space of memory in the exilic master narratives of Caribbean identity, and additionally the ironic cause of exile in the restricted opportunity of colonial hierarchies or unfulfilled postcolonial promise. Anglophone Caribbean fiction tends to open up the home to the world: from the home to the street to the nation, we often see a dynamic continuum of relationships that are not necessarily strictly gendered or spatially severed into separate spheres. The disorderly community of oddly likeable characters in V. S. Naipaul's *Miguel Street* animate an urban cartography in which the public and private is sometimes gendered and at other times challenge the domestic space as restricted to the house and involving only women. For all the amusing exploits that liven Miguel Street, the picaresque nature of the characters, the monotonous rhythm of disappearance, failure, and death, the chronic recurrence of departure, ending with the narrator's final brisk walk toward the airplane taking him out of Trinidad, presents a domestic/national plot that points towards the exit. Exile is not a simple gateway marking physical departure from national borders, but is infused into daily life on the street that in the final analysis enables domestic displacement, not collective kinship.

Like the street in Naipaul's story cycle, the house in anglophone Caribbean fiction embodies Freud's reversal of the uncanny, where the familiar and the "homely" are the locus of disturbance, the site of estrangement.[1] Sometimes the prevailing sense of angst is directly related to unhappiness in the individual home that spills over into national melancholy, resulting in flight from the islands by both men and women. The collapse of the postcolonial state is conversely figured through the domestic space that interactively stages familial and national breakdown.

Patricia Powell's *The Fullness of Everything* broadens the impact of domestic violence by focusing on the physical abuse of male children, not as visible in this context as their female counterparts, although this is not to say that abuse of women evokes national outrage either. Winston flees Jamaica and his father, blaming the sadistic family patriarch for the predicament that forces him into exile in Boston. After his father throws him against a wall and crushes his arm, the narrator reflects bitterly: "He [Winston] was fourteen years old, but he saw it clear as day, this great betrayal, and it was not just in his family alone, he saw it everywhere he looked now in the village; he saw it every day that there was light. He saw parents turning their backs, parents drawing a mask over their faces so as not to see, parents breaking their word, violating their own laws, perpetrating violence again and again against their own flesh and blood." Returning as a grown man to his dying father, all he perceives is "the smell of a man gone completely to rot."[2]

Velma Pollard, on the other hand, identifies the rot not in the parent, but in the disrespectful child:

> out of joint
> young men
> spit spite
> on fathers
> and on fathers fathers.[3]

As in Jamaica Kincaid's autobiographical works, narratives of dysfunctional parent-child relationships draw ripples of discontentment out into society and back into the home in compulsive cycles. Pollard turns apocalyptic with Shakespearean portents of familial crime and historical disaster expressed in natural phenomena. The poet continues:

> heaven
> through muted horns
> sounds us her warning
> rain where before no rain
> torrents and storms
> raging while
> good crops freeze and burn.[4]

The breakdown in traditional family codes of respect and mutual love causes climate change, the environmental crises signaling the interconnectedness of private and public, natural and cultural spheres. The implication is that the home—in both the individual and the national context—should provide secure foundations, but unmoored social conditions in the region threaten such idealized notions and create cosmic unrest.

This chapter argues for an expanded notion of the domestic that exceeds its conventional borders and relations, with continuing focus on the fiction of Shani Mootoo, Kincaid, and Naipaul. I also turn to

Easton Lee's poetry and Lorna Goodison's memoir to shift the dystopian emphasis of the previous three writers and provide more culturally diverse domesticities. A number of works besides the ones I discuss here portray domestic disharmonies, but this is not to say that intimate family networks and kinship bonds never provided a refuge from social turmoil, dehumanized labor, and racist exploitation. One can argue that in African, Caribbean, Middle Eastern, Asian, and other cultures, family counts for a great deal and can support as much as it hampers the individual, who is generally less important than the group. But what defines family, and even community, is itself representative of the ways in which diasporic mobility puts down a different set of roots (or rhizomes, some would argue) that wander. The "pumpkin vine" family of the Caribbean traces multiple relationships that are not always consanguineous and which can commonly be interracial, even when not publicly acknowledged. As early genealogical family trees depict, bloodlines and ancestry can be broad and indeterminate, but they also map the exciting sweep of Caribbean precursors from various continents. These peripatetic creepers can make the family stronger and more flexible, but they can also choke individuals, as Naipaul and Kincaid show in their suspicion of romanticized myths of family.

It is perhaps predictable that anglophone Caribbean fiction is split by an ambivalent sense of home, since much of it was written by migrants and by their descendants who never quite overcame the volatility of migration, the violence of historic memory (including its repression), and the nostalgic longing of diasporas. But in the centuries following European settlement and the Middle and other passages, a gradual sense of nativization in the new communities emerged, although fresh questions about who could claim citizenship, economic power, and political sovereignty would dominate the nationalist movement of the early twentieth century and the subsequent period of independence. Despite the once prevalent binary of male-female, public-private orbits in nationalist debates and reimaginings, such a neat spatial division was no more possible than the traditional sexual division of labor in the work routines of slavery and indentureship, where women often toiled alongside men in the cane fields. Male dominance in the political/public sphere notwithstanding, men were deeply marked by the home space while women, particularly among the lower classes, had a visible presence in the market and on the street.

The traditional ideology of separate spheres, which posits the home and the domestic space as discrete units disconnected from the public realm, has been thoroughly challenged. Black feminism was central to the challenge of separate-spheres ideology, since its distinct racial and class modalities complicated homogeneous gender identities. But even in a conventional Indo-Caribbean context, Naipaul's *A House for Mr. Biswas* incorporates men in the domestic space, and he conversely reads the family, albeit critically, as the site of ethnonational identity. Elsewhere, he announces, "Cruelty, yes: it was in the nature of Indian family life. The clan that gave protection and identity, and saved people from the void, was itself a little state, and it could be a hard place, full of politics, full of hatreds and changing alliances and moral denunciations. It was the kind of family life I had known for much of my childhood: an early introduction to the ways of the world, and to the nature of cruelty."[5] Whether one agrees or not with Naipaul's theory of disruptive family life seeping into and souring an entire community, his perception of "the clan" illustrates my point about the ambivalent politics of home in narratives by female and male writers, and figures alternative ways through which its structural and conceptual spaces are charted.

None of the prevailing conservative rhetoric about the insulated, affective private and the politicized, abstract public spheres "dislodges some of the accumulated sediment of cultural history," argues Lora Romero.[6] Not only was home not an escapist space from the turbulence of the market, but domesticity could and did travel, she insists. The domestic narrative written by American women had a unique role to play in civilizing the natives and widening the reach of national influence, as Amy Kaplan pithily sums up in her coined term "manifest domesticity."[7] Domestic fiction as a term generally describes the novel centered on women's lives, written between the late eighteenth and nineteenth centuries mostly by women, mainly in England and extending to the United States. A select group of male writers was included in subsets of sensationalism and the sentimental, of feeling and affect, but for the most part the domestic was a category reserved for women.

Early work on domestic fiction by major critics such as Nancy Armstrong, Nina Baym, Ann Douglas, Sandra Gilbert, Susan Gubar, and other scholars primarily focused on the role of white middle-class women, although later feminist work would include African American writing.[8] While the latter challenged limited notions of the domestic, other contexts can further expand this category. Current work now locates the female domestic worker in circuits of global capital, disrupting any singular notion of the domestic as immobile, reproductive labor within the household and highlighting the role of Caribbean women in transnational domestic work, as we see in the fiction of Paule Marshall, Kincaid, and Edwidge Danticat, and in a host of Latin American and Caribbean sociological studies. Such frameworks complicate the traditional gender divides of middle-class proprieties and present men and women in unexpected, shifting relations of power and agency that deserve more careful contextualization.

While challenging the dominant fictions of familial kinship by providing different histories of their formation, Caribbean literature also rewrites the Freudian family romance into a larger narrative of exile, a radical estrangement not from one's biological parents alone but from a dystopian nation run by dictators. Danticat, Julia Alvarez, and Junot Díaz present El Jefe, Rafael Leónidas Trujillo Molina, as a tyrannical megalomaniac and also as the self-appointed father of the nation who intrudes, to disastrous effect, into the lives of individual families, particularly those with beautiful daughters. His most dangerous side emerges when he is the suave, apparently idolized leader who is nevertheless responsible for the dissolution of multiple families in the Dominican Republic. What is striking, then, about this political figure is the seeming banality of his evil on ordinary, social occasions, in matters that might seem dislocated from the public sphere, but which emphasize the inextricability of state power and the sovereign's control over every aspect of life. He does not order the imprisonment, torture, or murder simply of his political opponents but also, for instance, of parents who do not oblige him with access to their daughters, giving his public persona private dimensions that cause more terror for his people.

In Alavarez's fictionalized account of the famous Mirabal sisters, Minerva Mirabal admits to feeling "a twinge of disappointment" when Trujillo asks someone else to dance with him, although she is well aware of his destructive gaze. She confesses, "This regime is seductive. How else would a whole nation fall prey to this little man?"[9] Hegemonic political power is often discussed with no reference to such moments, but the father's seduction applies to more than the incest narrative within the home. The entire nation, to put it bluntly, is screwed in this scenario. The availability of women upon demand with no consideration of their familial networks echoes the slave master's arbitrary sexual access to slaves, proving that dictatorships have something in common with slave regimes.

More ominously, I would argue that men do not always participate in domestic rituals surreptitiously, behind closed doors. Amabelle Désir discovers this to her peril in Danticat's *The Farming of Bones,* based on General Trujillo's sanction of the 1937 massacre of Haitians in the Dominican Republic. The biblical prototype of the slaughter forms one of the epigraphs to the novel. But in this specific, modern instance, the decisive marker of belonging to the Republic, and therefore the totemic charm for escaping death, is the "correct" pronunciation of *perejil*, Spanish for parsley. The Kréyol-speaking Haitian tongue is unable to trill the "r" and so treacherously gives away the hated immigrants who must be exterminated. Amabelle herself is caught, like other Haitians fleeing the pogrom, and forced to eat bunches of parsley (in some cases poisoned), thrust down her throat by a raucous mob, which then beats her unconscious. She reflects, "We used parsley for our food, our teas, our baths, to cleanse our insides as well as our outsides. Perhaps the Generalissimo in some larger order was trying to do the same for his country."[10] In the bio-logic of ethnocide, the intestinal functions of the body politic purge the unwanted waste, although many Dominicans are killed as well in the undifferentiated mode of such butchery. Ultimately, the medicinal herb is possibly a randomly chosen alibi, but its potency lies in the venomous appropriation of nature as an ethnic, linguistic, and national ID that domesticates the purgative slaughter.

Apart from expanding the operative domain and symbolic modes of the domestic, Caribbean contexts also suggest other spaces in which the public and the private intertwine and complicate gender divides. Far from being disconnected from such matters, male writers include a spectrum of family relationships that inevitably have ethnonational resonance, as Naipaul believes. For instance, Easton Lee's poems weave together sentimental reflections of China through ancestral memory and familial lineage, articulating a Chinese Jamaican subject constantly exhorted to be respectful to elders, to cherish family networks, to maintain cultural pride, and to appreciate women's work, particularly the endless labor of the mother, whose roughened hands and aged body the poetic narrator recalls with gratitude. Lee's poems augment the subjects of conduct manuals, inscribing men within regulated codes of behavior and domestic disciplines:

> Clean the halls
> sweep the dwellings of the living
> and the resting place of the ancestors
> cleanse your thoughts of anger, of malice and hatred
> as you wash your face in the pure dew of morning
> in thanksgiving pay respects to your Gods.[11]

Masculinity in the Caribbean is often figured in the stereotyped manhood of white male colonizers and the even more stereotyped hypermasculinity of black men. The patriarchal authority of Indian men within their homes is another unvarying motif, but Lee raises the possibility of Asian men disciplined by age hierarchy, spiritual equilibrium, and obedience to social codes symbolized in the inner and outer cleansings.

Several of Lee's poems describe the humdrum chores of keeping a grocery shop, where the narrator claims to have grown up. While other schoolchildren rush to play on Friday afternoon, he has to go home and take his place behind the counter.[12] The fact that the gender of the speaker is not always mentioned is in itself interesting, since one may assume that decorous behavior and restraint are not male prerogatives and that the voice is therefore female, even if pragmatic business tactics, not gendered expectations, are what codify his "welcoming," meek demeanor. But the male Chinese shopkeeper was portrayed as submissive to his clients even as he was believed to be a shrewd tradesman.

Although the speaker notes his father's affectionate admonitions, the mother's role is emphasized, as are family joys and a sense of community. Next to a poem outlining a parent's "instructions" to the son to hold his head high and to remember the glories of ancient Chinese culture, is another more mundane one about making paper funnels in which to sell various condiments and spices:

> My hands grow
> girl-delicate
> folding paper funnels. . . .
> Endless paper funnels
> each father-inspected for perfection.[13]

While these "girl-delicate" and "father-inspected" skills may reinforce stereotypes of feminized Asians, what is striking is the fact that they are inscribed against a framework of *patriarchal* Chinese culture, suggesting that what gets defined as patriarchal is also nuanced. The finicky attention to detail gravitates from the ritualistic father-son bonding in a close-knit family to the supervised inspection by the manager-father of the worker-child, not necessarily in adverse ways, even if playful Friday afternoons are sacrificed.

In extravagant rhetoric reminiscent of the tributes paid on Mother's Day, the boy more warmly recognizes the woman's acumen:

> My mother is
> a banker
> a financial advisor

an investment broker.
Just ask my father
for he doesn't know
how the little money stretches so far.[14]

Considering that predominantly male bankers, investment brokers, and financial advisors now exemplify profligacy and greed, the mother's thrift may in fact function as a more dependable financial strategy.[15] The mother's multiple functions within the home extended into a small business and petty trade confer national stature on the domestic woman who is generally overlooked and undervalued but is here romantically multiplied into "a people." The father oversees the making of paper funnels while the mother balances the books in an exchange of conventional patriarchal gender roles. What Lee's poems tell us is that constructions of masculinity even in decidedly male-dominated cultures do not always follow a predictable route.

In poems that recall the "dialect poetry" of Louise Bennett, the ordinary lives and conversations of the villagers are conveyed as "labrish," as neighborly gossip.

Say what?
Him beat you again? . . . .
You no tired fi teck lick.
You no tired of the shame
and batteration?
Why you don't leave
the old mampala man
and go look you owna living?[16]

A brief biographical blurb to the collection of poems tells us that Lee grew up listening to his mother's stories. The poems themselves often situate the youthful speaker as an eavesdropper on conversations between customers and perhaps his mother as she attends to them. In the above dramatic monologue framed as a series of scolding questions in the vernacular, the reality of domestic violence impinges itself on the boy's consciousness, situating, as Powell does, male children within its reach. At the same time, it also describes a rural community looking out for each other, as the advice advocating economic independence to break the cycle of violence suggests. Interestingly, the masculinity of the batterer is challenged by the term "mampala," a Jamaican Creole word meaning "effeminate." Although this compromised critique reasserts the negative connotations of men who behave like women, it suggests that men who beat women are weak, not strong.

The shop is also an ambivalent social space that might foster community for the largely black customers, but in its economic role, could generate tensions between them and the Chinese families that run these small businesses, leading to acts like burning down the shop.[17] Anne-Marie Lee-Loy points out that "one of the most common tropes of Chineseness in West Indian literature is that of the distanced and disengaged Chinese shopkeeper," who is often written out of national space by both Afro- and Indo-Caribbean writers.[18] Lee-Loy's observation that the shop sometimes figures as a "prison" for the children entrusted with its daily business complicates the notion of a domestic carceral, with the shop's double duty for residential and commercial purposes.[19] Its twin functions render the shop-dwelling families more vulnerable to hostility, and emphasize the economic aspect of domestic arrangements, particularly in abusive relationships that trap dependent women.[20]

Trauma studies have gained traction in recent years, the sustained critical attention resulting in a wider scope from the initial emphasis on genocide and the World Wars to include transatlantic slavery, colonialism, and other collective traumas. Michael Rothberg urges an approach to trauma that does not seek it simply in catastrophic events of vast magnitude, but also in everyday forms and experiences.[21] Such a perspective can highlight the violence that women experience on a daily, even hourly basis, but that remains invisible unless it involves mass rapes as war crimes, once again relegating trauma to grand historic event. These daily experiences of terror may not include what E. Ann Kaplan calls "classic" trauma, but her investigation of "'family' or 'quiet' trauma" and "common traumas" expands the gendered focus from men to women, from public to personal, and from collective to individual.[22] Of course, these are dynamic shifts and not one-way patterns, as I have been arguing, each affecting the other such that violence in the home ultimately finds its way into the public sphere and vice versa.[23] As Kaplan notes, a number of scholars have cautioned against reading trauma into everything and thus reifying social wounds, but paying attention to specific situations can avoid the "empty empathy" of voyeuristic, decontextualized perceptions of trauma.[24]

"Female-coded trauma"[25] offers important insights into women's writing from the Caribbean and demands a specific feminist ethics of reading. But what I call toxic domesticity representing individual, everyday forms of violence and terror is pervasive in female- and male-authored works, and marks suggestive connections as well as important differences between men and women. I begin this discussion of trauma in domestic fiction with Indo-Caribbean women because the nuclear, patriarchal structures of traditional Indian households are commonly perceived to be more stable structures. The examples I provide below, particularly in my return to Mootoo's *Cereus Blooms at Night,* which I discussed in the previous chapter in another context, tell a different story.

Infected Prose: Transgenerational Trauma Narratives

In contrast to the saccharine qualities associated with femininity, Caribbean women's writing often describes the poisonous consequences of gendered incarceration. The literary legacy of women's traumas, including the very act of writing them, has ironically a Caribbean origin in modern feminist theory. One of the canonical texts of Anglo-American feminist theory and domestic fiction, *The Madwoman in the Attic: The Woman Writer and the Nineteenth-Century Literary Imagination,* takes its title and even its trope of female mental instability from Charlotte Brontë's infamous Creole woman, Bertha Mason, imprisoned in her husband's English manor and immolating herself in the end, enabling him to marry the proper, chaste, English governess, Jane Eyre. Despite their minimization of the Caribbean subject, Sandra Gilbert and Susan Gubar's analysis of the language of illness and insanity surrounding English women in the nineteenth century, both in literary and medical discourses about them, and in their own writing, has an amazing reach, resonating in Caribbean contexts (but with specific differences, as I will note). Gilbert and Gubar believe that

> in comparison to the "male" tradition of strong, father-son combat . . . this female anxiety of authorship is profoundly debilitating. Handed down not from one woman to another [since women writers were rare at the time] but from the stern literary "fathers" of patriarchy to all their "inferiorized" female descendants, it is in many ways the germ of a dis-ease or, at any rate, a disaffection, a disturbance, a distrust, that spreads like a stain throughout the style and structure of much literature by women, especially—as we shall see in this study—throughout literature by women before the twentieth century.[26]

Exploring what they call the literary psychohistory of women, they claim that a pervasive malaise "infects" women's literature of the time, inherited from the poisoned apple of male-authored "fairy tales" about women. Such a sickness is not restricted to the women of their study but, as in Jean Rhys's *Wide Sargasso Sea,* can be revisited in Caribbean women's trauma. Suggesting a wider provenance and literary dialogue than Gilbert and Gubar envisage, Mootoo's *Cereus Blooms at Night* helps us situate the phrase "infection in the sentence," which Gilbert and Gubar borrow from Emily Dickinson, in an Indo-Caribbean family setting.[27] Contrary to the disciplined and contented image of the Indo-Caribbean "angels in the house," the minutiae of these women's lives in much of the fiction and poetry rarely exemplify a uniformly sanguine routine. Instead, there are several instances of intense toxicity in the supposed sanctuary of the home.

Although as subjects they have come a long way from their status as "the most under-researched aspect of the East Indian presence,"[28] inciting Ramabai Espinet's famous protest about "the invisible woman in West Indian fiction,"[29] the long absence of Indo-Caribbean women in literary and historical texts is yet to be fully remedied. Indeed, as Dionne Brand observes, women in general may have been *present* in the once dominant fiction of male writers, but they were rarely *subjects* in it, despite their ubiquitous and even overwhelming role in the lives of these writers.[30] Indo-Caribbean women became ethnic markers of difference, generally seen as more docile and pliable participants in a patriarchal system brought from India and only momentarily interrupted by the disruption of their passage to and settlement in the Caribbean. It is important to note here in the interest of contextual specificity that the term "patriarchy" also has to be revised and only provisionally applied to the Indo-Caribbean male. Indo-Caribbean women writers often demonstrate that the term does not (nor should it in any case) imply the unilateral power of all men, particularly when ethnic, class, and sexual contexts shift their status.

As the Subaltern Studies collective insists, dominance and subalternity are relational categories, so that the wife-beating, alcoholic husband of Indo-Caribbean fiction may be subservient and marginal outside the domestic threshold. Ranajit Guha explains that, in the colonial context in India,

> the same class or element which was dominant in one area according to the definition given above, could be among the dominated in another. This could and did create many ambiguities and contradictions in attitudes and alliances, especially among the lowest strata of the rural gentry, impoverished landlords, rich peasants and upper-middle class peasants all of whom belonged, *ideally speaking*, to the category of "people" or "subaltern classes," as defined below. It is the task of research to investigate, identify and measure the *specific* nature

and degree of the *deviation* of these elements from the ideal and situate it historically.[31]

Even as women writers expose the injustices of fathers and husbands, they situate them as figures deserving sympathy in colonial and postcolonial structures of inequality. At the same time, they are also unapologetic about stressing the particularly subjugated lot of the women.

So dramatic has been the rate of domestic violence on the islands that feminist historian Patricia Mohammed traces the contemporary women's movement in the Caribbean primarily to domestic violence activism.[32] Wife murders, in fact, became a dominant symbol of Indo-Caribbean identity, and although domestic violence is as pervasive in the Caribbean as in many other cultures, it achieved a notorious place in Indo-Caribbean history. In contrast to idealizations of the nuclear household controlled by a patriarch whose masterful presence in the household is fundamental and desirable, Mootoo's *Cereus Blooms at Night* presents the vile side to family relations when the girl is trapped by cultural expectations of rigid obedience to her incestuous father and by her lethal empathy for his grief and rage over his East Indian wife's flight with her white female lover.[33] Mala's breakdown is rendered in the language and images closest to her reality, which is in the unusual mélange of cooking and violence.

In her discussion of artistic production by Indo-Caribbean women, Rosanne Kanhai identifies the masala stone as at once the millstone of grinding domestic labor and the emblem of culinary creativity.[34] The song of the masala stone is certainly an ambivalent one, since a singular reading of domestic labor as drudgery makes mindless victims of the women whose task it mostly is to grind spices. Fragrant and delectable curries are cooked with the ground masalas, but once again the infection hovers menacingly. Perhaps the most intense evocation of the insanity lurking behind the domestic quotidian is in the pungent spices that Mala, reacting to her continued violation, ferments for days. I quote at length to provide a sense of their tumultuous consumption, peppered with verbs that are sprayed violently across the passage: "She thrust her finger into the bottle, scooped out a heavy clump of raw pepper and shoved the finger into her mouth. She scooped up more and then more, wiping her finger on the sensitive tip of her tongue, and then again, scooping more, shoveling it into her mouth. The skin underneath her fingernail tingled. She didn't swallow, keeping the fire on her tongue, by then so blistered that parts of the top layer had already disintegrated and other areas had curled back like rose petals dipped in acid."[35]

While it is true that one keeps a watchful eye on hot spices, who would imagine that such deliberate delirium lies in them? In a grotesque twist, the engorged, seared tongue seems to turn phallic, but not in simulation of the fiery mother-goddess Kali's tongue—defiant, bloodied, and threatening to men like the apotropaic head of Medusa. If this is resistance to patriarchal authority, then it is a ferociously self-destructive one. Mala stops speaking after this episode, but the painful cost of this aphasia only confirms Gayatri Spivak's uneasiness with too ludic a celebration of paradoxical subaltern agency, as I discussed in the previous chapter.[36]

Much has been said about the unrepresentability of trauma, the silences and distortions it records, because, as Toni Morrison reminds us, they are not stories to pass on. But women's literature in the Caribbean seems to suffer from no such diffidence, and in fact often describes trauma with remarkable clarity, even if the characters in the fiction are sometimes silenced in a typical consequence of being traumatized. Women's texts also draw sustained attention to individual trauma, even if they link it to the structural violence of gender, class, racial, or sexual discrimination.[37] Far from being stories not to pass on (the seeming disinclination a ruse to emphasize that the unspeakable is eventually spoken because the incredible must be believed), such narratives are related in multiple ways and demand equally flexible reading strategies.

The vivid account of Mala's self-mutilation strikingly presents both a symptom of trauma and the imperative to tell the story she makes it impossible for herself to tell. As Sandra L. Bloom explains, memory systems in the brain vary, and can be verbal as well as nonverbal. "Speechless terror" is a physiological response, the freezing of certain functions and reactions a defense mechanism under severe stress, leading to the inability to find words or meaning to express or make sense of the trauma.[38] Mala enacts and enforces this speechlessness, but this is not the case with the narrative itself, which does not mimic her symptoms here but instead steps in to speak for the silenced subaltern. Many scholars insist on the significance of verbal and visual representation, on the importance of telling the story and of the reader or listener "bearing witness," a phrase that is repeated in the scholarship. "Like lancing an abscess, the toxic memories and emotions must be drained—or as a nineteenth-century pioneer, Pierre Janet, described it, 'liquidated,'" says Bloom.[39] What seem to be acts of silencing, then, are revelatory, critical interventions in feminist texts such as *Cereus Blooms at Night*.

Daily violence in everyday contexts is not restricted to Indo-Caribbean fiction. Across anglophone Caribbean women's writing, in domestic scenes of terror, innocuous utensils turn into instruments of brutality. Audre Lorde's *Zami* and Edwidge Danticat's *Breath, Eyes, Memory* (where mothers who migrate to the United States are both nurturing and demoralizing figures) transform the mortar and pestle from resourceful kitchen tools to phallic menace. In Lorde's "biomythography," the pestle is at first reminiscent of fertility, of West Indian cuisine (women carry their culture in their condiments), of mother-daughter camaraderie in the homely rituals of making souse, and finally of their island home. But the "*thud push rub rotate up* repeated over and over" changes its tune to a sinister note as the first-person narrator is overwhelmed by a memory of rape.[40] The sounds and strokes of preparing a comfort food dissolves into a rape script whose grammar of violence is all the more disconcerting for its familiar echo in housework, a reminder that rape is a more common and repressed occurrence in the household, not in lonely alleys. Here the narrative is traumatogenic in the classic sense, where the memory and understanding of the experience of rape is belated, resurfacing to consciousness much later.

While Mala burns her tongue in response to the disintegration of her bodily integrity, in Danticat's novel, Sophie Caco drastically circumvents the "virginity cult" that is enforced when mothers test their daughters' virginity by thrusting their fingers inside the vaginal passage. Sophie breaks her hymen with a pestle in order to stop further tests by her mother, who throws her out in anger for disobeying the injunction of malleable femininity, which is to be pounded or pried into submission. "My flesh ripped apart as I pressed the pestle into it. I could see the blood slowly dripping onto the bed sheet."[41] Mala's mutilating use of spices and Sophie's disciplinary employment of the pestle is a refusal of consent to their subjection, but the victory is a Pyrrhic one.

Even as the mothers in *Cereus* and *Farming* are spectral presences for the most part, they often have a direct role to play in other novels and not always as protective nurturers. Despite Martine Caco's attraction to African American spirituals, particularly the one about the "motherless child," the pathos of her character lies not in being orphaned, but (like Kincaid) in her uneasy relationship with her mother. And it is not a singular one. In one of the Santeria rituals that Sophie turns to for therapy in New York, she and other women like her, one of them an Ethiopian circumcised by her grandmother, write the names of their "abusers" on pieces of paper and burn them: they turn out to be the names of mothers and grandmothers.[42] When she is confronted later by Sophie, Martine's justification of the virginity tests is starkly simple: "I did it . . . because my mother had done it to me."[43] It is hardly surprising that women writers antagonistically turn against mothers in such cases, if only to slash them with their pens. Like Martine's breast cancer, the legacy that passes between women is sometimes deadly transgenerational trauma. In Danticat's novel, the possibility that the granddaughter will be disconnected from their fraught inheritance is seen as a cause for triumph, in opposition to uncomplicated celebrations of bonding in female genealogies of grandmothers, mothers, and daughters.

Of the multiple sources of infection in literature, Gilbert and Gubar discuss in some detail the contagious effects of women encountering numerous images of themselves as angels, monsters, and other creatures of a male writer's imagination fashioned to suit his literary mastery. In order to write, they argue, women writers must overcome the paralysis of seeing themselves, thus, "through a glass darkly," and invent their own, presumably more affirmative portraits. But as they and many other feminist critics have noted, misogyny, matrophobia, and somatophobia are not the exclusive terrain of male writers whose "infantile dread of maternal autonomy has historically objectified itself in vilification of women."[44] Apart from the examples I mentioned above, in the anglophone Caribbean, Jamaica Kincaid is one of the most typical, if complex, examples of a female writer who does not comfortably inhabit the skin of warm, fuzzy sisterhood. She resists comparisons with other women writers, professes not to have read any West Indian fiction until late into her writing career, and, like Naipaul, claims literary antecedents in Western canonical texts, including the King James Bible. Critics have also noted her solipsistic self-referentiality, so that, unlike the explicit parallels between Phyllis Shand Allfrey and Jean Rhys, or Rhys, Michelle Cliff, and Mootoo, for instance, Kincaid tends to draw upon and repeat her own accumulated images.[45]

Similarly, her sense of self in permanent exile, her pungent reflections on the worsened state of Antigua after independence, her impatience with victimhood, her politically incorrect pronouncements on the many people she dislikes (such as the Lebanese in Antigua), the contemptuous descriptions of native incompetence, her unconcealed relief at having left her island of birth, her growing comfort with her American identity—all these might make Kincaid more akin to Naipaul than she herself is willing to acknowledge. Unlike Naipaul, however, (although Naipaul's fans will find this arguable), she is far more explicit in her condemnation of colonialism, slavery, and racism, and less generously inclined toward the Western world. But there is little doubt that Naipaul would agree with her on what it takes to become a writer, even if, like Kincaid, he returns again and again in his writing to the very space he renounces. Kincaid says, "I could not have become a writer while living among the people I knew best, I could not have become myself while living among the people I knew best."[46] The home is conceived of as a dysfunctional space from which to flee for different reasons, in this particular case in order to pursue the vocation of writing and to gain selfhood.

The claim that invention is stifled in the domestic (personal and national) space and that it takes the alienation of exile, the going forth, the living among strangers, to generate writing is one that Naipaul would find attractive. It took travel, he insists, to liberate his tethered talent, even if his return home (not always physically) was also essential. Kincaid seems to feel even less guilty than Naipaul about turning her back on home and family. In her words, she wonders "what my own life would have been like if I had not been so cold and ruthless in regard to my own family, acting only in favor of myself."[47] In both cases, their aloofness is attributed in part to the cruelty of family, the cruelty that a defeated people share in common. Kincaid's memories of having been beaten up as a child by her schoolmates, of obeah used to bring ill will and harm, of local contempt for Indigenous peoples of the Caribbean, of Antiguan indifference to AIDS, are interspersed with instances of her protagonists' sadism in her works, illustrating the victims-become-victimizers syndrome that is the bane of Third World politics. While a range of Caribbean writers have critiques to make of their island countries, Kincaid strikingly condenses her accusations in the biographical and fictional image of the mother. Such a tactic allows her to launch layered attacks against different "maternal" bonds, from biological mothers to the colonial "mother" country of England.

In a sympathetic reading of mothers as they appear in literature, Susan Rubin Suleiman notes, "*Mothers don't write, they are written.*"[48] In Kincaid's curiously titled *The Autobiography of My Mother* (perhaps borrowed partly from Gertrude Stein), a fictional novel that is written in the form of a memoir, the plot seems to require the death of the mother not just *at* the birth of the daughter, but *for* her birth and growth. This autobiography begins with the literal death of the author implied in the title. The daughter, as unofficial amanuensis, constructs her identity—and her text—through the absence of her mother. In contrast to the unloved Mr. Potter (based in part on Kincaid's father),[49] who is deserted in his childhood by his mother when she tires of him and walks into the sea one day, Xuela's mother dies in the throes of labor. But while the mother's disappearance seems understandable in the context of Mr. Potter, who is apparently a child that not even his mother could love, Xuela's feeling of abandonment comes from a more arbitrary intervention, the occupational hazard of reproductive labor. However, as Marianne Hirsch argues, the eviction of the mother from the plot is a calculated move by women writers who want to "separate their heroines from the lives and the stories of their mothers."[50] From this perspective of textual necessity and psychic individuation, the pathos of the mother killed in reproductive labor, dying in the act of giving birth, seems a contrivance in *Autobiography.* In some ways, Kincaid enacts both in fiction and in her life the classic Freudian model of hostility and separation from her mother. Moving from intense love, to ambivalence, to outright loathing of the mother in her oeuvre, her later works correspond not to the reparation narratives of feminist tradition, but to the "Mommie Dearest" type of denunciation.

Yet challenges to the Freudian model may emphasize the differently perceived black mothers in Black Atlantic cultures as opposed to genteel, middle-class, white European women. Black mothers tend to have stronger ego boundaries than their white counterparts, and are more likely to be immasculated rather than feminized figures.[51] But their undeniable strength is not always presented as castrating force, and they bond with daughters to protect and teach them survival skills in a racist and sexist world.[52] One of the lessons the daughters also learn, as the men-at-risk account bemoans, is that their men will let them down and they need to rely instead on a dependable network of women. If in the Freudian account daughters' hostility to mothers lies in their recognition of phallic lack, what are they rejecting when mothers are seen as stronger than fathers? Is it one more archetype of the devouring mother that is also prevalent across cultures, one more strategy of punishing and taming tough women?

Despite Xuela's claim that this account is as much of her mother's as of her own life, the mother, who is more an evasive "X" than her daughter's namesake, remains as mysterious and partial as her appearance in her daughter's dreams, where only the edge of her skirt is visible. She is available to us only through the daughter's gaze and even then in piecemeal fashion. The puzzle of the incremental portrait of an unnamed woman, who acquires a few more features each time she appears in the text, remains unsolved even after it is completed. The intermittent and gradually more detailed picture of a Creole woman in a head wrap, with an enigmatic Mona Lisa smile and one of her arms akimbo,[53] renders Xuela the mother no less marginal or fragmentary despite her centrality to the title. The appropriation of the mother's "autobiography" ultimately displaces her own voice and, following a condensation scenario, the mother as dream object stands eventually for various pejorative associations in Kincaid's reflections on her own mother.

Several critics have ascribed Kincaid's hostility against her mother to her replay of the unequal power struggles of colonial history. Moira Ferguson argues that the "doubled articulation of motherhood as both colonial and biological explains why the mother-daughter relations in [Kincaid's] fiction often seem so harshly rendered."[54] Echoing this view, Simone A. James Alexander even more explicitly argues that the mother-daughter relationship in Kincaid's work "can be classified as a . . . relationship between the colonizer and the colonized in which the (powerful) mother fits the profile of a colonizer and the (powerless) daughter is the colonized."[55] While Kincaid herself has encouraged this intriguing subversion of the Freudian account of mother-daughter object relations in her fiction and interviews, I am reluctant to take her at her word. However justified her sense of vulnerability, she is very much the one in control of the way her mother is represented.

Kincaid has somewhat organically figured her mother as "fertile soil" for her imagination,[56] and one reviewer claims partially in jest that her entire family can also be included as textual sources. "Jamaica Kincaid seems to be working her way through her family tree, and those of us who appreciate great writing pray she never runs out of relatives," begins the review of *Mr. Potter.*[57] In *Mr. Potter,* the first-person narrator, once again the daughter, expresses her resentment not of the mother but of the father, and of being a subject *sous erasure,* an illegitimate, ignored offspring of a man who has produced many children through different women. But his propagative power spawns a meaningless multiplicity, a fatherhood that is not even in name. The line that runs blankly through the space for the father's name on her birth certificate is the withheld line(age) that crosses from father to daughter.[58] The daughter's revenge is to pen her own lines on the illiterate Mr. Potter's life. In a rancorous reversal of the customary literary inheritance, she says,

> And Mr. Potter had no patrimony for he did not own himself, he had no private thoughts, he had no thoughts of wonder, he did not have a mind's eye in which he could wander, he had no thoughts about his past, his future, and his present which lay between them both—his past and his future—and he was not ignorant, he was not without a conscience, he could not read and he could not write and he could not render the story of his life, his own in particular, with coherency and I can read and I can write and I am his daughter.[59]

The adult narrator jeers at her father in extended and derogatory interpellations: "See the motherless Roderick Nathaniel Potter, but he did not know himself to be so, motherless. See him a small boy, vulnerable to all that is hard and without heart, to all that is hard and without love, to all that is hard and without mercy."[60] Potter's vulnerability is rejected by the daughter, beside herself with a rage not entirely without compassion but too aggrieved to forgive her father's abandonment. His obscure burial is an appropriate end to his equally insignificant life, she says later, and if he has any importance at all, it is as a subject of her writing.[61]

Contrary to Gilbert and Gubar's theory of the anxiety of authorship for women writers, here the daughter appropriates literary power while the father is rendered "storyless." Both Kincaid and Naipaul paradoxically conceive of home, family, and nation as the stony abyss that stares back at the writers and paralyzes them but also as the creative matrix of their authorial inspiration, although it shifts in Naipaul to a father-son exchange, which I will discuss later. For all Naipaul's insistence on travel as a cosmopolitan liberation of the insular imagination, as with Kincaid, the intrusion of the personal narrative and memoir into his prose continually draws attention to the significance of the domestic.

Kincaid has often credited her mother, Annie Richardson, with literary influence. Analogous to Naipaul's sense of initially echoing his father's voice, she claims, "My mother wrote my life for me and told it to me."[62] The "to me" could well be a "for me," when Kincaid is resentfully discussing her mother's control over her life. But if she is something of a ventriloquist's dummy, the mother must have conveyed extreme self-loathing. So sickening is her mother (a severe example of momism[63] in Kincaid's portrayal) that she is unable to love her children who are healthy or independent, claims Kincaid in *My Brother,* where, as in most of her other work, the author is largely the focus of the text.[64] While Devon Drew's body and his self-destructive promiscuity become the fertilizing compost for AIDS, his mother is projected as a contaminating gardener, although elsewhere Kincaid admits that she has inherited her talent for gardening from her mother. Unlike Alice Walker's tender image of mothers' nurturing potential passed on to daughters, Kincaid's mother wreaks as much havoc as the parasites and fungal growths that Kincaid describes in unnerving detail, culminating in the mother's destruction of various plants. The latter's untiring nursing of her son is viewed appreciatively neither by Kincaid nor, in her account, by her dying brother. And, unlike in Naipaul's case, it is not the pressure of writing that gets on her nerves but her mother herself who leads Kincaid to a nervous breakdown, initiating a recurrence of a childhood illness.[65]

Nevertheless, aligning the mother with the colonial mother country of England neglects the specific relationship that Kincaid's mother had to England, which, even if she was a light-skinned anglophile, was hardly one of equivalence. However "powerful" she might seem to a rebellious daughter, she too was once a colonized subject. Apart from the risks of congealing the conventionally gendered conflations of woman, land, and home, the colonizer-colonized binary is not an accurate fit for her relationship to her mother. Without expecting Kincaid to play up to the "No anger, just rum and rhythm. Happy wit' plenty o' nuttin'"[66] image, as Hilton Als accuses some of her critics of doing, I want to suggest that Kincaid's anger is not always that of a powerless victim, in much the same way that she reads her mother's rage.

Motherhood has evoked a wide and contradictory range of nationalist signifying practices across different colonies. Despite the sociological reality of female-headed households in the Caribbean, or perhaps because of it, the mother seems less idealized as a surrogate for the nation than, say, the chaste, demure, self-sacrificing Mother India myth of Indian nationalist discourse. Although one may note the "mobility and volatility of the mother as a discursive sign"[67] in any given context, in Kincaid's rhetoric the mother largely figures as a corrosive, pathological agent. Both metaphorical substitutions, of course, do violence to the embodied subjectivity of individual mothers, and neither should be accepted without suspicion.

Contrast Kincaid's account, for instance, to Lorna Goodison's various poetic tributes to her mother, as in "For My Mother (May I Inherit Half Her Strength)," and other poems in the collection *I Am Becoming My Mother*,[68] a possibility that gratifies Goodison but would horrify Kincaid. It would be impossible to read Goodison's mother as a colonizing agent or allied with the mother country of England. There is something calculating and individual, then, in the rejection of parental authority and the hostility toward the land of Kincaid's birth. Both disavowals are not simply symptomatic evidence of colonial damage, although the rage against history certainly plays a part as it does with Naipaul, equally fierce in his denunciations of family and nation. As in the case of Naipaul, Kincaid's inspiration is the native material that she claims to reject, the bedrock of her formidable skills as a writer. Ironically, the dysfunctional family and state become productive, if conflicted, sites of authorship, the traumas they inflict generating creative work.

Like many others of his generation, Naipaul was convinced that his future as a writer depended on his departure to England, even if he would find, with other exiles, that his arrival there would present its own enigmas. He has never been coy about his desperate anxieties over writing—to the point of shattering nervous breakdowns—despite his conviction that against all odds he was destined to be a writer. While Gilbert and Gubar diagnosed "infection in the sentence" for white, middle-class, English women writers in the nineteenth century torn between the reiterative two spheres of home and world, private and public, motherhood and vocation, "the anxiety of authorship" for a writer such as Naipaul was neither the Oedipal struggle between male writers and their overpowering predecessors traced by Harold Bloom nor what Gilbert and Gubar identify as the "profoundly debilitating" sickness induced in women by patriarchal literary traditions.[69] Rather, as George Lamming argues in an essay aptly titled "The Occasion for Speaking," the fact that Caribbean writers even existed in his time was a miracle in itself.[70]

If writing was a struggle for white authors in the period of early settlement and slavery, for the rest of the Caribbean population it was an even more unusual activity. The material demands of slavery and indentured labor hardly encouraged literary pursuits and, for years after, the absence of a strong foundation of creative writing or a sense of established, unbroken history stretching back through the ages would be deeply felt by the descendants of such laborers. Naipaul's "Prologue to an Autobiography" is full of affectionate details of his father's sadly curtailed writing life, including mundane paraphernalia such as his bookcase and desk made partly of packing materials; old papers; letters; and perhaps the most telling image of the working context of modern Caribbean writing by men such as his father. Not bound in fine leather but pasted into an estate wages ledger are articles from the *Trinidad Guardian* written by Seepersad Naipaul—part of the legacy of writing that he bequeaths to his son.[71]

Even in the years leading up to independence, the rupture of compulsory migration, the smallness of the islands, their economic and cultural dependence on the various colonial metropolises, the drudgery of unimaginative, derivative education, the scarcity of independent publishers: all these factors complicated the development of Caribbean writers and added to their personal insecurities even as they produced an outstanding body of work. Significantly, Naipaul's Nobel lecture, "Two Worlds," continues to stress the schizophrenic divide that allegedly afflicted his ascent to a remarkably successful career. Much of the oratorical acceptance of the crowning international recognition that he had arrived as a writer is still haunted by what he did not know—the India of the past or present, the Muslims from India, his father's side of the family in Nepal, his black neighbors, the history of the Caribbean, even the origin of Chaguanas, where he had lived during his childhood. His grandmother's house was "shut-in," excluded, "shut out" from what lay beyond the "fierce kind of privacy" of an East Indian Brahmin extended family residence. "So as a child I had this sense of two worlds, the world outside that tall corrugated-iron gate, and the world at home," Naipaul declares, echoing, with probably unintended irony, a grievance of the disaffected woman writer of nineteenth-century England.[72]

Providing the foreword to Seepersad's *The Adventures of Gurudeva,* the son, in a reversal of Bloom's anxiety of influence, enables the republication of his father's obscure work and pays homage to a career "stalled" by the father's limitations of personal and historical circumstances. The Parker pen with which the son writes the foreword to his father's disinterred work, he reveals, was bought with the modest reading fee paid by Henry Swanzy of the *Caribbean Voices* radio program for which Naipaul read one of his father's stories, at Seepersad's request.[73] The seminal implications of the pen, which seems both a genealogical/literary inheritance and a mutually exchanged gift between father and son, reveals the peculiar nature of gift exchange in this post-indenture father-son relationship and complicates the specific gendered tensions outlined by Bloom's study of literary paternity as well as in Gilbert and Gubar's analysis of domestic fiction.[74] It signifies an important shift away from a unilateral assertion of the father's power and makes it misleading to transpose gender relations and feminist theory in the Anglo-American context on to a Caribbean one without signaling differences.

At the same time, there is not too much exaggeration in Naipaul's acknowledgment of his father's influence on his early work. *A House for Mr. Biswas* was inspired not just by his father's difficult life and his unceasing in-law troubles, but Seepersad himself had invented a character named Biswas in one of his short stories. In a twisted chronology, his father's stories reemerge in 1975 in a new edition that Naipaul finally introduces and dedicates in a belated fulfillment of his father's wishes, more than a decade after *Biswas* was published and long after his father's death. Naipaul's revelation of literary "cannibalism," which would more sympathetically be called influence by Bloom and intertextuality by postmodernists, is perhaps deliberately phrased in the language of culpability and consumption. It ironically enables Naipaul's desire to ingest and "continue" his father's life, but unlike his less successful father, to also "fulfill" it, as he writes in a letter to his mother after his father's death.[75]

Naipaul inherits not just his father's flair for prose, however, but his psychological fears, particularly his father's dread of unproductivity. His fears of having no significant story to tell and no material worthy of putting in print shadow his early writing. Both father and son share a common panic about wasted potential and stifled opportunity and to some extent react to that panic similarly by a turn to absurdity. Naipaul says in his 1983 foreword to *Biswas* some twenty years after its first publication, "It is that anxiety—the fear of destitution in all its forms, the vision of the abyss—that lies below the comedy of the present book."[76] While he ties it in this instance to the overarching fear of creative paralysis, "to have written no book," in the novel the anxiety is partly managed by filling in the "void" with the material structure of the house. Both Biswas's obsession with the house and Naipaul's with the book embody the particular fears of the colonial subject. Aware of being represented as rootless in space, ungrounded in history, and diminished in culture, even sharing that dismissive view, Naipaul's yearning, like Virginia Woolf's, for a metaphorical room of one's own in order to write is not disconnected from Biswas's literal longing for a house of his own.

The germ of infection haunts the son not, as in Bloom's paradigm borrowed from Freud, because the competitive son fears he will not live up to the father's achievement, but because the son is terrified of becoming his father. "When I get to your age I don't want to be like you," says Anand in a cruel but honest rejection of his father, a rebuff Biswas accepts because he agrees with his son.[77] Anand's eventual departure to England, "surely where life was to be found," fulfills that wish.[78] While Kincaid kills the mother figure, Naipaul does the same with the father in his novel, which begins with the death of Mr. Biswas. Naipaul's confession in an interview in 1991 comes as no surprise. He says, "I knew I was writing a very big book. If my father was alive, clearly, I wouldn't have been able to write it. I wouldn't have wanted to do it. . . . I don't know whether his death wasn't a kind of creative liberation for me. No one was looking over my shoulder."[79] Somewhat differently from the disturbingly comical account of the death and funeral of Biswas's father, for which Biswas is haplessly responsible, Naipaul's admission here that the novel would not have come into being had his father been alive—"looking over [his] shoulder"—is also haunted by the son's contrition. Naipaul's guilt about leaving his father behind (not just on the island but also in his writing career), of distancing himself from the family, and not returning immediately after his father's death underwrites his various tributes to him.

The virtually invisible mother is not the castrating figure here, although both in *Biswas* as well as in his nonfiction, Naipaul accuses his mother's family of symbolically castrating his father, who came from less affluent origins.[80] But castration is an inadequate term for the sheer force of familial and historical factors that subsume Seepersad and compel the son's desperate flight is an attempt to save himself from a similar petrifying fate. Likewise, the father's mirror stage promises not the recognition and replication of patriarchal law or the emergence into language but the horrifying lack of both. It is not coincidental that during the father's mental breakdown, one of Seepersad's paranoid delusions involved looking into the mirror and not seeing his face reflected in it.[81] This gaze into the mirror makes clear the collective kinship between Indo-Caribbean male and female subjects (Mala's gaze into the mirror revealing her own isolation), although they also have very different, gendered experiences of terror. Unlike the narcissistic gaze of psychic assurance and ego ideals, both men's and women's gaze into the mirror triggers the anxiety of insecure selfhood.

In a fraught but understated exchange between mother and son, the dread of the father's gaze into the abyss of absence is folded into family archive. But it is clear that Naipaul finds in the return of the repressed, in its uncanny revelations, the stuff of his cultural capital: the rawness of wounds, the urgency of panic, the masochistic pleasure of pain that, according to him, is the inevitable lot of the colonial subject. He finds out in a trip to the library that his father had been forced to conduct an animal sacrifice to Kali, the "black mother-goddess," not in order to appease her but, as it turns out, in response to threats by his in-laws who seek to discipline him for criticizing the "superstitious" ceremony in print. The sacrifice to the Gorgon-like, fierce, dark-skinned maternal deity is just one, in Naipaul's view, of many degrading compromises made to his in-laws by Seepersad, whose Arya Samaj sympathies would consider ritualistic animal sacrifice an abomination of pure faith. Naipaul reads about the entire incident many years later in the private-public space of the *Trinidad Guardian,* where, as he has revealed, family affairs find political relevance and public revelation. He subsequently returns from the Port-of-Spain library to demand an explanation from his mother. He narrates:

> She said, simply, "I didn't remember." She added, "Some things you will yourself to forget."
>
> "What form did my father's madness take?"
>
> "He looked in the mirror one day and couldn't see himself. And he began to scream."[82]

The mother's neutral, unemotional tone (at least as rendered by her son) makes his father's humiliation a commonplace.

In order to compensate for the treachery of abandonment, the repression of memory, *the father's loss of face,* Naipaul offers the very act of writing out trauma and thus to some extent exorcising it. His "going back" home entails not the literal act of return but the literary act of "the exercise of the vocation": the creation of a corpus that combats not just homelessness but the father's "fear of extinction" that the son has inherited.[83] Naipaul's fame will now certify his father's existence. His success will reflect its radiance on his father's dimmed ambitions and restore visibility to his face. Filial sickness and infection are revealed and "worked through," if not precisely healed, by the son who seeks greener literary pasture in exile. And yet notwithstanding Naipaul's repudiations of the land of his birth, supported by attempts to locate him as a cosmopolitan writer entirely free of national affiliation, many of his personal observations on his emergence as a writer tend to acknowledge the significance of his Trinidadian upbringing. *"Sixteen years later, in London, in a darker time, when I had grown to feel that I would never get started as a writer, I remembered the street and the people, and they gave me my first book,"* he admits.[84] Even in his travel writing, he returns again and again to memories of his formative childhood and adolescence in the Caribbean.

The general complaint, particularly by writers of the fifties generation who tended to move away from the Caribbean, that their vocation came at great cost must certainly be taken seriously considering grievances about difficult writing conditions, but it is only part of the story. The rich yield of Caribbean literature suggests that the region is anything but arid in creative inspiration. If one portion of the literature portrays toxic domesticity both in the individual family and in the nation at large, another lovingly glues together the shards of Caribbean identities (to borrow Derek Walcott's famous metaphor)[85] and roots itself, however ambivalently, in stories of community, kinship, and social bonds, as in Easton Lee's poetry.

In the previous chapter, I dwelt on the resistance to naming and to genealogy, due in part to the fragmentation of spatial dislocation and broken heritage. But with the passage of time, a more settled habitation and more stable memories reveal a different sense of domestic life, never completely blissful, but embracing more positively the fullness of daily Caribbean existence. Goodison's *From Harvey River: A Memoir of My Mother and Her People* presents a more conventional picture of aspiring middle-class domestic fiction, while also showing the complexities of its location. Beginning with a family tree but not retaining the patrimonial aura of the traditional genealogical script, the memoir is a deep, sustained homage to Goodison's mother, who was not just a loving parent but a strict one. Doris ("Dorice") Louise Goodison née Harvey also forged strong bonds with her community both in the small village of her birth and in the tough neighborhood in Kingston where she was forced to move in less affluent times ("Hard Life," as Goodison refers to it) with her many children. While Goodison's father is also an ideal figure, he takes second place to the mother, whose people and land, Goodison says, "was to shape my imagination for the rest of my life."[86] Despite touches of nostalgia and sentimentality, family and community are revealed in all their complex shades and eccentricities.

Almost in direct response to Kincaid's condemnatory account, Goodison's "autobiography of [her] mother" reinstates the strong woman as a productive influence rather than devouring fiend, and more generously claims a literary kinship. The memoir begins with dreams of her mother nearly thirty-five years after her death, when Goodison pictures her mother in heaven and claims that the latter gave her a book, which is the memoir she writes. It ends with a resolute image of inspiration and a more complete picture of the mother that historicizes the woman's significance in the Caribbean as a source of productivity. In the last line of the memoir, Goodison says of her mother, "She dipped her finger in sugar when I was born and rubbed it under my tongue to give me the gift of words."[87] While Mala's compulsion to mutilate herself by maiming her tongue with fiery spices is one toxic aspect of domestic fiction, a loving dab of sugar bestowed by a mother in her daughter's mouth suggests that the shadow of the plantation does not lead to deathly silence, and the history of slavery and servitude was not devoid of sweetness amid the suffering.

Historical trauma, by no means unique to the Caribbean, forcefully expresses itself in Caribbean novels in ways that specify the catastrophic consequences of colonialism and slavery. Kincaid and Naipaul's works, in particular, present these melancholic histories, but their rich literary output belies their emphasis on catastrophe and reveals the curative effects of writing. Like the other authors I present here, they stage national and diasporic tensions in domestic sites and within family circles, which are both dysfunctional and nurturing spaces. Freezing an entire population into endless mourning ignores the potential of their historical lives and shuts off the future by entombing them in a chronically diseased past. While we need not resort to clichéd recovery in the therapeutic models of opening, healing, or closing wounds,[88] messages of hope and healing cannot easily be dismissed in such contexts. Goodison's conversion of sugar's value from its exploitative industrial scene of production to the generative power embodied in her mother's multiple connotations of genius, including guardian spirit, family (gens), and place (genius loci), emancipates Caribbean genealogy from a singularly toxic domestic heritage without excising its traumatic history.

3 "Disasters in the Sun"

Crime and Carnival

Stick a shovel into the ground almost anywhere and some horrible thing or other will come to light. Good for the trade, we thrive on bones; without them there'd be no stories.

—Margaret Atwood, *The Blind Assassin*

Those who ought to know better nourish our crazy dreams of resurrection and redemption; those safely beyond the borders of our madness underwrite our lunacies.

—Shiva Naipaul, *Black and White*

One of the most striking aspects of representations of the Caribbean is its schizophrenic quality, particularly in the jarring contrast its circulation as a carefree paradise offers to the history of violence and terror depicted in the literature. This is not to suggest that the converse is impossible: that tourists are unaware of threat and danger in the contemporary Caribbean and that anglophone Caribbean literature is devoid of carnivalesque ribaldry, trickster humor, and irrepressible *jouissance*. My dwelling here on the bipolar contrast in representation is not intended to reinforce a stereotype either of untroubled holiday carousing or of irreversible deviance and dysfunction. Rather, incidents of crime and violence have their own stories to tell, and fictional and nonfictional accounts of these and other kinds of Caribbean social turmoil reveal—or, as the case may be, obscure—a history that can be neither crushed by the juggernaut of calamity nor buried under enabling myths of triumphant survival. They portray a complex and dynamic web of cultural conflict spun in specific historical conditions of trauma and survival, conquest and resistance, failure and achievement, joy and grief, tragedy and comedy.

Murder is a common occurrence, and regrettably no culture or region can claim a history free of such crime. The Caribbean is no different in this regard, but what makes it distinct is the pattern of crime in my subjects here: who is killed, why, and how shapes a universal experience in very specific ways. As the first epigraph suggests, the specter of "some horrible thing" roams all over the earth, haunting virtually every national history. In the late capitalist age of cynical commodity culture, there is a thriving market for the gory and the macabre and, as Margaret Atwood pointedly observes, on occasion there is nothing as good for "trade" as scandalous disasters sensationalized for a ghoulish spectatorship. But the marketing of the Caribbean through the schizophrenic qualities mentioned above is tied to lurid images that are dangerously superficial. I hope to undertake a deeper excavation.

Shiva Naipaul dryly refers to a Guyanese man who seeks dubious comfort in the 1978 catastrophe of Jonestown, where more than nine hundred Americans died after consuming a potion of Flavor Aid and Kool-Aid laced with cyanide. Now, the Guyanese man can claim with probably gloomy satisfaction that he is unlikely to have his uninformed English friends ever ask him "where Guyana is located."[1] Here, as we know, is the familiar Janus face of the Caribbean in metropolitan news accounts. When not reporting sunny skies and virgin beaches, they dish up hurricanes, coups, and mass suicide or murder. While immediately identifying Guyana on the map through the singular memory of the Jonestown tragedy is perhaps understandable, one would prefer a sober grasp of the deaths and their relationship to a particular history of the Americas, rather than a flattening of Guyanese culture through the metonymic appropriation of mass deaths.

As I have discussed in a previous chapter, the very soil of the Caribbean absorbs "disasters in the sun," a Shakespearean phrase expressing Horatio's fears for Denmark after the specter of Hamlet's father, the murdered king, is sighted.[2] Both the Naipaul brothers, V. S. and Shiva, share Hamlet's discourse of intellectual antipathy, the sharp anger of disillusionment in their observations of Caribbean polities. As Hamlet exclaims in his context, "Fie on't, ah fie! 'tis an unweeded garden/That grows to seed, things rank and gross in nature/Possess it merely."[3]

Other writers also echo this sense of anomie, although some stress productive social movements for change in the region. The particular specters that I raise here, the bones I unearth from the soil (to expose how they got there in the first place), tie regional causes to the historical effects of British and U.S. racial and class inequalities. While the "garden" of the Caribbean is occasionally bewailed as a "rank and gross" (post)colonial wilderness, George Lamming's phrase "the empire and the garden" suggests—and the delinquents here demonstrate—the intimacy between this pair and a long history of violence.

Jonestown and the Michael X murders, the main subjects in this chapter, continue to resonate in the present well after the official end of British empire and American racial bias. I discuss these events at length in order to locate them as specifically Caribbean crises, but also to note their wider implications. Various journalistic commemoratives on the thirty-year anniversary of the suicides appeared in October and November 2008, and a recent film, in the genre of a crime caper, includes a character playing Michael X with intriguing charges involving the British royal family. The fictional renderings do not tell a story of unmitigated disaster, however, notwithstanding their necessary critiques.

In analyzing what the different stories have to tell, I use the notion of caper not to dismiss the tragic consequences of the crimes, but to dwell on the possibilities of its different senses of play and masquerade as well as of frauds and audacious swindles. It may be unseemly to consider illegal acts and multiple deaths as associated with crime capers, especially considering that the entire Caribbean has been stereotyped into one big caper, a site of carnivalesque escapade or even a thrilling lark. Behind this consumerist dreamworld lie many others, including the weightier theological and messianic sense of Paradise, as this book has been tracing, as well as the socialist utopia that was used to legitimize the Jonestown commune. The betrayal of the messianic project and the utopian dreamworld sought within Jonestown ultimately led to its catastrophe. I will turn momentarily not to the historical materialist as Walter Benjamin advises but to literature, specifically Wilson Harris, to salvage a constructive sense of dreamworlds from the rubble of utopia, while the next chapter on magical realism more concretely focuses on the reenchantment and liberation of the imagination held hostage by postcolonial crises. Play as invoked here involves not simply mindless recreation or crass consumerism of spectacular disaster but theatrical aspects of performance and masking, which have serious consequences.

Jonestown was built in Guyana as a not playful but deadly earnest, if eventually misguided, escape from American adversity that ended in mass suicide, or, as some might flatly argue, murder. The Reverend Jim Jones in his final sermon (played on various television excerpts) referred to it as "an act of revolutionary suicide protesting the conditions of an inhumane world." Jonestown, to quote from Susan Buck-Morss's analysis of Stalinist techniques, was "the dreamworld of happiness promised to the masses and the nightmare awaiting those who were banished from it, that became the effective instrument of mass control."[4] Although she refers to two separate events in other contexts, one celebratory and one belligerent, in Jonestown they merged, and those who were in Jonestown rather than "those who were banished from it" experienced the nightmare after the promise.

Among the many commemoratives, scenes from an NBC documentary (a reporter and a cameraman from NBC lost their lives in the events leading to the suicides) show images of a number of followers, both black and white, giggling and singing, "We're a happy family, yes we are," recalling the popular children's song "If You're Happy and You Know It." This glimpse of elation reflects back with savage irony on the opening sequence that provides a view from an airplane circling the commune, which shows on the soil below hundreds of multicolored strips and patches of the corpses seemingly arranged, as one witness notes, like a "quilt": a colorful, chillingly intimate extended family locked together in the final embrace of death. Meanwhile, a portentous voice-over likens the thickly scattered bodies to "strange fallen fruit rotting in the tropical sun."[5] The quest for happiness had deadly consequences for the people who bought into Jones's performance as savior and believed that the commune would welcome a new heaven and a new earth. Instead, it became indelibly associated with apocalyptic disaster.

Although the poetic narrator in Fred D'Aguiar's version of the Jonestown events in the ironically titled *Bill of Rights* castigates himself for being the dupe of Jones, he is also quite facetious about the latter. As he cheekily puts it:

> Jim Jones doesn't know his okra
> From his bora;
> His guava from his sapodilla;
> His stinking-toe from his tamarind.
>
> He will get us all into a jam,
> A terrible pickle,
> A big muckle,
> An awful stew.[6]

Accentuating the incongruity of garden cultivation and pastoral nostalgia by urban Americans who knew little to nothing of the intense Guyanese landscape ("Mosquito nine mosquito ten/Mosquito nyam us all to death"), D'Aguiar borrows the English nursery rhyme "Ring a Ring of Roses" (itself recalling the medieval plagues) to deflate the idealism of the venture: "And all o' we is one,/And we all fall down."[7] The hint of paternalism toward the players tumbling down at the command appears more explicitly in the commune's obedience to the delusional patriarch:

> You see, Father had a vision, God help us.
> He said what paradise
> Was not; it was not this.
>
> Temple members, he went on, would be first
> To sample this
> Actual paradise.[8]

Instead, fleeing from one part of the New World to another in search of this elusive Eden, Jones's faithful abide by his lethal final orders to "Fall" down together. Paradise and anti-paradise are thus entwined in narratives of Jonestown. The Carnival slogan "all o' we is one" and the creolized "pickle," "muckle," and "stew," ironically reproduced here in their metaphorical meanings, distort communal play and social harmony into the shocking performance of mass suicide, where black and white bodies, male and female, adults and children, and even animals, do indeed attain a fatal, "mashed up" community.

While D'Aguiar has recourse to caustic humor, Wilson Harris's eponymous novel on Jonestown recuperates the seemingly irredeemable horror through the Carnival, not reductively, but as one of many historic episodes with restorative potential "shot through with chips of Messianic time."[9] Harris is not mocking in his use of Carnival, although this tactic is not unusual in the Caribbean. Some decades after Jonestown, the Jamaat al-Musilmeen coup in Trinidad of the A. N. R. Robinson government at Red House in 1990 and the looting that followed would be rendered in calypso form as a "Bakrnal," after the Jamaat leader, Yasin Abu Bakr.[10] Similarly, in the grotesque humor that characterizes Trinidad (discussed in more detail in a later chapter), Lord Kitchener's "One to Hang" and the Mighty Chalkdust's "Hang Him" were popular calypsos that cheerfully celebrated Michael's death sentence.

While politics as a pappyshow and death as a carnival may not seem to bode well for the region, bacchic irreverence seems a fairly healthy way of dealing with calamity, although it can never fully repair the trauma. Even as Michael X is finally characterized as one grand hoax, the jest is never too far away from the sinister and the tragic. If the Naipauls are correct in attributing the suicides and murders to lunacy, the insanity, I argue, is not a matter of inexplicable or characteristic frenzy in the

Caribbean, but of the destabilizing consequences of unaddressed social grievances. While Jonestown structures were dismantled (said to be carried away by neighboring Indigenous people) or allowed to rot into the wilderness, the final trial of Michael reminds Naipaul of a dummy Judas whipped in a carnival parade, clearly indicating that the Caribbean landscape and public culture find their own ways of absorbing social crises.

Jonestown in Nonfiction: Shiva Naipaul and Gordon K. Lewis

Shiva describes his reluctant arrival into Guyana to assess the aftermath of the Jonestown deaths as the beginning of a "jungly nightmare."[11] What Michelle Cliff perceives as Caribbean ruination—the agency of the rebellious wilderness fighting attempts to subdue it—he reads more negatively as the inevitable confluence of untamed landscape and uncivil politics. Not an island like Trinidad, Guyana assumes a menacing aspect, overrun by savannahs and jungles, huge waterfalls, and rivers that dwarf the smaller islands. After a brief description of this intimidating terrain, Shiva switches unsurprisingly to an account of the Guyanese political scene: the exacerbation of Afro-Indian tensions after the removal of socialist leader Cheddi Jagan in 1953 and the subsequent ascendancy of Linden Forbes Burnham with British and U.S. support, an ironic shortage of sugar, looting and plundering, "choke and rob," death squads, fear and paranoia, the deterioration of Georgetown, its regression to a Hobbesian state of nature: "Ruined people in a ruined setting."[12] More noteworthy than the allusion to the foreordained Fall is just how *natural* political chaos seems in such a "ruined setting." The people of Guyana supposedly live in an ungovernable wilderness that cannot be civilized by the legal decrees and civic compromises of the social contract.

Despite Shiva's frequently astute and occasionally compassionate analysis of the events leading to the Jonestown suicides, his disapproval of the rebellious character of the colonies and his reservations about the turbulent sixties—which his older brother shares—skews his perspective. The conclusion this leads him to is that there is something endemic not just about apocalyptic violence in the Caribbean but in the Third World at large that lures its victims with dreams of redemption only to devour them. Unlike the hysterical white woman who is convinced that she has been brought to Guyana on false pretenses and that she will die like the residents of Jonestown,[13] the natives of these regions willingly, if naively, walk into the voracious maws of delusion and death. Tossing socialism, anticolonial insurgency, sixties revolts, black radicalism, and feminism into a diabolically intoxicating mix, Shiva construes all participants in such societal strife as Jonestown residents in the making, propped up by reckless white liberals in the First World and black radicals in or from the Third World. Shiva's largely negative assessment of Black Power in Trinidad sums up his opinion of the larger political and regional turmoil the movement exemplifies for him: "Cynicism, calculation, genuine conviction, downright lies: all would be hopelessly confounded. Together, they would create a typical—and deadly—Third World potion."[14]

So established is this reading of willingly consuming poison that "drinking the Kool-Aid" now stands as a colloquialism for being gullible, for swallowing messianic, socialist, or any other kind of propaganda. (The fact that what was ingested or forced down the throats of those who died in Jonestown was mostly poisoned Flavor Aid, a cheap imitation, would probably be just as telling of Third World realities, where even the method of dying has to be substandard, a mere replica of the real thing.[15]) Jonestown residents in Shiva's figure of speech are not unique in willingly swallowing the hype of their leaders and the poison the latter offer them as they did on that critical "white night" after a series of rehearsals and preparations for suicide. Their ill-fated community serves as an uncanny emblem of the Sisyphean suicidal path Third World revolutions hurtle toward.[16]

But much as many Americans would like to disown Jonestown as indeed a typical Third World phenomenon or blame it on crackpot socialist dogma, Shiva's narrative travels from Guyana to the United States in an attempt to reexamine the metamorphosis of the People's Temple of Jim Jones in California to Jonestown in Guyana. The American edition of Shiva's *Black and White* was titled *Journey to Nowhere: A New World Tragedy* (Simon and Schuster, 1981). Like other Caribbean skeptics, Shiva is unwilling to exonerate American politics in the sixties and seventies, and although he sees in the fatal end of Jonestown many ingredients of Guyanese origin, he is also determined to read the recipe for disaster as a peculiarly North American one. He suggests that Jonestown techniques of controlling restless residents were no different from U.S. prisons and asylums. The Jonestown philosophy that everything "is justified in the pursuit of total human happiness" was part of the national myth.[17] In a poignant passage, he describes the unwanted remains of the dead even as government agencies, politicians, journalists, writers, librarians, sociologists, psychologists, and "taxonomists of all kinds" on either side of the Caribbean Sea hurried to categorize the tragedy.[18] Obsessively scrutinized, analyzed, and written about, the actual subjects of study were unsolicited scrap, or, as the NBC announcer might prefer, "strange fallen fruit rotting." The drastic comparisons may be deliberately dehumanizing to convey the sense of human waste, the bitter, unfruitful harvest of cumulative social marginalization and unbelonging.

Camera shots of the dead usually dwell on the innumerable corpses crowding the scene, many of them face down and linked together in poignant final embraces, and then move on to the hundreds of crumpled, used paper cups of poisoned fruit drink and the discarded syringes that litter the landscape. In one bizarre clip, two colorful parrots perch on a fence, surveying the ghastly scene like Benjamin's Angelus Novus in an almost parodic signification of the Eden-Hell configuration that has haunted the region.[19] Guyana "did not want those nine hundred bodies to enrich its soil . . . in death they had become hopelessly American. Nobody wanted them, not even family and friends. Scores of bodies remained unclaimed in the cold storage chambers of an Air Force base in Delaware," declares Shiva.[20]

Gordon K. Lewis, the noted political scientist, is even more caustic than Shiva about U.S. influence on Caribbean misfortunes, although his point of view is sympathetic to the socialist aspirations of the Jonestown community.[21] Shiva, for instance, is not as hostile to American capitalism as he is to American narcissism, escapism, promiscuity, extremism, patriotism, militancy, and hysteria, all of which he sees large doses of in the revolutions and counter-revolutions of the sixties.[22] But he reserves his harshest language for what he believes were the self-indulgent and self-absorbed motives of those turbulent times. The very notions of "tripping out" or being "into" something, he argues, betrays the errant nature of political, emotional, and intellectual investment in this era. "They were absurd, these men and women; they were also, most probably, quite harmless—as harmless as the germs that go to make up a common cold. But a common cold, given a suitable twist of fate, can turn into bronchial pneumonia. In this hot-house atmosphere of pampered self-consciousness, ideas—or what passed for ideas—floated like viruses. They were a disease you caught."[23] If we are to reverse climatological and regional stereotypes, following Alfred Crosby's epidemiological track of a Western source of disease, California, the western end of the American frontier, the whimsical space of dreaming, and at one point the alluring site of the gold rush, becomes the source of regional infection.

In another strange twist, this new quest in Guyana—or, in D'Aguiar's telling phrase, the "budding El Dorado" of Jonestown—turned out to be literally toxic.[24] Jones obtained a jeweler's license to stock up on cyanide, used to clean gold; those stockpiles were eventually used to create the nightmare of the Jonestown massacre. "America's wilder dreams have always rolled to the Far West. Fantasies flourish best in a warm, sensual climate," concludes Shiva sententiously, and perhaps with deliberate irony, given American stereotypes of a dysfunctional Caribbean that intermittently needs occupation by the U.S. military.[25] Lewis, like Shiva, also sees both the United States and Guyana as infected, but his estimate of the vectors of disease and his prognosis vary significantly from Shiva's.

While Shiva tends to read farce and revolution as misshapen twins, Tweedledum and Tweedledee in the fantastic Wonderland of the New World, Lewis identifies Jonestown ("from a Caribbean Viewpoint") as one of a series of universal human tragedies. Invoking Voltaire's satire of Panglossian faith in divine providence, he interrupts a complacent narrative of Reason and Enlightenment with reminders of natural disasters and human holocausts. One may speculate on the reasons for the frequent eruptions of the macabre and the murderous in our societies. In the case of Jonestown, however, Lewis has specific answers. In direct opposition to Shiva, he ascribes the implosion not to the apparent shenanigans of the sixties radicals, the hippies, and the feminists, but to the inescapable pincers of capitalism and racism in U.S. society at the time. The hundreds who followed Jones and fled to the Guyanese wilderness for refuge were not merely dupes, but desperate people who turned to the evangelical leadership of a white man to save them from intolerable conditions at home.

In her imaginative assessment of "the passing of mass utopia," Buck-Morss locates the twentieth century as the time of modernity's crisis, when Benjamin's wind-borne angel blown backward might survey, like the parrots on the fence in Jonestown, the debris of progress. Rather than target one or the other, Buck-Morss implicates both the Soviet Union and the United States in the loss of socialist and capitalist utopias. She explains, "It is here that Western capitalism and Soviet socialism need to be thought together as systems of power. Capitalism harms human beings through neglect rather than through terror. Compared to the personal will of a dictator, the structural violence of market 'forces' appear[s] benign. Those individuals (or groups) excluded from capitalism's dreamworlds appear themselves to be to blame. The fate of the poor is social ostracism. Their gulag is the ghetto."[26] Far from being the preferable alternative to Soviet dictatorship, the United States in the seventies also seems a place its residents find unlivable for various reasons, not just poverty or racism.

A quick contextualization might be in order here. After a fairly undistinguished career, Jones grew into a mystical leader with his community-building enterprises and church in Indianapolis in the mid-fifties. Driven away partly by local objections to his mixed-race congregation and partly by his own fears of a nuclear holocaust in the event the Cold War heated up, Jones moved his church in 1965 to Redwood, California. Now an ordained minister in the Disciples of Christ denomination, Jones drew large numbers of black people to his church, which retained, along with him at the center, a white, educated, middle-class leadership. Facing growing criticism and negative press reaction in California as well, what was now after a series of mutations the Peoples Temple shifted residence to Guyana by the mid-seventies, acquired land to raise crops, and introduced a self-supporting community of immigrants who were welcomed by the Forbes Burnham government in its avowed espousal of socialist enterprises.

We may stretch the American frontier now to include the Caribbean, which has long been employed as plantation partner, tourist haven, defensive base, and offshore factory when it suited its more powerful neighbor. Whereas official U.S. occupations have been rationalized as keeping the best interests of the Caribbean in mind, here the settlement by American citizens was intended not so much to save the Caribbean from itself but to protect the migrants from the country they fled. Threatened with legal action involving Jones's parental rights over his illegitimate young son, John-John, and harassed by family members who wanted their relatives back in the United States, Jonestown became the focus of possible U.S. congressional investigation and state intervention. After some of the residents attacked a visiting U.S. delegation and the few families who had decided to return with the delegation, killing Congressman Ryan, a cameraman, and a press reporter among others, the people in the commune, fearing harsh retaliation and deportation to the United States, killed themselves, some willingly, many likely coerced.

If Lewis sees nothing inexplicable about either the exodus to the Caribbean in search of refuge from U.S. society of the time or the subsequent self-destruction of the failed utopian experiment, it is because he does not fall into the usual characterization of socialism as crazy and totalitarian. Reminding us of the heritage of American socialism (now sternly repressed) and tying it to the activism of the American churches that took Christ's concern for the downtrodden and the underprivileged seriously, he condemns, instead, the crass materialism and competitiveness of American society that forced people either to run the rat race or simply to run away. Echoing Thoreau's sense in the nineteenth century of the urge to withdraw from "lives of quiet desperation,"[27] Lewis sees in the community's flight the extreme measures to which the misfits and rejects of capitalist and racist society are driven.

The flight into the wilderness to test one's sense of identity, to face one's innermost demons, to shuffle off the worldly coil, is an almost universal archetype, particularly in spiritual allegory. But in colonial societies, the wilderness functioned as actual sanctuary from the shackles of coerced industrial modernity in more immediate ways, as Indigenous people, runaways, and maroons fled into remote, inaccessible areas and lived undercover in swamps, woods, and mountains. The stereotypes of Guyana in its entirety as a jungle ignore its urban development. But more to the point, they overlook the historical significance in plantation societies of untamed land that tantalizingly held the promise of freedom and inspired slave flights.[28]

The flight of Jones's black following signified the modern connotations of the slave trajectory, the underground that bolted southward. But middle-class, white Americans who believed they were captive to an unwanted lifestyle also accompanied the many black people who felt they were noncitizens. Lewis was probably right in surmising that the rationalistic, consumerist, modern urban lifestyles drove this community to what was perceived as "nonrational" ends, which he distinguishes from the unproductively irrational. He observes, for instance, "that American society as a whole is in deep crisis. The rationality of its economic and technological apparatus stands in stark contrast to the irrationality of its ideological superstructure."[29] Ironically, this very contradiction explains the ultimate failure of the Jonestown community to find alternatives other than suicide. The crisis Lewis is alluding to is an offspring of two strange bedfellows, American capitalism and American evangelism, suggesting that the stresses of the former lead to the frequent convulsions of the latter, including the national obsessions with cults, aliens, and messiahs.

Initially, the Jonestown community's flight may have been nonrational in a system of radically different values and objectives, but all it was doing was putting into practice what Voltaire's Candide had learned the hard way. The inhabitants of the commune might argue that they were simply trying, like Candide, "to cultivate our garden."[30] In the Marxist theory of alienation, estranged labor, alienation from nature, and alienation from one's society are trussed together in a triple whammy.[31] The commune, beginning a process of de-alienation with socialist and spiritual undertones, ultimately sank under the weight of what might be called vanguardist leadership and messianic faith. In trying to escape the alienated character of capitalist life—by trying to forge a close community, doing manual labor, growing and selling their own produce—the Jonestown residents ultimately replaced the commodity fetish with the fetish of the messiah in the figure of Jones. Regardless of how disturbing or aloof the drug-abusing, mentally unstable, physically weakened Jones had become to the community before he was found shot in his quarters amid the ruins of his dream project, he held a dangerous charisma for his supporters. Both the downfall of the redemptive leader and the community's submission to his domination reveal for Lewis the hubris of Greek classical tragedy, not the farcical element perceived in Shiva's disenchanted version. In D'Aguiar's long poem, Jonestown acquires characteristics of both farce and tragedy, while Harris finds a carnivalesque renewal and affirmation through a classical sense of comedy.

However, Shiva carefully avoids the overwrought condemnation of bizarre cults that influenced most media accounts of Jonestown. His more thoughtful analysis includes a genuine attempt to understand the motivations of the supposedly brainwashed victims. "Exaggeration, humbug, downright lies—all existed in Jonestown. It was not a paradise. But nor was it the hell on earth that its enemies made it out to be."[32] Like the Nation of Islam, an equally controversial enterprise in a predominantly Christian nation, Jones's American church worked actively on behalf of the community, offering food, legal and medical assistance, structure, and comfort to drifters, troubled youth, the elderly, and the poor. Countering the "atrocity stories" of the critics of Jonestown are those by witnesses and participants who believed in the idealism of the project.

What is baffling about Shiva's retelling, however, is his indifference to the civil rights movements of the sixties, which leads him to parody and downplay their struggles and achievements. If poor black people were driven by their paranoia about imminent genocide, and the white (despite claims of Native American ancestry) middle-class Jones played on these and other fears, just what were the social conditions that led to such hysteria? What led hippies to rebel against the social mores of their parents; students to agitate against the Vietnam War and for university courses with more of a sense of cultural diversity; women, black people, gays, lesbians, and other minorities to demand equal rights?[33] Shiva seems curiously uninterested in the very legitimate reasons for the civil rights movements that raged across the United States, firing up other countries as well, or even in the momentous civil rights legislations that came out of these conflicts. Like all other movements for change, they had their risks and pitfalls, but they were hardly the drug-induced frenzies of a mindless mob of misfits. The demonization of all these groups in his book unnervingly echoes the discourse of the conservative right, which tends to find in the revolts of the sixties the beginning of social decay, rather than the inevitable reaction against an exclusionary national structure.

Chaos, Genesis, and Apocalypse in Jonestown: Wilson Harris, Lakshmi Persaud, and V. S. Naipaul

If Shiva attributes events in both the United States and Guyana to social chaos in its most negative sense, Wilson Harris's novel *Jonestown,* published almost two decades after Shiva's nonfictional account, reintroduces chaos as a positive and dynamic principle. Beginning with several epigraphs on Mayan civilization and on chaos theory, the novel offers multiple and sometimes contradictory readings of history at both the cosmic and the local level.

Time, space, mind, and matter explosively fuse together in the novel so that centuries collapse between Mayan sacrifices and the Jonestown suicides, between Walter Ralegh's search for El Dorado and Jones's quest for utopia in the wilderness. They all become part of parallel universes, an enigmatic "memory theatre" in which the specters of the past don't just haunt the present, they coexist with it. In obvious allusions to Ahab's narcissistic obsession with the whale, Francisco, the lone survivor of the self-destructive enterprise led by Jonah, Jim Jones's fictional counterpart in the novel, is the only one left, like Ishmael, to tell the tale. His last name, Bone, implies the resurrection of the word, the survival of human creativity, and the immortality of art: "What curious memorials a bone inscribes, draws, paints, builds, sings in the mind, the exiled mind, the solitary mind and soul on the margins of doomed civilizations."[34] Harris would agree with Benjamin that art has a redemptive value that is different from and exceeds an instrumentalist rationality, a thesis I will pursue at more length in the next chapter, on magical realism. But what is striking in Harris's resurrection of the bone is the specific approach that characterizes his work: from the grisly remains of death and disaster, he retrieves salvific potential, a usable past of not just psychic but geological resilience.

Harris repeats many of the themes and concepts of his earlier novels. The riffs in plot, figures, and narrative structure exemplify his philosophy, which is strongly influenced by an experimental new science. The concept of simultaneity, of something being many things at once, of someone being many entities in different places and times, he creatively adapts from quantum physics.[35] Thus, not only are his characters interchangeable within the same novel, such as Francisco and his East Indian alter ego Deacon, or Francisco and his mother, or Deacon and his bride, and so on, but stock characters such as the Dantesque guide and mentor, the dreamer-narrator, the confessional figure of W.H., the mother-son duo, the male pairs who are twinned in often hostile and competitive relationships (factually presenting Guyanese ethnic conflict in this case, although as a rule Harris is not invested in realistic sociohistory), recur through many of his novels.

As a result of these fertile, phoenix-like revivals, Caribbean history, like Harris's fiction, embodies a constantly renewed plenitude despite the constant depredations. Harris goes beyond merely avoiding polarities; he actively severs and reassembles bodies, souls, and contexts, sculpting bizarre reformulations from different perspectives. The effect of his prose is different from the stimulations of Kamau Brathwaite's video Sycorax style, not a mobile, visual collage of manipulated computer graphics and lexia, but nevertheless conceptually dynamic and disorienting. Multiple personality "disorders" seem to embody more accurately for Harris the schizophrenic nature of reality. But the curative factor for its possible ill effects is always at hand: despite destructive acts across time and cultures, he inevitably retrieves "the seed of value" in the agents as well as in the victims of violence.[36]

For example, the bone that signifies the epic possibilities of (re)creative art is both a mundane precursor to technological literacy and a restorative tool. It is also the hard evidence of survival—the rem(a)inder of life and the power of the word—despite several evolutionary cycles and technological revolutions. In his brief discussion of "transubstantiation," Harris asks, "How can one begin to revise the technologies in which we lodge our furies, technologies that we have planted around the earth and which seem immoveable? How can we begin to revise them unless one looks very deeply into the capacity of fiction by way of its imageries and textual perspectives to 'consume its own biases'?"[37] Francisco Bone thus embodies the generative "capacity of fiction" to renegotiate the traumatic past and appease its "furies."

The religious overtones of resurrection and redemption are not strictly Christian, since Harris borrows myths and beliefs from many cultures. The metaphorically cannibalistic consumption of the body of Christ has a different connotation in the ancient Carib story of the bone flute that Harris describes on more than one occasion. He says, "The ancient Caribs possessed a bone flute that was made from the body of the enemy.

They consumed a morsel of the flesh of their enemy and they thought thereby they would understand the secrets of the enemy, what the enemy was planning to do, how he would attack them, how he would ravage their villages. The peculiar thing is that the bone flute also became the seed of music."[38] What begins as a primitive cultural superstition with all its macabre inferences to controversial Carib cannibalism ends as a source of poetic imagination, a thing of beauty. The sublime aspect of terror is not without its attraction for Harris, but in this dramatic shift from its brute nature to the beauty of artistic creation in the above passage, the enemy literally becomes one of us. Whatever little consolation the enemy may derive from being consumed in such transubstantiation, Harris clearly imbues the process with a regenerative aura.[39] If in Christ's predestined murder there lies the providential seeds of human absolution, in the legacy of violence in the Caribbean there is still a potential for "*La Pénitence* and *Le Repentir,*" the names of two French estates in the novel with historical resonance.[40] And not just for repentance, but also for great art that surmounts the murderous specificity and materiality of the quotidian in order to achieve a more enabling, forbearing cosmic perspective.

In thus exonerating "mystical dismemberments,"[41] Harris may seem perilously close to Pangloss's "metaphysico-theologo-cosmonigology," which assumes that "everything is necessarily for the best purpose."[42] But whatever the risks of cosmic idealization and rescue through fossil memory, Harris is as deeply committed to an earthly ethics of forgiveness and reconciliation as he is to a genuinely cross-cultural dialogue and exchange. His model of the poet-singer is not Medusa but Orpheus, whose celestial music moved beasts and stone, and who continued singing even after his head was severed from his body. Harris's supple language and flexible, shape-changing characters express what he calls the "*limbo-anancy* syndrome," inspired by the material limits of slave movement on the ships of the Middle Passage. Attributing, like Brathwaite, the origin of the limbo dance on slave ships to encourage exercise on cramped decks, Harris reads in the bodily contortions of slaves as they slide under a gradually lowered stick the promise of a "far-reaching new poetic form" that is both specifically Caribbean and inspiringly universal, "an activation of unconscious and sleeping resources in the phantom limb of dismembered slave and god."[43]

Quoting Brathwaite's depiction of "knees spread wide" in the limbo dance, Harris maps the graceful and deceptively fragile motion of a spider's legs onto cultural survivals and reinventions such as stilt dancers and African Anancy folktales.[44] But given his cross-cultural imagination, he does not limit the dynamic metaphor to Africa or to slavery. He includes "the Egyptian Osiris, the resurrected Christ and the many-armed Goddess of India, Kali, who throws a psychical bridge with her many arms from destruction to creation."[45] Embracing death with arms "spread wide" involves a particular "poeticist" consciousness that obviously grates on a rational-secular-historicist perspective. Harris, as Paget Henry states, is a poeticist who "breaches the ego's conventions separating life and death," reconciles extremes, heals ruptures, and converts the void into a gateway.[46] For Harris, the minutiae of violent events are transfigured by the power of the imagination, which transforms the darkness of the former into the luminosity of the latter. The spirit survives the assault on the flesh, mortal error is redeemed by a vigilant grace. Harris refuses the absolutism of death and thereby rejects the negativity of most accounts of Jonestown. The novel instead ends with Bone/Deacon hurtling down the abyss of death but falling, along with the Predator, into "the net of the huntsman Christ."[47] In thus finding a literal space for both the Predator and the victim to face each other, to share intimacy, Harris encourages, as he does in his embrace of many contradictory and antagonistic cultures, the possibility of the reunion of diverse, even hostile, elements.

While the "jungly" surroundings rattle an already nervous Shiva Naipaul, "wilderness music" offers the wise Mr. Mageye the lessons of acceptance, survival, and ceaseless transformation, or to use Harris's phrase elsewhere, the universal recycling of "infinite rehearsal." Guyana therefore neither is defined/defiled by the Jonestown slaughter, nor does it merely transcend it. Out of the void emerges a new consciousness; out of chaos, genesis. The apocalypse signals if not a new heaven then certainly a new earth. Harris implies that the soul awakens by "coming abreast" of the carnage of the past, thus making the contemplation and transformation of "Injustice" more significant than "mechanical Justice."[48]

By contrast, *Escape from Jonestown,* the CNN special by Soledad O'Brien that aired on November 13, 2008, commemorating the thirty-year anniversary of the mass deaths, showed few supporters of the theory of renewal. Most of the interviewed survivors still seemed severely traumatized, and the extraordinary footage of the period, including the dramatic assassination of Congressman Ryan, the horrifying images of hundreds of dead bodies, among them children, and the now virtually abandoned site with its ominous air of emptiness tend to emphasize stark tragedy and the waste of lives, suggesting that Shiva's reactions are not isolated. Even D'Aguiar seems not to share Harris's reconciliatory approach, characterizing Jones as the hypnotic snake in the garden: "*I resembled Medusa/But lacked her appalling power . . ./He looked me straight in the eye/I was the one who turned cold as stone/He slithered away in the razor grass.*"[49]

Deborah Layton's biographical account of her involvement with Jones's church at a young age and her nerve-wracking flight from Jonestown years later similarly endows Jones, who believed he was Lenin in his past life, with mesmerizing seduction. Her account of her rapes by her "Father" has overtones of incest, and, as the second chapter of this book discusses, the relationship with the patriarch becomes "infected." Layton reveals disturbing details of Jones's vituperative responses to his enemies, imagined and real, which include ordering his loyal staff to send letters saturated with leaves of poison oak to those he wished to punish for insubordination. Like Michael X, Jones in his heyday was courted by the powerful and the famous with plenty of capital, and he used these contacts for leverage. However, Layton also wonders if her repeated warnings to American authorities were ignored because the majority of his followers were black. She moves from ironic titles like "Exodus to Paradise" and "Guyana—the Promised Land" to a total disavowal of the project: "It is not the dream world they [the followers] came to so willingly. Jonestown is not the Promised Land they envisioned."[50]

There is something woeful about the signs that hung in the covered sheds of Jonestown: "Black is Beautiful"; "Love One Another"; and one particularly unsettling legend: "Those who do not remember the past are condemned to repeat it." More similar to the Naipauls' perspective than Harris's, Lakshmi Persaud's bleak novel *For the Love of My Name* includes a section on Jonestown, although the focus is Forbes Burnham's dictatorship and the ethnic conflagration between black and East Indian Guyanese in this period. Unlike Harris's evocation of masks as creative art or enigmatic psyche, the purple masks worn by the supporters and enforcers of the regime emphasize violence, kinship, and sacrifice tied to allegiances of blood and ethnic absolutism. The purple mask covers over the Levinasian face of humanity and imposes the frozen visage of terror, as Afro- and Indo-Guyanese are caught within Forbes Burnham's spider web.[51] The scorched earth policies as they turn on each other recall Shiva's condemnatory analysis of Georgetown. One of the characters in Persaud's novel says tersely, "I see abandoned grey houses, gardens and yards gone wild. Weeds seed."[52] Meanwhile, the narrative of flight from the country provides an ironic counterpoint to the flight from the

United States into Jonestown. But East Indians are not the only ones who feel compelled to flee the country: the long lines at the airport include a wide cross-section of people leaving probably for Canada and the United States. As someone rhetorically asks, "Who has a future here?"[53]

Persaud changes names of historical figures and refers to the East Indians not as an ethno-national category but as a rural group, the "country Mayans." The novel is set in fictional Maya, but the Guyanese connections are clear. In what seems to be an allegorical plot twist, the dictatorial president is murdered by his sister, who rejects the blood loyalties demanded by the mask and poisons her brother to end repression. In adding to the various theories that circulate about Forbes Burnham's death under somewhat mysterious circumstances in a hospital, this account suggests that Guyanese genealogy needs to cast aside racial or ethnic consanguinity in favor of a broader national sense of family. Despite this message, Persaud's sympathies for East Indian tribulations tend to predominate from time to time, even as she presents the unraveling of the entire nation. Although not named as Jonestown, the commune in the novel becomes yet another site of torture, rape, and abuse and its members are believed to instigate riots in the city. Vasu, the East Indian who decides to spy on the commune and who finds incriminating evidence, is tortured and almost killed. He loses his mind as a result.

The Jonestown legend on being condemned to repeat history from colonial catastrophe to postcolonial crisis seems to hang over the entire country as a long line of Mayans shuffle through the "Departures" area of the airport: "These weary feet are not chained. It is not 1682. It is 1982."[54] The novel opens with the literal enactment of Revelation 16:20—"*And every island fled away and the mountains were not found.*"[55] The island of Maya has sunk into the ocean and what we read of the novel is a flashback to the past, an archival memory that is opened up by a researcher. We are therefore not in Harris's messianic but in apocalyptic time, in which societies with shaky foundations will collapse, a biblical prophecy that Persaud uses to heavy didactic effect. Although she is by no means as pessimistic as the Naipauls, in some ways the novel echoes their judgments on postcolonial societies that seem bent on implosion, not Harris's mystical reconciliation and faith in fossil survivals.

Harris makes multiple references to Carnival in his novel. The interchangeable roles, the masking, the "theatre of enigma," the fluid identities (breaking conventional ego boundaries) fold the texture of life itself into the brilliant scenes of Carnival, which, like the natural seasons, exhausts itself and then begins a fresh cycle. Not all interpretations of the mutability of Carnival view it as enabling the "digesting of trauma," as in Harris's parables of seasonal regeneration.[56] V. S. Naipaul, whose stark realism, lofty understatement, and crystal-clear prose presents a direct contrast to Harris's style, also tends to read certain events in the Caribbean as echoes of Carnival, but less sanguinely. Carnival, Harris would say, reenacts significant moments of world history—quite different, as we will see, from Naipaul's perspective. Where the imaginative life of fantasy is the saving grace of the Caribbean for Harris, fantasy is precisely the millstone that weighs down the past and blights Caribbean futures for Naipaul. Rather than enhancing human consciousness, carnivalesque elements infantilize and retard the region: Harris's superego, to put it somewhat facetiously, regresses to the id. While some of Naipaul's early novels such as *The Suffrage of Elvira* tend to see politicians in picaroon societies (Trinidad being one example) as latent criminals, he later combines this affinity between politics and crime with a popular culture seduced by the deadly cool of American gangsters.[57] The odious kinship between politicians and the thugs whose strongholds are guarantees of party votes has certainly created problems, particularly in Jamaica.

But the difference ultimately lies in the terrain of action. The deadliest consequences of European colonial power play, until the imploding World Wars, were wreaked overseas. Western Europe itself seems to have recovered and carried on, building a great culture and civilization. So, too, the United States. The Caribbean has no such happy outcome, according to Naipaul. It is doomed to echo in falsetto the deep and meaningful booms of weighty revolutions elsewhere, the painfully inadequate mimic of the American, French, and Spanish wars.

The failed mimicry survives in the twentieth century. A title like "A Handful of Dust: Cheddi Jagan and the Revolution in Guyana" expresses Naipaul's later views of Jagan's socialist aspirations for Guyana.[58] A handful of dust—borrowed from the title of a Waugh novel, which ends with the hero imprisoned on the savannah, doomed to read aloud the works of Charles Dickens—is what Jagan is left with, frozen as he is in the mausoleum of what is for Naipaul the outmoded ideology of Marx. Naipaul's remarks on the legacy of Jagan's archrival and nemesis, Forbes Burnham, are even more telling. In the Botanical Gardens of Georgetown, established as a seat of learning by the British, he adds, is a monument to the black leader after his death. "It is a spiderlike structure, with a low central pavilion with an outer colonnade of concrete brackets that look like spider's legs. The intention was that the founder of the Cooperative Republic should be embalmed and displayed for ever, like

Lenin; but something went wrong and the body decomposed before it could be treated."[59]

Dust and decomposition are pretty conclusive scenarios for Naipaul, unlike Harris's regenerative use of them. The Anancy-like memorial signifies mummification, and a botched one at that; not the enlivening gateway of limbo or fossil survivals but the deluded fancies of a backward-looking mentality. The section in *The Writer and the World* titled "Africa and the Diaspora," a collection of essays and articles written through the years, returns again and again to Black Power and Afrocentric movements, a preoccupation that drove Naipaul to write one of his most disturbing novels, *Guerrillas,* which, he claims, "lost [him] about half [his] readership" in England.[60]

In an article titled "The World and the Home," Homi Bhabha reflects on the relationship between history and literature and comes to conclusions that seem similar to Harris's theories on the subject. The concurrent discussions of history and literature in most postcolonial criticism, including within the Caribbean, stirs unease in some quarters, particularly when creative writing is seemingly rendered hostage to historicist conventions. Literature is not merely a crude reflection of history, the argument goes, and vulgar historicism reduces it to a puny adjunct rather than to a creative force of its own. What makes the task of separation difficult, though, is that most of the writers in this field deliberately tend to use historical events with literary license quite overtly in their fiction. Historians would no doubt share the nervousness for other reasons given the different disciplinary backgrounds of both. How can literature be capable of doing justice to the scientific objectives of history? What does history mean—what is its outcome—in the literary imagination?

In Bhabha's argument, as with Harris, fiction trumps history *precisely because it displaces and distorts* the latter, and thereby produces a more "profound understanding of what constitutes human necessity and agency."[61] Toni Morrison's incoherent version of slavery (what Paul Gilroy terms the slave sublime), the "undecipherable languages" of her novel *Beloved,* expresses, in the most appropriate manner for Bhabha, the unspeakable, repressed history of slave infanticide.[62] For Bhabha, then, if the task of history is to shine the light of blinding clarity on worldly events, the work of literature is necessarily to dim that light, and paradoxically to make the events more perceptible and perceptive by placing them in shadow. Fiction manages "to both 'obscure' [the] political role and to articulate it the better."[63] Harris, in particular, would appreciate Bhabha's point that this interpretation makes the literary subject "the nest of the phoenix, not its pyre," the latter a disagreeable reality that presumably the historian cannot evade in the disciplinary attention to fact. "When historical visibility has faded, when the present tense of testimony loses its power to arrest, then the distortions of memory offer us the image of our solidarity and survival," Bhabha concludes,[64] an assertion that might just as well apply to Harris's evocation of Jonestown, which pays hardly any attention to actual events or accurate chronology.

Without wanting to minimize the enabling, suggestive force of Bhabha's argument, I want to consider more critically the ability of fiction to shadow, to render diffuse and indistinct "the present tense of testimony." What of the possibility that fiction can dim the light of history with the insistence on pointless self-immolation, not on rebirth? Naipaul's use of historical events in *Guerrillas* tends to do just that. My point here is not to assess how accurate Naipaul's historical memory is or even to maintain that Harris's creative distortions are preferable to Naipaul's, but to consider the potential effects of Naipaul's calculated expropriation of Trinidadian and English social realities in this particular novel. Unlike Harris, Naipaul represents his views through a realist frame, making the task of sifting through his interpretations difficult in a different way from Harris's more abstract rewrites.

Michael X and the Killings in Trinidad

In 1972, a mere six years before the Jonestown deaths, just two years after the Black Power revolution, a sensational court trial was under way in Trinidad after a couple of murders were discovered in a particularly strange concatenation of circumstances. In mid-February of that year, the local police had responded to a fire reported at Christina Gardens, a seemingly innocuous suburban property rented from its owner, Mrs. Mootoo, by self-styled Black Power radical and activist Michael X, alias Michael Abdul Malik ("Servant of God"), alias Michael de Frietas, at that point visiting Guyana with his family. Patrolling the grounds, the police, possibly acting on a tip, discovered below a bed of lettuce, under the shade of flowering trees, the badly decomposed body of a young black male, later identified as Joseph Skerritt, a twenty-five-year-old resident of Port-of-Spain and Michael's cousin. A few days later on the northern side of the house, another body, this time of a white woman identified as Gale Benson, the twenty-seven-year-old English companion—the converted Muslim wife—of one of Michael's American associates, Hakim Jamal, was discovered beyond the coconut tree–lined boundary of the fence. She had been killed even earlier than Skerritt, more than a month before her murder was discovered. The court trial attracted attention across the Atlantic, not just in England from where, after fourteen years, Michael had fled back to Trinidad under the shadow of threatened arrest, but also in the United States. Among the many scribes attending the trial was V. S. Naipaul, recording it as a special feature for the *Sunday Times*, which had, like other English newspapers, created Michael's celebrity status and then exploited his notoriety in England.

One of the accounts of this figure, *The Life and Death of Michael X* by James Sharp, (mis)identifies "the novelist V. J. [*sic*] Naipaul" at the murder trial, adding that he was "a fellow countryman of Michael's and as such presumed to understand his peculiar mentality more clearly than his abashed former apologists."[65] With the bonus of the perspicacious insider added to his role as objective outsider (having left Trinidad in his late teens and never ceasing to announce his alienation from it), Naipaul does indeed claim the ability to understand the "peculiar mentality" of his compatriot, who inspired him to expand the journalistic pieces into the essay "Michael X and the Black Power Killings in Trinidad: Peace and Power" in 1973 (with a long postscript in 1979), and to write the fictional version, *Guerrillas,* in 1975. The pointed articulation of individually planned executions with an entire social and political movement personalizes and criminalizes the latter. Just as Jonestown comes to reduce Guyanese history into the nadir of mass suicide for many, Michael's murders are the flashpoint for Trinidadian ethnic and political ignition in Naipaul's account of "Black Power Killings."

But what made Black Power *not* irrelevant in regions that were dominated by a black majority, if not numerically, then by political advantage? What were legitimate grievances in the social justice movement that Naipaul links to the isolated criminalized figure of the condemned killer? He decisively asserts that Black Power invents and fights its own bogeys. "But there is no enemy. The enemy is the past, of slavery and colonial neglect and a society uneducated from top to bottom."[66] However, in the seventies, not just in Trinidad but also in black majority Jamaica, the past and present were not as severed from each other as Naipaul would like to believe. To quote an opposing point of view, "One hundred and sixty years after emancipation, the culture of slavery still casts its shadow over the entire Caribbean. . . . Despite significant advances in educational levels, employment policies and, to some degree, ownership patterns, the African heritage is still largely devalued in a region with a population—with the exceptions of Trinidad and Guyana—which is overwhelmingly of African descent."[67]

Black Power was also about more than just black cultural image. The riots and demonstrations of that period snowballed to impressive numbers with the involvement of other citizens in what began as a small university-driven event.[68] Far from being a simple export of Black Power from across the Atlantic, as Naipaul and like-minded critics claim, there were local grievances that both majority communities in Trinidad shared (and, of course, others they did not). The march to Caroni that was accomplished under threat of ethnic riots proceeded without such a feared outcome, and while rural East Indians did not exactly rush out to embrace the black marchers, water and other refreshments were placed along the route, an important gesture of hospitality where direct solidarity may not have been forthcoming. More important, Black Power, despite its categorical label, was hardly the homogenous, united movement it was made out to be. While the Williams administration eventually made a series of concessions to ease tensions, and the movement enabled more access to the public sphere for many black people, opinion is still divided on whether the movement was revolutionary or not.[69] Naipaul is not alone in parodying the excesses of Black Power. Both Samuel Selvon and Caryl Phillips have done so, although these authors have also been far more critical of racism than Naipaul.[70] Earl Lovelace's more ambivalent portrayals of the Black Power movement incorporate elements of commodified carnivalesque culture and electoral politics that merely paraded and performed resistance. But he also believes that it did challenge, however temporarily, the official regime of the neocolonial elites.[71]

Michael X's autobiography begins not with race but with the modalities of class in a stereotypical Caribbean family: an unobtrusive grandfather, a "sturdy black bridge" of a grandmother, a dominating mother, and an absent father, whose Portuguese background provided the light skin that was so cherished by his mother. Soon after revealing that eight people lived in the three rooms of his grandmother's house where he was raised in Belmont, a poor neighborhood just a step up from Laventille, he recollects, "My mother would point out the Governor's house, the Botanical Gardens and how clean and neatly painted the houses of white folks were. 'One day when you're grown up we're going to live around here,' she would say."[72]

Michael's later struggle with housing in England, his succession of different ghetto residences, his association with racketeering landlords, his pimping and poncing in dicey neighborhoods of Cardiff and London are all related to what Lamming, adapting the phrase from Derek Walcott, would call "the castle of my skin": where and how one lives is determined by one's perceived color (the light-skinned de Freitas was labeled black in England). Whatever Michael's trials and tribulations in London, however, he was no political dissident, outraged citizen, or disgruntled worker, at least, not for very long. His organization, the Racial Adjustment Action Society, or RAAS—with its ultimately unfunny pun on "rassclot," a Jamaican obscenity meaning "blood-cloth" or used menstrual pads—was seen as something of a joke, however serious its origins in combating English racism. So while his various attempts to seize the day are the flotsam thrown up by the vortex of his troubled background, he is not the singular embodiment of Black Power or any other ideology even if he claimed to be influenced by it. If anything, despite his various contradictory attempts to participate in anti-white rhetoric, he lived the high life when he did mainly because of wealthy white patronage. Ironically, he became one of the first targets of new laws against inciting racial hatred, a trial he ultimately fled.

Sharp notes several instances of suspicion toward the prodigal son by the Trinidad locals who were less easily taken in, unlike some white liberals and aspiring radicals in London, by the various messianic postures adopted by someone who, it was said in his childhood, was clearly headed for the gallows. "In Trinidad itself, a small island, none of the political parties had welcomed him and even the resident Black Powerites denied him, saying that their organizations were in no way affiliated to any of Malik's groups."[73] The initial chilliness turned out to be justified. Sharp adds that the general public feeling during the trial, in contrast to the various celebrity sympathizers in England and the United States, was quite hostile. "The fact that this man, [who] many people thought ought to be in jail in England, had the nerve to come back, set himself up in a posh house, scatter cash about like autumn leaves, stick his nose into all sorts of affairs that didn't concern him, and pose as some Oriental prophet leading his children to a promised land was enough to persuade the ordinary citizen that he probably did kill Skerritt, and if the truth be known, others besides."[74] And yet, despite the obvious tension between the national and the diasporic, this is the self-proclaimed savior who is seen as so quintessentially the *Trinidadian* Black Power radical by Naipaul.

Guerrillas, however, is unable to sustain the strain of such alignment for long. In fact, Naipaul's portrait of the fictional counterpart to Michael X, Jimmy Ahmed, is on occasion unnervingly accurate in revealing the latter's alienation, his solitary brooding, his febrile ramblings in various prose fragments (apparently based on Michael's foray into writing), and his only sporadic interest in social progress or political activism, despite his poses and affectations. But it becomes increasingly clear that to the unsympathetic third-person narrator Jimmy is a parody of the parody that the black revolutionary already represents for Naipaul. With the ridiculously inflated titles, the inept allusions to English classics, the pose of the Haji, the grandstanding, even his claims of being black or alternatively focusing on his Chinese shopkeeping background (when neither community claims him), Jimmy is a pathetic yet sinister figure. His right to be called a revolutionary is disputed by Harry: "Jimmy was always washed up here. I don't know who told him otherwise. I don't know what they told him in London."[75]

While Naipaul is severe in his disfigured characterization of the black revolutionary, he is not much kinder to white liberals and is as uncompromising as Shiva about what he considers the metropolitan tendency to encourage the wrong sort of "other" and confer upon him an entirely misguided celebrity status. If Jimmy is marked by the repeated sense of "desolation," Peter Roche, the exhausted and exiled white South African, haunted by memories of torture and hopelessly committed to his barren vocation, is a "calamity." It is hard to tell who is the puppet and who is the little hunchback (to adapt Benjamin's powerful image in another context),[76] since both warily exploit each other, and Jimmy's title of "Massa" for Peter is not without mockery. Just like Shiva, V. S. Naipaul is convinced that the collusion between misguided do-gooders like Peter and confused neurotics with messianic pretensions like Jimmy have the worst consequences not on the metropolis but in postcolonies. Meredith acidly tells Peter, "But what a nice world you inhabit, Peter. You have so much room for error."[77]

Although those more sympathetic to the enigma of Michael X may see Naipaul's novel and his stringent analysis as further evidence of Naipaul's bias and careerism, Joan Didion identifies precisely the critique expressed by Meredith as proof of Naipaul's legitimate adversaries here. She claims that the author "reserves a kind of tragic sympathy for the buyers of" the radical cause marketed in the First World by, and she quotes Naipaul here, "'the revolutionaries who visit centers of revolution with return air tickets.'"[78] What Naipaul fails to acknowledge is that revolutionary work is done even if it not up to the speed or the kind that he prefers. His archetypal character in the postcolonial world is the "diminished man"; in *Guerrillas,* it is Jimmy, surrounded by "English mementos," the vacant symbols of his borrowed life. But rarely are we given a sense of London in the sixties and seventies, which was rocked by race riots,

Teddy Boy hooliganism, housing and employment discrimination, and Enoch Powell's infamous anti-immigrant outbursts.

Jimmy is an amalgam of Michael X and Hakim Jamal (born Alan Donaldson and, like Michael X, an erratic convert to Islam), although the latter's background is also selectively appropriated. Anticipating Shiva's oblique view of the virulent racial injustices of an earlier period in American history, Naipaul picks up only on Hakim's hoodlum tendencies. But as with Michael X, the debris of Hakim's autobiography is not entirely worthless or tangential even if it proves he is no ideal hero. Part 1 of *From the Dead Level* is titled "Out of the Grave," and Hakim provides grim details of the poverty, drug abuse, violence, and social collapse of his teenage years in the Roxbury ghetto of Boston. "My generation was intellectually dead, spiritually dead, economically dead, politically dead and there was nobody around to give hope to the hopeless nor help to the helpless. So, in we plunged," Hakim concludes. What he describes is a different version of the socially dead followers of Jim Jones's church, for whom actual death awaited. "We were too busy challenging death . . . and death wins," Hakim adds rather prophetically, since he was to be gunned down, just a short time after Gale's murder, upon his return to the States.[79] But the deadly violence of the 'hood seems self-inflicted, if it appears at all in Naipaul's different reports. Just as with the sixties in the United States, the prurient gaze can be directed to the manic aspects of English popular culture, which include alcoholic parties, dope, sex, and the complicated class and interracial dynamics that explode in the novel.

Diana Athill's memoirs of her employment at André Deutsch often corroborate and sometimes contradict Naipaul's assessments of that tempestuous period in London and its confused racial, class, and sexual politics. Athill's narratives are candid and discomfiting, revealing her own complicity in the convoluted relationships, particularly her liaison with Hakim, which hinges on the sexual patronage of black men by older and more affluent white women. While crude discussions of sex for money offend Athill, there is no doubt that Hakim and his allegedly besotted white lover, Gale Benson (who changed her name to Hale Kimga as an anagram of both their names), knew just what it took to gain funds from white socialites eager to establish their compassion and understanding for the colonized peoples. In return, the "progressive" patrons expected to be cleansed of their guilt and to enjoy with good conscience the casual sex that came with the turf. Hakim was quick to distinguish between patronage and being patronized, and, like Michael, he exploited liberal guilt with much enjoyment. "Everyone in this story was at some time or another at least a little mad," confesses Athill, including herself in this jumble with devastating honesty, but none, she demonstrates, as "lunatic" as Hakim, who showed increasing signs of delusional grandeur, and Gale, "a crazy girl in love with a crazy man."[80]

Explaining her dislike of *Guerrillas* despite being a great admirer of Naipaul (who likewise thought highly of her), Athill locates her discomfort not in his caricatures of Michael, whom she distrusted, or even of Hakim, who for some reason she thinks inspired the character of Roche in the novel,[81] but in his unfair portrayal of Gale in the character of Jane. While she believes that Gale was quite demented in her hero worship of Hakim, who unabashedly exploited it, Naipaul's rendition of Jane as a flirt who liked playing with fire was unfair to her actual counterpart. Athill says, "The people she [Gale] had most in common with were not the kind of secure Englishwomen who had it off with black men to demonstrate their own liberal attitudes, but those poor wretches who followed the American 'guru' Jones to Guyana in 1977, and ended by committing mass suicide at his bidding. She was so lacking in a sense of her own worth that it bordered on insanity."[82] Athill sees some dubious affinity between the socialites in England and the socialists in the United States who, she believes, felt rootless, lost, and devalued in different contexts.

In the film *The Bank Job,* which claims to be based on "true events," Gale Benson is presented not as a dupe or even as someone entirely lacking in self-esteem, but as a sharp English spy, giving some truth to what people thought were Michael's paranoid accusations against her in Trinidad and providing a rationale for her murder. The film alleges that the reason Michael was able to get away with many of his shenanigans in London was because he had possession of compromising pictures of Princess Margaret (apparently getting her groove back while on vacation) engaged in an interracial, bisexual threesome in the Caribbean. In the film, Gale's task in Trinidad is to recover possible copies, presenting a different angle to the idea of a slavishly devout follower who is trying desperately to belong to the Michael X inner circle. (Athill confirms that Gale disliked Michael but seems to agree with Naipaul that she was nothing more than a Hakim groupie.)

As reviewers have noted, there is no real way of knowing what is fact and what is fiction in the film version. One of the statements in the credits says with deceptive blandness, "The names of many of the people identified in the film have been changed to protect the guilty," alleging a continuing cover-up despite the scandal of the 1971 Baker Street bank robbery (one of the "true events"), the resignation of important political leaders, and the indictment of corrupt policemen. Another note at the end of the film intriguingly states that the Michael X file is in the British National Archives and remains classified until January 1, 2054. The film has Peter de Jersey playing Michael X, looking the part but mystifyingly endowing the Trinidadian with a Jamaican accent.

The film's plot revolves around a real-life bank heist of the contents of a safe deposit vault to recover the damning pictures. The crime caper presents a sleazy but realistic picture of sixties and seventies London, with promiscuous and kinky white politicians, corrupt law enforcement, shady spies, and posturing black radicals wooed by the "pinko" press. The unflattering references in the film to Michael are confirmed by Gale's character, who seems intelligent and aware of the risks of spying on him even as she laughingly dismisses him: "He's a crazy, dopesmoking, pimp extortionist is what he is!" The film continues to present her sympathetically, and the burning of Michael's house in Trinidad is attributed to the vengeance of the MI-5 agent she is working with when he discovers her murder.[83]

However pathetic Athill finds Gale, she believes that Hakim was an intelligent man whose nerves were wrecked by his upbringing, his unstable life, and his anguished sense of racial inequality; some of her insights into his behavior are quite Fanonian. Her book ends with an elegy for a man with potential who eventually self-destructed. For Michael, though, she has no sympathy: "whatever label he was given by whites, Michael was considered a joke by most blacks in England."[84] Dilip Hiro and Stephen Fay, who give a serious and positive account of black activism in London in the sixties, have this to say in their caption of a photograph of Michael: "Took to politics after an unedifying career as a brothel-keeper, procurer and property racketeer. Muddled thinker, but natural flair for self-advertisement."[85] Whatever Athill's own failings in this cauldron of race, sex, and politics, she is more nuanced in her analysis of character and in her understanding of what prompts men like Hakim and Michael to act out as they did, even if she ultimately finds them absurd. Nor does she mistake the men for the movement.

Athill is also correct in intuitively sensing Naipaul's fury in his rendering of Jane. If Naipaul's depictions of Jimmy Ahmed and Peter Roche are unforgiving, they are mild in comparison to his portrayal of Jane, whose last name is significantly never revealed. While he draws on the stereotypical rape-as-revenge scenario of Black Panther icons such as Elridge Cleaver, one wonders how much of Naipaul's own nervous tension guides his account of this fictional character and that of her historical counterpart. The narrator in *The Enigma of Arrival,* for instance, a close autobiographical equivalent to Naipaul, confesses, "But my life in England had been savorless, and much of it mean. I had taken to England all the rawness of my colonial's nerves, and those nerves had more or less remained, nerves which in the beginning were in a good part also the nerves of youth and inexperience, physical and sexual inadequacy, and of undeveloped talent. And just as once at home I had dreamed of being in England, so for years in England I had dreamed of leaving England."[86] There is something here of Jimmy's confessional angst revealed in his fragments and notes, which show him as intoxicated by his construction of the repellently desirable figure of the white woman.

Patrick French's biography adds a significant dimension to one's reading of *Guerrillas* and to the equally disturbing *A Bend in the River*[87] in the unsparing portrait of Naipaul's demeaning treatment of his late wife, Pat, a white Englishwoman; in the allegations of physical abuse that Naipaul denies; in the revelations of trysts with prostitutes that devastated Pat; and in the violent sex between Naipaul and Margaret, his Argentinian lover whom Naipaul was to reject for his current Pakistani wife.[88] The troubling loyalty of his former wife and lover and their helpless dependence on a man who treated them badly seem to have leaked into his fiction, and the sexual violence is transferred from his erotic abuse of Margaret, who admittedly showed some degree of consent to the sadomasochistic relationship, to the fictional characters.

Jane/Clarissa/Marjorie, the interchangeable white women in *Guerrillas,* are literally "common" names (two of them at least recognizably intertextual), casually engaging in sex with men made exotic by their class or race, prostituting their frivolous political views along with their bodies. Together they coalesce into the "succubus" the novel mentions early on, further augmented by images of the Rabelaisian orality of Jane, whose avid sexual and gustatory appetites the narrator mingles in the cleft/mouth image.[89] She gobbles food, plants sloppy wet kisses on the lover of the moment, and lets drop some trivial comment or other that infuriates the sarcastic Roche, who by now is as disillusioned with her as she is with him. Unlike the wounded Jimmy, however, Naipaul's wish to leave England remains unfulfilled, and the narrator in *Enigma* provides us with a possible reason. Returning to the island, he says, he finds it unsettled by racial tensions—the Black Power movement—and he decides not to stay. This too is revealed in Naipaul's biography, along with his anger at the expulsion of Indians during the so-called Africanization of Uganda.

Naipaul's rage, then, is most focused on the black man and the white female temptress or seductress, and it is no coincidence that the sexual angle, not really a significant part of the Michael X scenario in Trinidad, ultimately dominates the novel. (Although there had been charges of rape against two of the men in the commune, one of whom was Skerritt, they had nothing to do with Gale.) Both these figures condense castrating anxieties. Their entangled downfall is the consolation for the missing angle, the inconspicuously intrusive third-person narrator of the novel, whose ethnicity and gender are significantly undisclosed, but whose distanced yet damning voice often echoes that of the long essay. Hardly any mention of multiethnic tensions is made in the novel, the focus largely being the binary of black and white. In one of many passages that deform landscape and character, the narrator describes Bryant, Jimmy's lover and eventual partner in crime: "His face was oddly narrow, and twisted on one side, as though he had been damaged at birth. The eye on the twisted side was half-closed; the bumps on his forehead and his cheekbones were prominent and shining. His hair was done in little pigtails: a Medusa's head."[90] The paralyzing glimpse of female pubic hair evoked by Freud in his reading of Medusa's head[91] resonates in the dreadlocks of the black male—a feature that Naipaul prefers to call "pigtails"—and emphasizes the double menace that unnerves the narrator.

One of the first descriptions of Jane shows her striding along with her usual clueless indifference to the possibility of danger, as it becomes apparent to Peter that she is a misfit in her surroundings: "The flowered blouse, through which her brassiere could be seen, the tight trousers that modeled stomach, groin, and cleft in a single, sudden curve: that could pass in the city, and in the shopping plaza of the Ridge would be hardly noticeable, but here it seemed provocative, overcasual enough to be dressy: London, foreign, wrong."[92] Throughout the novel, Jane is also a parody of the canonical Jane Eyre. She is the modern deviation, a descent from the demure, disciplined, sexually chaste nineteenth-century angel of the house to the unanchored, "loose" white woman who drifts from one meaningless relationship to another and whose very existence threatens the Victorian morals of now ironically more conservative middle-class brown and black communities.[93]

The notorious "sweet man" is emasculated neither by the white male of colonial regimes nor by the employed black woman in this case but by the affluent white woman of the metropolis whose "keep" he becomes. Mrs. Stephens hints as much. "That is the only sweetness he [Jimmy] know. That is what they feed him up on and then they send him down here. Parading through the town with their tight pants sticking up their crutch. They stink, Mr. Roche. They stink like rotten meat self."[94] As does the narrator, Mrs. Stephens moves seamlessly from Jimmy to the "they," the multiple, cheaply available Janes.

This striking reversal of racial and gendered embodiments of morality indicates a crucial shift in the individual agency of the white woman, but in troubling ways. Daryl Cumber Dance, considering different factors behind the derogatory portrayal of white women in what is now a commonplace in Caribbean fiction, says that one "possible explanation for the wholesale acceptance of the myth of the white woman's lust for the black man may be the black male's need to avenge himself against the white man and white society in general by ravishing and thereby degrading and destroying that society's symbol of purity while at the same time asserting the black male's superiority over the white male."[95] But the "symbol of purity" has since the period of nineteenth-century imperialism and early twentieth-century lynching deteriorated steadily to quite another symbol rivaling, as is evident on the covers of popular magazines, in music, television, pornography, and in various denunciations of the state of Western society, the lascivious image once foisted on nonwhite women.

As Benita Parry notes in her analysis of the rape motif, "That colonialism engendered a sexual pathology in both black and white, women and men, is not in question. What is at issue is how texts speak these psychoses."[96] While Dance may be correct in partly attributing the image of the sexually aggressive white woman to the perceived experiences of the writers, an antifeminist backlash may also have something to do with its excessive virulence. Stereotypes shift with changing social conditions. Now fears of the corruption of chaste women from traditional societies in or from the postcolonies by the decadent West are channeled through the deviant white woman who assumes an identity separate from the white man and whose authority she seems to have overpowered. White women are no longer the passive latecomers to imperialism; they are in this account imperialists in their own right. Naipaul's ferocity toward Jane and Gale indicts both for their exploitative use of black men, not just the other way around.

Jimmy's confusion about being "playboy" and "plaything" is actually quite appropriate—he is both predator and prey in England, just as Michael claimed of himself, despite confessions of sexual insecurity. The ominous warning about black boys who no longer want to play, Jane's queasy sense that she is "playing with fire," heighten the sinister undertones of carnivalesque excess, the critical threshold when the punitive effects of the morning after impinges on the overnight recklessness of throwing caution to the wind. Indeed, Carnival is often the scene of rapes, particularly when inebriated women are made more vulnerable to assault. All four of them, Michael and Gale, Jimmy and Jane, are performers in the negative sense of the term, fluidly slipping from one role to another. Naipaul, for whom such impersonations are absurd and shallow, does not share Harris's lyrical celebration of changeability. Michael "is only a haphazard succession of roles," both in his life and in his rambling writings. Even if Hakim was a "true American," he is one insofar as he is a hustler par excellence, a gangster parading as a radical. "Benson was, more profoundly than Malik or Hakim, a fake" is Naipaul's merciless epitaph for the woman.[97] His sense of Jane as a tourist, wandering into perilous situations with the complacent conviction of being able to withdraw at will, ultimately shapes the rape script in the novel. What might seem Cleaver's rape-as-politics formula or Frantz Fanon's conversion of white women into cultural currency or proxy for power in *Black Skin, White Masks* is also, I argue, a postcolonial scenario with grim implications for the supposed agency of the white woman who "asks for it."

The illusion of a tourist who calls the shots and can quit when the going gets rough is destroyed in *Guerrillas.* In the unsettling end to the novel, Peter reads to himself the skimpy details of the Canadian-born Jane's passport—still not revealing her last name—obviously aware that she has come to a bad end. Having slipped through immigration in the company of rich Americans, her passport is never examined or stamped by the authorities. "Officially she's never been here," as Harry meaningfully points out.[98] This obliteration—this voiding—of Jane, who from the very beginning is marked as "white enough to be unreadable," a blank page like the one in her passport, is in accord with her abrupt murder in which, unlike Gale, she dies soundlessly and without a struggle shortly after being brutally raped and sodomized by Jimmy in a reckless second sexual encounter.

In the island's rumored rape fantasy, an unnamed white woman is gang-raped and then offered water in the cupped hands of one of her rapists. Jimmy incorporates this fantasy as his own, imposing his obsessions onto the anonymous face of the raped woman in a foreshadowing of Jane's violation. His visual depiction of the prone white woman jarringly interrupts and literally inflicts itself on the picturesque, mass-produced Edenic litany of the Caribbean islands:

> But to Jimmy it [the offer of water] was the most moving part of the story, and it had stayed with him, in a setting that had grown stylized as a tourist poster: the soft light and blurred shade below the coconut palms, the white sand, the sunlit breakers, the olive sea and blue sky beyond the crisscross of the curved gray coconut trunks, the bleeding girl on the front fender of the old Ford, the cupped hands offering water, the grateful eyes, remembering terror.[99]

The shocking intrusion of a "bleeding girl" in a familiar landscape that ought to outline a bikini-clad sun worshipper running carefree on the beach aggressively maps, in Sara Suleri's phrase, the "geography of rape," which she later calls "colonialism's master narrative," even as it parodies the banal formula of tourist posters.[100]

Jane's kinky penchant for abusive sex, her self-destructive pursuit of a clearly dangerous man, does not lessen the horror of her gruesome murder. But as disturbing as the erotic hazard she wagers is the plot of gratuitous sexual violence against the white woman that is proposed as symbolic evidence of the bankruptcy of the Black Power movement. Whatever exhilarating potential there might have been in the huge mass demonstrations for Basil Davis's funeral (after he was shot down by the police) is lost in its retelling in *Guerrillas* as Stephens's funeral peters off into ominous stasis with a state of imminent Emergency and military intervention.

Significantly, Gale's later murder is hitched in the novel to the Black Power movement of Trinidad in 1970, so that the movement is defined not by any productive goal but by the pointless rape, slash, and burn at Christina Gardens. While Gale and Jane are not directly implicated or even interested, like the white women in Jonestown, in the utopian agricultural commune supposedly in progress at Christina Gardens and Thrushcross Grange, respectively—Jane refers to it as "All that shit in the field"[101]—their indifferently casual presence in these locations comes across as even worse than the susceptible Jonestown women.

In his critique of fantasy and the twilight worlds of slave grotesque, mimicry, and festivity after the daily grind of plantation labor, Naipaul claims that the foundational subculture of Carnival trivializes the seriousness of revolution and reduces it to farce. The slaves' dreamworld of masquerade and Rabelaisian laughter that enabled their psychic survival in the grim period of slavery manifested later in the period of independence is an absurd anachronism rather than the abidingly resourceful play of the imagination, as Harris clearly believes. But it is precisely this essentially comic vision—the ability to find space for mirth and play in the most trying times—that not only survives, but also ensures the psychological stamina of different post-plantation cultures.

Despite his disavowals, Naipaul himself recognizes the creative conversion of villain into a failed con man unable to deceive the percipient local public, but taking the colonial "massa" for a ride:

> To the Trinidad crowds Malik had become a "character," a Carnival figure, a dummy Judas to be beaten through the streets on Good Friday. Which was all that he had been in London, even in the great days of his newspaper fame as the X: the militant who was only an entertainer, the leader who had no followers, the Black Power man who was neither powerful nor black. He wasn't even black; he was "a fair-skin man," half-white. That, in the Trinidad phrase, was the sweetest part of the joke.[102]

Naipaul admits later that "a black Trinidad dancer who was in London at the time, says, 'When I heard about this X guy I thought, 'There goes one of our con men.' And I wished him well, because he was in England and because they told me he was Trinidadian.' It was the West Indian attitude: the jester was recognized and accepted as a jester, but was otherwise kept at a distance."[103] Naipaul's irrepressible enjoyment of the hoax, of the picaroon, locates his sense of humor firmly in Trinidad, as I will argue in the final chapter.

In some ways, Jimmy and Michael begin as subversive Fridays but then turn into the Bohbolees (the Judas effigies that are beaten on the streets on Good Friday). As Jackson Phillip warns Harry Trewe in Walcott's *Pantomime,* the shadow and the mimic take on a life of their own: "He [the massa] cannot get rid of it, no matter what, and that is the power and black magic of the shadow, boss, bwana, effendi, bacra, sahib, until it is the shadow that start dominating the child, it is the servant that start dominating the master. . . . And that is why all them Pakistani and West Indians in England, all them immigrant Fridays driving all you so crazy."[104] While Naipaul is more ambivalent about the role of farce, Walcott's sense of its subversive potential predicts the frustrated "boss, bwana, effendi, bacra, sahib" who is made to look foolish by his mimic men.

The carnivalesque, defined by the ethos of Carnival cultures, engages multiple elements: official and unofficial, revolutionary and anti-revolutionary, playful and serious, traditional and innovative, mindful of the status quo and a menace to it.[105] Politics and parody are not inseparable, and their convergence was undeniable in Black Power as Selvon, Lovelace, and Phillips also show to humorous effect. But elements of parody need not diminish the entire movement. Michael, only seemingly a revolutionary figure who did little to challenge the system but exploited it instead, was also carnivalesque. He was not so much a political activist but a manipulative trickster who cashed in on colonial guilt at the very heart of the colonial center. One begins to see why Naipaul thought the novel rather funny despite the murky, depressing plot.

What Naipaul might concede, however, is that the joke is not really on either Trinidadians, who knew better than to take the circus seriously, or the Black Power movement in Trinidad, which was, unlike Michael, at least partially concerned with political transformation. John Williams's biography is one of the more complex accounts of Michael X's life in London. In his account, Williams expresses surprise that Michael's guilt was so easily accepted by observers like Naipaul. He does not try to make Michael out to be completely innocent, but provides various alternatives that suggest the case was not as clear-cut as it seemed. Williams gives Michael the same sympathy that Athill reserves for Hakim, presenting him not as a cold-blooded murderer, but as a charming man of shaky morals determined to make the most of the countercultural underground and the racial dynamics of London at the time. He identifies the turning point as the first of Michael's prison experiences in England on charges of petty theft, and surmises that the latter became increasingly disturbed and paranoid in subsequent years, just as Athill believes of Hakim.

Although Geoffrey Robertson, one of the lawyers who fought against Michael's death sentence, is less convinced of the latter's uninvolvement in both murders, he provides a poignant account of Michael on death row in Trinidad and the latter's concern for his fellow inmates.[106] What both Williams and Robertson suggest is that far from being a hardened villain, Michael was in many ways a muddled victim of his time. Caught up in the heady and mutually exploitative relationships of black and white, impecunious and wealthy in London's riotous counterculture of the sixties, Michael's devious aptitude for role playing led him ultimately to the gallows. The joke that Trinidadians recognized in the story of Michael X, then, is not without its tragedy. As I will suggest in a later chapter, grotesque humor may seem to belittle figures such as Michael, but it paradoxically allows us to understand their complexity.

4 Magic, Science, Fantasy, and Religion

Humanity seems destined to oscillate forever between devotion to the world of dreams and adherence to the world of reality. And really, if this breathing rhythm of history were to cease, it might signal the death of the spirit.

—Franz Roh, "Magical Realism: Post-Expressionism"

He was a hardcore sci-fi and fantasy man, believed that that was the kind of story we were all living in. He'd ask: What more sci-fi than the Santa Domingo? What more fantasy than the Antilles?

—Junot Díaz, *The Brief Wondrous Life of Oscar Wao*

Scientific and technological advancements are often implacably invoked to distinguish the First from the Third World, white Euro-American populations from nonwhite others, the advanced "culture" of Western(ized) societies from the backward "nature" of non-Western peoples. Within each of these categories as well there are various levels of hierarchy between science and the humanities, technology and the arts, reason and imagination; between the rational views of the urban industrialized elites and the irrational superstitions of the rural folk. It goes without saying that vast differences in industrial prowess, information technology, and scientific knowledge are correspondingly tied to significant inequalities in individual and national wealth, class, race and gender divides, state power, and international status. Without dismissing the invaluable contribution of science and technology, we might ponder the implications of a world that tilts toward educating its young mainly in these disciplines, since anything else is considered less useful and certainly less lucrative.

Wilson Harris counters the goal of science with that of art in perhaps an understandable overstatement. "Absolute knowledge is treasured as the literal goal of science. What is the goal of art? Profoundest self-confession, self-judgement is the supreme goal of art," he declares.[1] Dismantling the usual binary between religion and science, Harris does not exempt science from fundamentalist certainty and even arrogance. He believes conversely that the "theatre of the arts"[2] in its cosmic experience of masking—with multiple roles assumed by human and animal, victor and vanquished, self and other—refuses the desire to pursue "any irritable reaching out after fact and reason."[3] Art, not in the limited sense of painting but as an entire domain of the imagination, becomes a corrective to "technocratic and utilitarian realism."[4]

There is some basis to Harris's distrust of technocratic science. Although early science was a distinct practice from applied science and technology, increasingly the latter are tools in the economic and political connivance that intrudes into minute aspects of everyday life and spreads its tentacles from the transnational to the local and from the systemic to the individual in the so-called Age of Terror. The defused explosive ending to Zadie Smith's *White Teeth* comically involves an aspiring Islamicist radical and a Jewish scientist with the French geneticist Dr. Marc-Pierre Perret, who once worked for the Nazi regime. While Millat stands for the dangers of religious extremism, figures such as Perret and Marcus Chalfen assume the mastery of purposive rationality, the Faustian collusion between controlling nature and asserting dominance in a global biopolitics.

In Harris's view, giving the scientific, technical, and related disciplines an imperialist status in hierarchies of knowledge, far from encouraging a healthy sense of reality, actually reifies it, and has a deleterious effect on human values that are unsuited to a rigid grid of "Titanic Reason."[5] We need not romanticize the "savage" and the "primitive" societies whose beliefs in magic and religious faith were generally studied as archaic oddities from the combined perspectives of Western anthropology, philosophy, sociology, and psychology. But there is little doubt that with the advent of modernity, "philosophical inquiry and applied science appeared to have raised Western thought to a commanding height from which the thought systems of others could be confidently measured."[6] Such dominating heights inevitably led to the categorical descent and time lag attributed to "the thought systems of others."

Bronislaw Malinowski, from whom I adapt my title, complicates strict oppositions between "the power of reasoning" and the "acts and observances. . . . associated with beliefs in supernatural forces, especially those of magic."[7] He provocatively suggests that its desire to control the often-chancy forces of nature (in contrast to propitiating gods) makes magic "akin to science."[8] He obviously does not conflate the dominant ideologies of reason, observation, classification, experiment, and verification that allegedly drive the scientific mind with the mystical belief in magic, but he challenges Lucien Lévy-Bruhl's initial contention that "primitive man" was wholly dominated by mysticism.

Additionally, Malinowski believes that despite the recognized difference between the "knowledge and reason" required for agricultural labor and "the unhallowed garden made without magic"—between the profane practice of science, however "rudimentary," and the sacred faith in the divine—magic, science, and religion were irretrievably mixed in primitive life. Such fluid interactions constitute not just primitive but contemporary life in the Caribbean and many other parts of the world where indigenous religious, magical, and spiritual beliefs and medical practices are not predicated on the body-mind dualism that led to the gradual secularization and "disenchantment," to use Max Weber's term, of the increasingly rationalist post-Enlightenment world.[9] As several studies of obeah, Vodoun, and Ifa demonstrate, "religion" is an elastic term in cultures where philosophy, psychotherapy, pharmacology, performance, art, music, mythology, magic, and hermeneutics are part of such belief systems.[10]

Resurrecting Bones, Reviving Speech in Pauline Melville and Wilson Harris

While magic is distinct from magical realism, the shared worldviews and the persistence of magical beliefs in contemporary society dominate the literature of magical realism. In her short story "The Parrot and Descartes" (note the irreverent placement of the renowned seventeenth-century philosopher and mathematician after the tropical bird associated with unthinking mimicry), Pauline Melville attributes the disjointing of hitherto entwined epistemologies, ways of life, and beliefs to Descartes's meditations, which forced "magic and technology . . . to go their separate ways," "and science and magic to march in opposite directions."[11] Inserting the fictional parrot into the life of the historical figure amid one of Europe's many internecine wars, this particular one in Prague in 1619, Melville parodies the emphasis on reason and skepticism that marked Descartes's influence on rational philosophy and the then-developing schools of natural science, and tells the story from the insightful South American parrot's point of view. The parrot's twin loathing of *The Tempest* and Descartes is prescient, since it recognizes the link between the anthropocentric imperatives of the *cogito* dictum and the imperialist, racialized hierarchies separating Prospero, the learned philosopher-aristocrat-magician, from Caliban, the monstrously brutish, colonized slave.

At the end of the story, which finds the parrot ornamentally chained and his wings clipped by a new set of human captors, his worst fears are realized and he is trapped by his "appetite for fruit" into becoming a prop in the play, although not a mechanical one. He recites Prospero's final epilogue together with the actor before "bemused audiences," performing as percipient chorus rather than as conventional echo. Even the echo is not mere reflex. The parrot's shriek of terror upon coming face-to-face with Descartes repeats his screech just before he is captured by an English courtier traveling up the Orinoco in 1611 and sent into "unhappy exile" in Europe. In keeping with Melville's insistence on the parrot's ability to reason, he is able to prophesy his own fate as well as that of his kind, given the incipient practice of taxidermy that would provide Flaubert, among others, with his proverbial stuffed parrot a couple of centuries later.

As I discussed in an earlier chapter, not just birds but human inhabitants of the tropics were classified and, if not mounted in quite the same way (the Greek word for arrangement being the root for taxidermy), displayed concomitantly as outlandish zoological specimens and freak shows before a marveling European audience. Trinculo craftily calculates the worth of Caliban and surmises that in England "would the monster make a man" and provide some "silver" for his entrepreneurial exhibitor. Terence Hawkes, like Peter Hulme, asserts Caliban's terminological ambiguity, but he specifically interprets this line to mean also ambiguously that in England, the monster would be classified as human; and the monster would make (money for) a man willing to display him to the curious. In either case, concludes Hawkes, "classifications which we assume to be settled, objective and definitive appear to fluctuate with the tides of the 'making' market-place."[12]

Reminding us that Trinculo's first question upon sighting Caliban on the magical island is to wonder whether he is man or fish, Hawkes notes that as a "European signifying system" began to separate the human and nonhuman (and differentiate between races), any grotesque hybrid was "bound to smell fishy."[13] Melville's playful use of magical realism as a mode to challenge the vaunted irrationality and bestiality—the nonhumanity—of the "lower" orders and species poses a powerful counter-narrative to the supposedly infallible archaeology of knowledge and stable scientific systems of classification that underpinned the exploitative practices of colonialism. As my later discussion of Nalo Hopkinson will imply, her transformation of humans into seal-like creatures will provide the slaves imaginative oceanic sanctuary that is not available on land, while at the same time exposing their historical status as chattel, as disposable cargo rather than as full human beings.

Lois Parkinson Zamora and Wendy Faris introduce their collection on magical realism by citing Julian Barnes's interdiction against the mode in his whimsical *Flaubert's Parrot.*[14] Incidentally, his narrator's additional prohibition of incest themes is quoted in one of the epigraphs to Melville's *The Ventriloquist's Tale,* a novel that cheerfully breaks both proscriptions and to which I will return shortly. Acknowledging the relevance of the witty "parrot(ie)s" in Barnes's attack on the formulaic excesses of the mode, Faris and Parkinson Zamora nevertheless go on to present the multiple yields of magical realism, and insist on its "replenishing force."[15] In her own book on the subject, Faris attributes to magical realism "a certain visionary power," claiming that it reverses the bourgeois secularization of nineteenth-century realism through narratives of "reenchantment or remystification."[16]

The paired language of exhaustion and replenishment is borrowed from John Barth, in two eponymous essays, the first of which speculates on the "used-upness" of the novel as a contemporary form and the later one assigning to postmodernist fiction the replenishing potential sorely needed in this age of exhaustion.[17] While there may be some kinship between postmodernist and magical realist techniques, the magical realism of the authors I consider here has a particular anxiety more concerned with replenishing denuded life forms rather than remedying the fatigue of a genre. Speaking parrots and articulate slaves display not just the reviving skills of magic but also the dialogic potential of the inanimate and mute. More stories come alive when (stuffed) objects become ventriloquists.

The first-person narrator in *The Ventriloquist's Tale* provides another version of the skills of ventriloquism. Rather than merely projecting his own voice, "Macun . . ." boasts of being able to "reproduce perfectly the mating call of every bird and beast in the Amazonas[,] . . . sometimes with the help of certain leaves or grasses curled around my fingers. It seems magical, but then magic is always related to desire. . . . Magic is private. It deals in secrecy and disguise."[18] Like the South American figures of ultimate wildness, the *aucas,*[19] who possess the "occult" skills of animals when moving through the forest, tracking and smelling, moving stealthily at night, and communicating through birdcalls, the narrator claims the chameleon's power of magical mimesis. He coyly refuses to disclose his full name despite offering many clues to his identity, but even the incomplete signifier is an intertextually labyrinthine one, as Barth (drawing from Jorge Luis Borges) would point out. Melville's first narrator claims divinity like his namesake Makunaima (or Canaima) of Guyanese Indian myth, but he also evokes the folk antihero of the Brazilian novel *Macunaíma,* which inspired other versions in theater and film.[20]

"Macun . . ." exudes the irrepressible garrulity of Salman Rushdie's characters, along with the carnivalesque vigor of Rabelais. Dredging one word from primal slime, he finds more words that tumble into sight "and as the babble grew louder, as the throng of words grew and approached along the forest trails, the savannah tracks, the lanes and by-ways and gullies, the words, some declaiming, some whispering, were joined, firstly by laughter and ribald whistles, then by rude farting sounds and finally by an unmistakable clattering that could only be the rattling dance of bones."[21] The grotesque embodiment of bare (but noisy) bones in a prolific lexical swarm is a death-defying act of survival, indeed of regeneration, not in flesh but through utterance—sacred and profane, miraculous and morbid.

Contrasting it to the hysterical proliferation of meaning in Euro-American postmodern fiction, which ironically concludes with the vaunted absence or nonsense of meaning, Kumkum Sangari argues that the generative narration of magical realism in Gabriel García Márquez, for instance, stands for a very different grammar of excess. "The long sentence is an index of the *fecundity* of the repressed, of the barely begun and unfinished—not uncertain—stories simmering beneath the strident sounds and tight enclosures of dictatorship, and so gestures toward unopened possibilities." Stressing the process of "struggle" inherent in the eruptions of different voices, fragmented and incomplete though they may be, Sangari concludes that the "collective, digressive quality of an oral narrative . . . invokes the submerged life of a ravaged people and marks their glimpsed resilience."[22] While Sangari's notion of resilience seems to echo that of Barth's replenishment, the former emphasizes more the traumatized stories of this embattled collective whose storytelling is both endlessly creative and unromantically related to private and collective neuroses. Magical realism as a mode seems eminently suited to their expression, their telling and retelling in a kind of manic Third World talking cure.

García Márquez, in particular, has implicated magical realism in a violent history, dispelling any wistful reading of the magical as a process of enchantment granting a happily-ever-after to the ingenuous believer with the wave of a wand. His explanation for the existence of magic in Colombia is similar to Michael Taussig's description of the "appalling and senseless brutality in a theater of sensual cruelty" played out in that country.[23] Given the historical procession of tortures, death squads, mass killings, disappearances, and so on, not only was lived experience fantastic by its very nature, but colonialist and nationalist accounts converted these atrocities into "objectivist fiction" by a narrative sleight of hand.[24] Despite the rationalist search for free labor, the waste of human and material resources beggared reason, notes Taussig. Entire villages could be razed to avenge one attack and acres of rubber would be destroyed in a wanton destruction of habitat. Rather than reflect on this Conradian "horror," however, paranoid colonial mythology accumulated stories of dismemberment, devil worship, cannibalism, and other "uncivilized" behaviors on the part of the Indigenous peoples who were being decimated.

Ceaselessly repeated, embroidered stories of savagery were "indispensable to the formation and flowering of the colonial imagination," feeding into its hysteria and establishing, in a self-fulfilling prophecy, the colonial allegory of justified domination. As if the spooky tales of the jungle and its even more fearful inhabitants—the "colonial work of fabulation"[25]—were not enough, the physical repression of any resistance sometimes turned playful, torture a grisly diversion for the bored mind trapped in alien surroundings. Such unbelievable experiences continued into the postcolonial era. In Melville's macabre short story "The President's Exile," the ghostly dictator of a country that bears some resemblance to Guyana under Linden Forbes Burnham insists he deals with "realities" while spinning "an elaborate web of lies and deception" to cover up his misdemeanors and crimes.[26] As his sister bitterly notes, "We must be the only country where the government is elected by the dead. Half the names on the [electoral] lists are taken from tombstones."[27] "Democratic" governments stay in power through such absurdities, so when the dead can seemingly vote, why can they not dance and speak, magical realism seems to demand. Its reanimation, however, is meant to challenge social enervation and expose national crises.

The "joyous assembly" of Melville's chattering, skeletal crew in *The Ventriloquist's Tale* is a less sublime expression of Harris's phrase the "*live fossil nursery of language*,"[28] which variously expresses "the technology of the resurrection" in life cycles: from a seed, in the fall of a bird's feather, sedimentary rock, and other organic remnants "fused with the murmur of threatened species that still arise and address us."[29] Harris speaks of "the book of the living landscape,"[30] a critical formulation in his oeuvre of the silent, often murderous, void of Guyanese history becoming articulate through such live fossils, at least to the "literate imagination."[31]

In the 1998 preface to *Palace of the Peacock,* Harris also invokes the bone-flute or the bone-spirit, another one of his richly symbolic concepts drawn from the practice of ritual cannibalism, where a morsel of flesh from the bone of the conquistador was cooked and consumed by Carib Indians. Rather than the sacro-cannibalism described by Malinowski, an act of love toward the dead (also expressive of dread and repugnance toward death itself),[32] this is more a totemic "sacramental eating,"[33] which seeks literally to implant the knowledge and tactics of a formidable enemy while also consuming the fruit of "bitter self-knowledge"[34] on the part of a conquering race that is now the conquered. The defensive aspect of the ritual is an archetypal precursor to vaccination, with a similar intention of injecting dead pathogens in order to create a memory safely in the immune system, deflect an attack by the viral conquistadores or stimulate antibodies upon invasion.

Harris also connects the bone-flute (and Canaima) to the mythical Quetzalcoatl, the Aztec bird-serpent deity whose lore stretches in a bridge or arc from "pre-Columbian Mexico" to the "post Columbian Guianas in South America."[35] Bones scattered by Quetzalcoatl play an important role in the complex repertoire of creation myths of the Aztecs, and Melville's lexical generativity may echo, like Harris, this mediation between words (myth) and bones (creation). Here too the worship of this deity has uncanny slippages from fantasy to fact, religion to science, reptile to bird, and prehistoric to historic, considering speculations that the deification of the feathered flying serpent may have transpired from exposed fossil remains of pterosaurs. One of these specimens, Quetzalcoatlus, in a peculiar reversal, is now named after the god in paleontology, and indeed, a natural history museum can certainly seem to be a site of fantasy. For Harris, "the winged serpent which flies in space" represents an animal riddle that dissolves absolutist boundaries between the animal and the divine, so "we find ourselves steeped in plural masks that break an addiction to power, that break a hubris or proclivity to enslave others whom we deem inferior creatures."[36] While dismantling anthropocentric classifications of other species, the statement embeds a critique of slavery, when humans were (mis)treated like animals.

Harris has developed in his long career an extraordinarily complex range of archetypes and tropes to confirm his avowal of vital rhythms of life and expressions of memory amid the cycles of conquest, death, revenge, and violence that have repeatedly plagued history, in a cosmic sense, and particularly haunted the Caribbean. In Harris's evocation, Silas Weir Mitchell's medical neologism, the "phantom limb," links the discourses of science and the humanities. Just as some amputees' neurological sense of the pain or pleasure from physically nonexistent limbs revises conventional notions of presence and disembodiment, visual perception and physical evidence, sensory feelings and material reality, what is and is not, the trope of the phantom limb as it appears in Harris's theorizations suggests different levels of reality. Andrew Jefferson-Miles explains this simultaneous if contradictory sense of past and present, of absence and embodiment, of visible and invisible realities as characteristic of Harris's "quantum fiction." He concludes, "For Harris, one of the chief demands of fiction is to raise provisional, yet viable, quantum bridges between ourselves and an unfinished past; a past in which, in the appearance of things [like the phantom limb], we seem not to reside," and yet that is always with us.[37] Hopkinson's hybrid writing, to which I now turn, implicitly embodies the trope of the phantom limb in its liquescent depictions of history and identity, time and space.

Migrating Ghosts, Ventriloquist Voices in Nalo Hopkinson's Speculative Fiction

The writer's ability to transcend linear chronology and breach bounded space, to piece the broken fragments together, to make the muted voice heard, to perceive vividly the unseen and the absent, is as magical a gift as that of Melville's narrator who witnesses and exemplifies the buoyant prolixity of language. As another of Melville's titles signifies, "the migration of ghosts" inevitably conjures ventriloquist tales. "The Soul is a solitary wanderer yet steeped in plural masks it may pluck from the fractured body of Death itself . . . curiously living Word or ventriloquism of Spirit," Harris muses.[38] Nalo Hopkinson's novel *The Salt Roads,* while embodying quite literally the time-traveling "plural masks" of the wandering goddess Lasiren, also identified as River Mumma and Ezili of the Waters, reverses Harris's Orphic vision to fracture and multiply a variety of subjects with a particular emphasis on the forgotten myths and tales of female seers and divinities.

In many cultures women have been forced to ventriloquize, to use other bodies and voices. In Hélène Cixous's view, denied a continuous, coherent, overtly vocal existence, they have always found other ways of expressing themselves: "Muffled throughout their history, they have lived in dreams, in bodies (though muted), in silences, in aphonic revolts."[39] The time-traveling spirit in *The Salt Roads* likewise leaps into different bodies, sometimes manipulating her intrusion, at other times unable to control her flight and landing. Not simply the misleading songs of seductive sirens, women's voices provide an ethical imperative for Hopkinson, often challenging what Harris would call the adversarial regimes of colonialism and anticolonialism polarized in Prospero and Caliban. Unlike the Canaimian "pathology of revenge"[40] that consumes Beatrice in *The Ventriloquist's Tale,* the enslaved Mer fights to prevent an all-consuming violence, the scorched earth tactics of the warlike Ogun/Makandal, both figures inaugurally associated with the Haitian Revolution.[41] Hopkinson often fuses a number of Vodoun deities in her work, although the syncretism is also a characteristic of the practice, which offers different versions or names for the same icon.

For instance, various manifestations of Ezili appear in the novel: Ezili Danto, the black country woman in Mer (in the novel specifically identified with Rosa Parks); Ezili Freda, the Creole seductress who loves the fine things in life in Jeanne or Lemer, the French poet Baudelaire's mistress in the novel. Ezili Freda could also have possessed the white plantation mistress who intervenes to save the runaway Patrice from summary punishment. The spirit/loa travels from the watery burial of an infant in pre-revolutionary Haiti to mid-nineteenth century Paris and also to fourth-century Alexandria where she inhabits a prostitute called Thais (Meritet), who speaks in contemporary slang and eventually converts into the dusky Saint Mary of Egypt. The deity's travels are appropriately figured as aquatic, in the rush of the river or the wave of the ocean, and the fragments of Mer in the alternative names of the characters across time and space emphasize the "quantum" sense of geography, individuality, and history.

Joan Dayan informs us "the loa live *en bas de l'eau,* under the waters, in an unlocatable place called 'Guinée.' Though clearly distinguished from *les morts,* the spirits of the dead, they share their home with the ancestors. When loa come to visit their 'children,' whether in a formal, public ceremony or in private times of dream or individual communion, they come by way of the *chemin de l'eau,* or water road."[42] The airy flights and falls of the loa or spirit in search of temporary corporeality are also significant but to those I will return shortly.[43] Significantly, the trajectory does not follow the "arrowlike nomadism" that Édouard Glissant critiques as the territorial, settled root structure of singular identity, but pursues the deterritorialized "circular nomadism" of a rhizomic "poetics of relation."[44] Or in the words of the time-traveling consciousness: "Time does not flow for me. Not for me the progression in a straight line from earliest to latest. Time eddies. I am now then, now there, sometimes simultaneously."[45] Despite Mer's sense of failure and exhaustion, the ominous warning that the salt roads are drying up, her desire for death at the end of the novel, and the truncation of her story and her tongue by Makandal (possessed by Ogun), the "I" in the novel splits and emerges in different moments as revolutionary female and male, gay, lesbian, and transgender activists, complicating the heterosexist male-centered heroics in conventional bourgeois and nativist narratives of national revolution.

Hopkinson's deployment of the "massa's tools" does not simply involve the predictable manipulations of colonial power, but engages head-on the gender politics of toxic domesticity I discussed in an earlier chapter. In *Midnight Robber,* Tan-Tan's coming battle with incest and abuse from the age of nine is foreshadowed when she assumes the popular garb and persona of a traditional figure from Trinidad Carnival, but decides to go one better. Historically, explains Tan-Tan's eshu to her, the Midnight Robber has always been male with the exception of Belle Starr, a Trini woman who borrowed the name and costume of an American cowgirl to play Mas'. In Hopkinson's characteristically syncretic work, the novel evolves into what Barth calls "Tales within Tales within Tales" strung together through an assortment of modes, including science fiction, folklore, fantasy, fairy tale, and magical realism.[46]

Thus, the Eshu of West African and Afro-Caribbean orisha worship appears here as a robotic but equally canny equivalent who guides Tan-Tan and, as it becomes clear in the end, is the narrator of all the interconnected stories to Tan-Tan's baby in the process of labor. The fairy tale and folklore elements are rewritten, as in many of Hopkinson's short stories, with a feminist orientation, where children, in particular young girls, live in a dangerous world and must learn survival skills. Even as a child in costume, fearful but defiant of the bogeyman, Tan-Tan comes to a decision: "The Midnight Robber, the downpressor, the stealer-away of small children who make too much mischief. The man with the golden wooing tongue. She would show him. She would be scarier than him. She would be Robber Queen."[47]

The Trinidad Carnival that eshu refers to is now the past of an Earth that can only be viewed from a screen on planet Touissaint, where Tan-Tan resides before the fateful events that lead to her flight in a shift pod to New Half-Way Tree along with Antonio, her father. The terminology of science fiction is enmeshed with the historical threads of the Middle Passage and even later migrations, although in this case Antonio is the criminal who will control his daughter. Like Chandin Ramchandin in Shani Mootoo's *Cereus Blooms at Night,* he perceives his daughter's incipient romantic interest as "tiefin'" what belongs to him. And as in that novel, he beats and rapes his daughter, who eventually stabs him with the knife gifted to her by her stepmother on the new planet. Her stepmother Janisette's repeated attempts to criminalize the on-the-run (maroon) Tan-Tan and bring her to book is ultimately stymied by Tan-Tan's gifted oratorical skills. She appropriates the bombastic "Robber Talk" of the Midnight Robber who sometimes mimics and parodies the master's speech and declaims the wrongs of history.[48]

Here the subversive postcolonial parroting fuses with the caged bird that sings, a Philomela who acts on her promise to tell the world of her rape not through tapestry, as in the classical version, but in spoken word performance. The oral, poetic revelation of Tan-Tan's rape and abuse in the midst of Carnival reiterates the historic and political role of this festivity in many Caribbean novels, and justifies Harris's insistence on the performative and cultural significance of carnival masks and masquerades.[49] The novel is crowded with figures from folklore and carnival costumes, the mako jumbie, the douen (here a friendly guide rather than the impish prankster-abductor of unchristened children), and the Rolling Calf included, which appear also as science-fictional beings who sometimes live in mutual hostility with the (post)human inhabitants of the planet colony where the cast-offs from Touissaint are exiled.

The controversial ascription of "Blackheart man" not to a villainous white slaver, but to the incestuous Antonio fleeing murder charges, stages a contemporary postcolonial gender politics where slavery and colonialism are not the only historical terrors to be resisted and there is not always a simple "us" versus "them," not even with gender conflict, as Janisette's complicity and projection of guilt proves. David Findlay's poem in the epigraph declares:

> I stole the torturer's tongue!
> man wouldn't recognize this dancing, twining, retrained flesh
> if it slapped upside the empty space in him head.

Unlike Mer, whose tongue is symbolically sliced off by Makandal, in this novel Tan-Tan opens her "magical mouth"[50] and finds her tongue, which, as in the poems of Marlene NourbeSe Philip, is the whiplike instrument of torture and the phallic weapon of fellatio and rape that has to be "retrained."[51] Tan-Tan offers her own "word science" against Janisette's account, entwining her name with "the N-AN-ny, Maroon Granny; meaning Nana, mother, caretaker to a nation. You won't confound these people with your massive fib-ulation!"[52] As is characteristic of magical realism, lies and truth, fact and fiction are hopelessly "confounded," not to assert that there is no truth, but to reverse the assumption that facts are all about truths that matter and fiction about fibs that don't.

The framing of the novel as a "tall tale" upstages both colonial and masculinist versions, leading to the eventual confusion of the witnessing crowds of Carnival as to whether the story is "old-time story, not real!"[53] or "is Masque that was, or real?"[54] These queries provocatively leave open the elusive gateway between fact and fiction, truth and lie that magical realism also unlocks. We cannot sentimentalize the novel's ending in birth, however, given that the new life is the product of incest and rape. But Tan-Tan's baby is gifted in her womb with an "extra limb" by Granny Nanny, whose nanomites keep all the new worlds running.[55] Grande 'Nansi Web becomes the science fiction permutation of Anancy the trickster spider in Caribbean folklore.

Unlike Tan-Tan, who was lost to planet Touissaint when she crossed dimension veils, her son is endowed with a literal "sixth sense," which will allow him to stay physically connected with the Grande Anansi Nanotech Interface. Like the phantom limb or filament that traces its delicate links from Africa to the Caribbean, the additional limb will keep alive other lost histories and the connection to the "mother, caretaker to a nation." Not surprisingly, Tan-Tan, reunited with Granny Nanny and her eshu, names her son after a woman: "Tubman: the human bridge from slavery to freedom."[56] From Nanny of the Maroons to Harriet Tubman, as in *The Salt Roads,* Hopkinson resurrects a diasporic genealogy of rebellious women obscured by the privileging of male revolutionaries who ignored the fact that some of these rebellions were against them.

However, in a move similar to Maryse Condé's refusal to romanticize Tituba, the "black witch" she resurrects from a historical silence, the heroic women in Hopkinson are also ambivalent if not complicit figures.[57] If Rudy in *Brown Girl in the Ring* is a cardboard figure of evil—a combined bogeyman of folklore, vampire of horror story, and wicked wizard of fairy tale—and Tony, Ti-Jeanne's lover and Rudy's weak underling, is the "sweet-talking sagaboy,"[58] Ti-Jeanne, Rudy's sulky granddaughter, is hardly the beloved heroine one roots for at first. Even as the refreshing openness of youthful imagination is said to characterize science fiction, fairy tale, folklore, and magical realism, the precarious position of children, particularly girls, is a frequent theme in feminist fiction.

Hopkinson's variant of the Fall in the genesis myth "How Tan-Tan Learn to Thief" as well as the folkloric rendition of "Tan-Tan and Dry Bone" in *Midnight Robber* pictures older male figures as mutations of the female soucouyant in Caribbean folklore, leeching off the innocent girl and exploiting her.[59] Likewise, Rudy is unilaterally presented as a power-obsessed source of potent evil, combining the malevolent ruthlessness of a slave driver with the threatening potential of the Haitian bokor, the priest-sorcerer of Vodoun. Although Hopkinson is clearly not demonizing Vodoun, giving it pride of place in her religious iconography, Rudy's brutal zombification of Melba and duppification of his own daughter, Mi-Jeanne, locate him within baneful mainstream stereotypes of the practice.[60] Gros-Jeanne, Rudy's wife and Ti-Jeanne's grandmother, occasionally distances herself from both Vodoun and obeah, and identifies herself primarily as a healer of the living and a servitor of the spirits, like Mer. Hopkinson's syncretic use of these practices and her fusing of religious icons despite these disclaimers may seem problematic to those who insist on the distinct cosmography within and between each belief system, whatever the admitted links. But her rejection of the binary of good and evil in characters other than Rudy and his henchmen, and of any rigid separation between religion, folklore, medicine, and magic, speaks more accurately for such Caribbean practices. "Papa Legbara, Prince of Cemetery. Her Eshu. The Jab-Jab"[61] is an open-ended conduit of life and death, truth and lie, sacred and profane, good and evil, female and male: a liminal crossroads figure.[62]

Hopkinson borrows the names of her characters from Derek Walcott's play *Ti-Jean and His Brothers* but converts them into females of three generations.[63] The feminized intertextuality does not vouch for a simple reversal of heroes with heroines, despite the clichéd features of male reprobates and female healers. Toxic domesticity is evident in this retelling, particularly in the evocative children's rhymes and ring games that frequently form the epigraphs to the novel. The exercise of violence is not simply that of white on black, or male on female:

> Rocking my baby, I know you are sad,
> Baby, you were naughty; Baby, you were bad.
> I'm sorry to whip you my darling, but true,
> My Mama whipped me, so I'm bound to whip you.[64]

This disquieting "lullabye" demonstrates, as Gros-Jeanne sadly acknowledges in the novel and as V. S. Naipaul has asserted elsewhere, the harsh legacy of family cruelty, violence against women, and child abuse in post-slavery and post-indentured societies.[65] Although the unnamed bolom baby is, unlike Tan-Tan's, not an outcome of rape and incest, he is still unwanted by Ti-Jeanne, who struggles with being a single parent whose absent mother is mentally disturbed and whose lover is considered "too flighty to make a good father."[66]

Children as unwanted waste or easily exploited subjects are a recurring thread in the novel, an ominous sign of not just the dysfunctional family but also the impaired postapocalyptic nation-state, here represented by a dystopian, futuristic Toronto, rocked by riots and ruined by blight in the city and flight into the suburbs. Feral children of varying ethnicities run wild in its underground, both precocious predators and hapless victims—the disappeared—of Rudy's illicit organ trade. Deprived of the gleeful innocence of childhood, their literal descent exposes children's vulnerability to the infernal. If magic occasionally breaks out from the "enclosed space of frustrated domesticity," it is not always liberatory for all concerned.[67] The mad duppy, the Diablesse, and the soucouyant manifestations of Mi-Jeanne are only extreme versions of Ti-Jeanne's own ambivalence toward her role as granddaughter, daughter, and mother. Not just folklore but also fairy tales reveal the complicated domestic scenarios that put women and children at risk.

Hopkinson's short story "Under Glass," inspired by Hans Christian Anderson but with a science fiction touch, unnervingly concludes with a mother hesitating over opening the door and providing sanctuary to her daughter caught outside in a hailstorm of broken glass.[68] Guilt, rage, and perhaps death are some of the consequences for the child and the mother in such situations. The horrific fallout of unwanted motherhood and resentment against the thankless labor of primary caregivers counters the exoticism, primitivism, and nostalgia in romanticized portrayals of nonwhite women as natural healers and caregivers.

Although science fiction is the genre most associated with imagining how newness enters the world, and is typically located in the future and on another planet, as if all these estranging techniques are necessary to imagine the world anew, in the narrative bridges Hopkinson builds between fairy tale, fantasy, magical realism, horror, and science fiction, the past and material reality are not always shed as easily as a soucouyant's skin. Hopkinson is comfortable with this "mashed up" mixture and is also amenable to the label "speculative fiction" to describe what she writes. Margaret Atwood characterizes the difference as essentially between future and present, with science fiction located in a yet-to-be and speculative fiction ensconced in a futuristic but recognizable earth.[69] Hopkinson, however, writes in the interstice, allowing for reappraisals of race, gender, and sexuality in a faraway planet or time, but also retaining current and even past earth-bound histories.

Recent theories of "the slipstream of mixed reality" may more productively characterize Hopkinson's work, complicated as it is by its porous or quantum mixture of time and space. N. Katherine Hayles and Nicholas Gessler use this adapted phrase to indicate the borderland between science fiction and mainstream fiction and to insist that given the rapid pace of scientific and technological advancement, "conventional distinctions between science fiction and ordinary reality become increasingly difficult to articulate and maintain."[70] While magical realism dispels the boundary between the ordinary and the magical by making the magical mundane, slipstream fiction renders the technological marvels and cognitive estrangement of traditional science fiction into a more everyday affair, particularly to a current generation that may not share an earlier generation's perception of reality, actual or virtual. Even in areas where technological interventions into quotidian life are less prevalent, exposure through Western media tends to take the edge off the defamiliarization common to science fiction, such that the distant future of even more technological marvels seems only a step away.[71] As Hopkinson has discussed in several interviews, estrangement in her fiction is just as likely to come from the Caribbean cultural and linguistic elements in her work for non-Caribbean readers. The hybrid Creole used in *Midnight Robber,* for instance, may just as well be an argot on a new planet for those unfamiliar with it.

This intermixture of past, present, and future, of earthly realities and unearthly elsewheres and other-times, challenges the tired schisms between a Third World lodged in the fantastic past and the First World speeding into the science fiction future.[72] Hopkinson's invocation of postcolonial history in her quantum fiction goes further to challenge the male ethos of conventional science fiction. Gender relations constitute a primary area of defamiliarization in feminist fabulation, and the family, anatomy, and sexuality are made radically alien in order to reimagine and potentially revise their taken-for-grantedness in the real world.[73] But in Hopkinson's fiction, Caribbean gender relations are examined through a corresponding estrangement of accepted racial and sexual categories, allowing each to probe and transform the other. Many writers and critics of science fiction have pointed out that the grotesque depictions of humans or alien beings were not always relegated to futurist extraterrestrial worlds but can be retrieved in colonial accounts of racial and cultural others. As Hopkinson observes, "One of the most familiar memes of science fiction is that of going to foreign countries and colonizing the natives, and . . . for many of us, that's not a thrilling adventure story; it's non-fiction, and we were on the wrong side of the strange-looking ship that appears out of nowhere."[74]

Sheree R. Thomas discusses the speculative fiction of black communities and labels the invisibility of black people in traditional science fictional scenarios as "dark matter," an astronomical term for an undetected form of matter. Yet from early colonialist accounts to contemporary racist narratives, "detected" blackness has been rendered bizarre and grotesque, essentially strange rather than deliberately estranged or defamiliarized. Thomas explains, "Blackness has exerted a power on the international racial psyche that is fantastical."[75] Fantasy, reality, and science fiction are therefore not mutually exclusive categories for Hopkinson, who uses these as well as magical transformations of human beings in a creatively grotesque (re)assembly. Such intermingling in alien forms opens up new possibilities for human interaction. Stretching the body in this protean fashion is in its own way a tall tale, but the resulting composites are not unrelated to social realities. Hopkinson notes a paradox in her flexible manipulations of racial and sexual possibilities: "By exaggerating them into the realm of the fantastical . . . the consequences conversely become so real that they are tangible."[76]

In her short stories, for instance, Hopkinson uses science fiction, fantasy, and magical realism to enable characters to change body parts, sexual orientations, and racial characteristics at will. Sexual relations themselves are explored with frank experimentation, not just through scientific breakthroughs in the future as with the Senstim wet suits that allow men and women to reverse sexual organs in "Ganger (Ball Lightning),"[77] but also in more magical settings such as in *The Salt Roads*, where, besides a range of sexualities, Baudelaire is an appropriate participant in the *jouissance* of raunchy boudoir games. (Jules Verne briefly and parodically appears as the earnest science fiction writer who has just discovered the writings of Edgar Allan Poe.) Like Samuel Delany, her onetime teacher whom she claims as one of multiple influences, Hopkinson challenges normative constructions from different angles.

But as Fredric Jameson speculates, utopian scenarios are never as radical as expected. Citing the image of the seemingly extraordinary Chimera, which is merely made up of different parts of actual animals affixed together,[78] Jameson is unable to conceive of imagining worlds "not somehow already in our historical experience. The latter necessarily clothes all our imaginings, it furnishes the content for the expression and figuration of the most abstract thoughts, the most disembodied longings or premonitions."[79] Even in science fiction or fantasy, therefore, the chimerical imagination can never quite escape the past or entirely leap the bounds of lived reality, assuming they so desired. In the critical dystopia of Hopkinson's making, the earthiness of the living and the rootedness of one's location are deliberately retained.[80] This is particularly evident in her retellings of the legend of the flying Africans, now a rich source of folklore and symbolism across the black diaspora and a cross-Atlantic literary trope.

Flight in the Diasporic Imaginary

I refer to the legend of the flying Africans as folklore, but in literature its appearance can be classified as magical realism, although as I will explain, not in any strict sense.[81] Flight, of course, has a rich symbolic significance worldwide. Piero Boitani begins his exploration of the trope of flight by announcing its universality: "Every culture has imagined flight—the flight of gods, angels, prophets and heroes; flight in science fiction; mystical, psychedelic flights; and finally flights in songs."[82] Focusing on the "western imaginary of flight," Boitani takes his readers on a heady trip from the Greek myths of Pegasus (the winged horse), Icarus (the briefly airborne human), Hermes (the flying god), the varying symbols of halcyons, butterflies, and eagles. He moves on to more historical references such as the Wright brothers' first flight at Kitty Hawk in 1903, the 1945 bombing of Dresden, the 1969 touchdown of *Apollo 11* on the moon, and finally the riveting moment when four hijacked planes in U.S. airspace proved that the exhilarating possibilities that flight has evoked in the universal imagination are quite uncannily laden with overtones of high risk and disaster. While winged words suggest poetry, music, and philosophy—art itself—borne aloft through the image of birds, Icarus's tragic free fall into the ocean, Walter Benjamin's apocalyptic angel of history, and the wreckage of the burning planes in 2001 demonstrate that flight and its various symbols—magical and technological, symbolic and literal—are just as likely to evoke the sublime aspect of terror.

The legend of the flying Africans, not mentioned by Boitani, has a purview that extends across the Americas, particularly located among black coastal communities, but now manifested in other populations.[83] Over and over again, the more formally educated interlocutors of the WPA seem bemused to find in South Carolina and Georgia in the 1930s generally a belief in all kinds of "conjure" and "root work," in ghosts and shadows of otherworldly presence, dream visions, witches riding people, and animist principles illicitly coexisting with Christian faith.[84] But particularly recurrent is the belief that some Africans actually flew away from slavery. The similarities in details and phrasing suggest that regardless of whether one wants to take the story literally as many of the subjects claim to, the folklore at any rate has been extensively shared between generations to the point of structural similarities and patterns (a particular ritual phrase, a specific physical movement) across regions. Most of the participants recorded in *Drums and Shadows* seem to accept it at face value by invoking other authorities, albeit largely familial sources—"my grand," "muh mothuh," "muh daddy used to tell me. . . ." Only one or two claim to have seen people fly away or disappear or to have witnessed something equally incredible that makes them more readily accept that some African people knew how to fly and they exercised that "technology" to escape the shackles of an intolerable slavery.

The connection between material reality and magical escape is very significant here. In almost every variant that goes into some detail, the instances of flight occur when the slaves are in the field, under insufferable duress. As one account goes, "My gran use tuh tell me bout folks flying back tuh Africa. A man an his wife wuz brung from Africa. Wen dey fine out dey wuz slabes an got treat so hahd, dey jis fret an fret. One day dey wuz standin wid some udduh slabes an all ub a sudden dey say, 'We gwine back tuh Africa. So goodie bye, goodie bye.' Den dey flied right out uh sight."[85] The unflinching faith in some African people's power of flight comes across not as foolish but as all the more pragmatic to those who tell the stories. If there is anything unreasonable here, they imply, it is that humans could actually enslave other humans without expecting such extreme responses. As Erna Brodber concludes, "To fly like a bird is a desire found anywhere there are prisons and problems. The enslaved Africans had four hundred years' need to engage this simile and the dichotomy associated with it."[86]

In Toni Morrison's *Song of Solomon,* Milkman Dead, who breaks into hysterical laughter when someone tells him he has seen a ghost, hears the story of Solomon his ancestor who just upped and took off one day. He asks his informant, "When you say 'flew off' you mean he ran away, don't you? Escaped?" The uncompromising response to his question from Susan Byrd is, "No, I mean flew. . . . He was flying. He flew. You know, like a bird."[87] Milkman's need to rationalize the belief and translate it into the realm of possibility from literal to metaphorical is understandable, because maroon flights into the wilderness often occurred in secrecy and stealth that did indeed seem like they had disappeared overnight, "flown away." But Morrison's refusal to satisfy Milkman's rationality reveals a system of beliefs that seems so at odds with the credible and the empiricist, particularly in Westernized, industrialized areas, as to qualify as something off the wall, impossible.

Arguing for an ontological marvelous in the Caribbean, Alejo Carpentier explains why he was converted by the "collective faith" of the slaves that "produced" the "miracle" of Makandal's flight at the moment when he is to be burned at the stake for organizing mass poisonings of planter families.[88] Unlike the virtuoso techniques of European writers and artists whose version of magic, according to Carpentier, rings of insincerity and lack of faith, because they are unable "to conceive of a valid mysticism or to abandon the most banal habits in order to bet their souls on the terrifying card of faith,"[89] the magical realism of the Caribbean is a creative aspect of the everyday where real life often seems unbelievable and extraordinary events seem mundane. In the account of the execution in *The Kingdom of This World,* the laughter and celebration of the slaves, both before and after the public spectacle of burning Makandal at the stake calculated by their masters to demoralize them, baffle the colonial authorities.[90] But the narrator explains the perceived incongruity as emerging from the very different worldviews of the masters and the slaves: "What did the whites know of Negro matters?"[91] Makandal's grotesque transformation into various winged insects, his ability to operate outside his bound and deformed slave body—"This was what their masters did not know."[92]

The secret shared only by the slave community—a radical difference in not just ontology but epistemology, according to the narrator's stress on occult, esoteric knowledge—is not always clandestine.[93] But it is a set of societal beliefs that challenges the skeptics to consider the social, psychological, historiographic, and philosophical role played by mysticism, magic, divination, and prophecy: the mnemonic devices, the subjugated and discredited knowledge through which an unofficial, popular history is revealed. Both the magical as well as the performative aspects here may be put down as "primitive," freezing such views into the arrested development of premodernity, the cultural equivalent of an embryonic stage. But these oral folktales and literary versions play a powerful role that cannot be so easily dismissed.

As García Márquez demonstrates in his disorienting account of the Banana Company massacre in *One Hundred Years of Solitude,* and as Salman Rushdie's satire on Indian and Pakistani news accounts during the war in *Midnight's Children* reveals, the lies of official colonial or nationalist history gain a commonsense, objectivist reality that must be unsettled and exposed through the seeming nonsense of magical realism.[94]

In the pithy formulation of Milan Kundera, "On the surface, an intelligible lie; underneath, the unintelligible truth."[95] When "straightforward" accounts of what "really" happened are distorted or inadequate, dream states, visions, hallucinations, and imaginary events paradoxically provide more legitimate explanations or responses to the terror of history. The fact that Milkman Dead's individual genealogy and collective legacy is revealed through children's rhymes and ring games and through the oral narratives and memories of his female guides is not accidental, since, like the primitive and the nonwhite, women and children are also underestimated purveyors and transmitters of cultural knowledge and history.

Hopkinson's account of Makandal's flight, however, is a decidedly ambivalent if not downright negative reading that refuses an easy slide into the magical or the revolutionary. Male flight in Morrison's novel has been critically reviewed.[96] It bears too disturbing a proximity to the negative stereotype of male abandonment in black families, whether through death, desertion, or incarceration. In Earl Lovelace's *Salt,* flight in general, from the trope of the flying Africans to mass migration from the islands, is powerfully if sympathetically challenged. But in *The Salt Roads,* the automatic correlation between flight and freedom, between marronage and revolution, is severed in the characterization of Makandal and his likely fate at the stake.[97] The narrative is in Mer's first-person account and by now the reader is already familiar with her dislike and distrust of Makandal, who she believes is putting too many people at risk for his own glory.

Unlike Carpentier's fictional account that leaves juxtaposed two diverging views of whether Makandal was burned or flew away without explicit editorial comment, here Mer specifically says she saw him burn and collapse on the embers. Then some witnesses set up a shout of seeing a "manmzel" fly away, and as in Carpentier's novel, they celebrate what they interpret as Makandal's metamorphosis and escape. But Mer insists, "I could not see it." She notices that the authorities have been feeding him salt pork in prison, a possibly deliberate attempt to break his spirit by breaking taboos, since the belief is that only slaves who do not eat salt can fly; and Makandal, being Muslim, is forbidden pork. (In following this speculation about Makandal's religion, Hopkinson does not account for his association with Vodoun.) Mer wonders a little later, "Did he eat the food? Or did he starve himself and fly free one last time? Mama, what just happened here? . . . In my head, I could still hear him screaming in agony. I wanted to believe that Makandal flew away, but my wishes can't fly freely so. They're rooted to the ground like me, who eats salt."[98]

By associating salt with humility and obedience to Lasiren, Mer, like Lovelace, suggests that eating salt is not the inevitable sign of resigned slavery any more than dreams of flight are necessarily revolutionary. Eating salt could well be a sign of creolization and a disavowal of a nostalgic return to Africa. Not that Africa is deliberately forgotten or slavery passively accepted. Mer's section, however, certainly ends on a note of critical dystopia: "It is ugly in this world, and when the killing starts, the same stick will beat the black dog and the white."[99] Her prediction of the killing fields in Haiti is as sobering as Ti-Noel's disillusionment when he finds himself under renewed bondage by a once revolutionary regime in Carpentier's novel. While Hopkinson is by no means subscribing to the demonization of postrevolutionary Haiti, Mer foretells the internecine violence of a predatory state encouraged in part by the neocolonial hangover of paramilitaristic regimes such as the Duvaliers. The critical reading of Makandal not only applies the brakes on Carpentier's mystifications of the Caribbean landscape, black folk, and the Maroons, it also demands that we understand the heroic and the revolutionary from Mer's grounded and gendered point of view.

While the desire to escape one's racially fixed (and bound) or gendered body is perfectly understandable, the interrupted trajectory of flight patterns suggests an alternative referral back to earth, to the specific historical situation that needs to change. Even in the case of the woman's desire for flight, Ti-Jeanne's eventual return to her body is telling. At the end of *Brown Girl,* Rudy rubs buff powder into a gash he inflicts on her skin, in an attempt to replace Melba and Mi-Jeanne, his earlier victims, with his granddaughter. He makes it seem an act of seduction, though, pointing out that people who "slash buff" feel like they are "flying," a hallucinogenic perception of reality.[100] But as Ti-Jeanne knows, buff (so named because it comes from bufo, the poisonous toad) paralyzes nerves and muscles to create zombies, a physiological state that precedes a process of "*indoctrination,*" as Rudy smugly adds.[101] Ethnobotanical and other sources of medicinal knowledge are used by Rudy for poison and Gros-Jeanne for healing, reflecting their traditionally divergent use in both obeah and Vodoun.

Rudy presents Ti-Jeanne's out-of-body experience as desirable and she momentarily allows herself to consider the temptation of shedding her skin and escaping her domestic carceral: "There would be no Baby constantly demanding her attention and her energy. *She coulda go wherever she want, nobody to stop she.*"[102] Her choice of anxious corporeality over unencumbered astral existence recognizes that the latter offers only misleading freedom from material responsibility and maternal care.[103] "The absolute absence of a burden causes man to be lighter than air, to soar into the heights, take leave of the earth and his earthly being, and become only half real, his movements as free as they are insignificant," notes Kundera.[104] As a healed Mi-Jeanne confesses later, she had felt the same resentment against Ti-Jeanne and abandoned her to regain Rudy's love.

While Ti-Jeanne's acceptance of the "burden" of motherhood might seem like capitulation to conventional patriarchal norms, she does it on her own terms, breaking the cycle of child abandonment and parental flight. With the help of the West African gods she calls up, Rudy and his evil minions are killed and Ti-Jeanne carries on her grandmother's legacy, even as the latter's organs are co-opted by the state in a poignant echo of slave women's lack of full ownership over their bodies. Africa makes its presence felt through Caribbean channels, but only to secure Ti-Jeanne to her Canadian location. The past, present, and futuristic societies scramble linear chronology; and magic, science, and religion present an alternate universe in which women become superheroes and saviors, albeit flawed ones.

Magical Metamorphoses from Sky to Sea

I had stated earlier that Hopkinson's critical reading of flight indicates neither a rejection of Africa nor a tolerance of slavery. What happens to slaves and their descendants in her novel *New Moon's Arms* might suggest yet another formulation of the desire to escape the intolerable past and present, although I would argue that the metamorphosis in the ocean, however fantastic, demonstrates magical realism's reengagement with the real, the tormented but not doomed historical predicament of the slave subject. As in the legend of the flying Africans, the unfettered imagination in the novel shows too poignantly the dire constraints of the enslaved body. The imagination explodes when the experience of bondage becomes unbearable.

The exuberant excesses of magical realism at times conceals, at times paradoxically draws attention to what is absent, spilling over the void it attempts to fill. "This may be an absent freedom, but it is not an abstract freedom: it is precisely that which is made present and possible by its absence—the lives that people have never lived *because* of the lives they are forced to live or have chosen to live. That which is desired and that which exists, the sense of abundance and the sense of waste, are dialectically related," argues Sangari.[105] When Africans were believed to have flown away from slavery, the narrative is less about what really happened in the past than what it might signify for their future: a sense of hope that their bondage would end even if took a miracle. A usable past is extracted from these magical narratives, the elixir to impel future action. Ceremonies such as Boukman's reputed Bois Caïman incantations are alleged to have provided psychological fuel to the fire of the Haitian revolution. Even if direct action does not result, how the story of their flight is told and retold, its very generativity, as Scheherazade's tales suggest, is a sign of life under threat of death. In such dire situations, bones become words and other magical metamorphoses occur.

The title *New Moon's Arms* aptly uses a scientific phenomenon to express a reverse fostering relationship between the past and future. The phrase is a folksy way of describing the astronomical term "earthshine," when sunlight reflected from the earth is visible as a thin sliver of the moon. The old moon, or the rest of the darker circle, seems nestled in this crescent, leading to the quaint saying "the old Moon in the new Moon's arms." Hopkinson seems to deploy this image from outer space to illuminate her approach to history: here the shadowed past is cradled by the newborn, more hopeful future. The distant light from above actually emanates from the earth, beaming back to it the glimpsed potential of a brighter future yet to come.

But what lies concealed for most of the novel beneath the ocean depths is nevertheless calamitous, even as it seems exquisitely paranormal. The narrative moves from what Amaryll Chanady would label fantasy to a gradual sense of magical realism[106] as the novel's feisty, fifty-three-year-old Chastity, who renames herself Calamity to more appropriately depict her life (and, as it turns out, the horrors of slavery), begins to accept the marvel of the sea people. Finding a little toddler with amphibian characteristics, a combination of fish and human by the seashore, Calamity adopts and finally returns him to the sea by the end of the novel. Some of the authorial reticence that Chanady calls for is exercised when it comes to Calamity's full knowledge of the existence of these fishy humans. But the omniscient narrator's italicized interventions scattered through the narrative reveal to the readers what is hidden from the inhabitants of the fictional island of Cayaba. The reverse metaphor of cradling implies not only that the child from the sea will play a role in Calamity's resolution of her unresolved filial and maternal tensions, but also that the telling of this childlike tale will restore a traumatic past into a convalescent if not fully healed future.

While Hopkinson uses science fiction to dismantle gender binaries, she is not quite able to escape them entirely, particularly in her insistence on women's perspectives. Evolutionary biology and sex differences have long been used to put middle-class women in particular in their place as keepers of the hearth and reproductive receptacles. As the second sex, women, it was argued, were genetically suited to the sensible socially prescribed roles of domesticity. Sociobiology used circular arguments to defend the latter state of affairs. Virtually universal taboos against menstrual blood and gloomy prognostications of menopause were among the supposed data commandeered as evidence of women's diminished productivity and questionable mental and emotional stability. Both organic processes tracking the woman's reproductive cycle attained bewitching and diseased qualities tied to social pollution and impurity, decay and disorderly hormonal syndromes. Conversely, menstruation and menopause have been incorporated by radical feminism as essential characteristics of the feminine, to be highly valued as such, leading to their romanticized portrayal. Intrauterine and mammary images have been part of some radical feminists' arsenal, French feminists such as Cixous, for instance, coining the term "white ink" to inscribe *l'écriture féminine.*[107] In the Caribbean context, Beryl Gilroy uses the "Long Bubbies" attributed to slave women whose breasts were elongated by the particular nursing tactics of their children to signify coming to writing and women's emergence into history.[108]

Hopkinson uses similarly recuperative biological images of the woman's coming to consciousness. Calamity's menopause, far from simply being the mortifying condition she complains of at first, is the empowering biological catalyst of material manifestations from her childhood. Unable to accept the child born from a humiliating teenage encounter with a school friend for whom the act confirms that he is gay, she initially rejects her role as mother and grandmother, breaking away from their sometimes prescriptive presence in black women's narratives. Her abandonment by her lover explains her bitterness over men and her homophobia, although it does not excuse it. The feminine mystique here is specified in a particular historical context, and Calamity's struggles are not over domesticity as such but over teenage pregnancy and abandonment by the male figures in her life.

Considering that women, nonwhites, and subjects of European colonies were derogatorily portrayed as being close to nature, the novel engages in a tricky negotiation of gendered and racial primitivist stereotypes, often risking reconfirmation. But they are also simultaneously challenged, since what exactly is considered natural and what is not, what is perceived as real and what is not, are interrogated. Calamity's brief adoption of the sea child allows her to revisit her childhood and review her life. Her fear of aging is put in check by the sense of regeneration at the end, echoing feminist challenges to the detrimental stereotypes of women's bodily changes.

Science, fantasy, and magic continually interact in the novel, ultimately providing a luminous account of what is at stake when Calamity's individual and historic pasts literally come back to haunt her.[109] The free-spirited, foulmouthed grandmother is having trouble coming to terms with aging, and the discomfort of her menopausal symptoms—hot flashes, tingling, irritability, loss of memory—do not seem to be helping the reconciliation. But as Benjamin famously put it, "To articulate the past historically . . . means to seize hold of a memory as it flashes up at a moment of danger."[110] With each biological hot flash or "power surge," as Hopkinson puts it, a flashback is catalyzed by a physical object from Calamity's childhood. A plate, a teddy bear, a truck, children's books, even an entire cashew orchard, explosively materializes into the present. If this is a literal, gendered version of the Proustian madeleine, what elusive past (or phantom limb) lies in these object-ive memories seems initially related only to the individual memory or more precisely to remembrance, to a personal retrospective movement from present to past.

At first a baffled Calamity is the skeptic who finds these uncanny manifestations "horripilating," but with each piece of the puzzle and the incredible evidence of the hitherto rumored sightings of sea people in the form of the lovable toddler whom she names "Agway" (signifying Agwe, Ezili's consort and lord of the ocean in the Vodoun pantheon), Calamity is forced into disconcerting insights about the nature of the real and the return of the repressed. The increasing shakiness of the world she no longer finds understandable or rational exposes her aversion to people on land who are different from her: gays, bisexuals, and Rastas, for example. The play between the derogatory epithet "aunty man" (signifying homosexual) and being "anti-man" becomes obvious as the "unnatural" child from the sea inspires an evaluation of what makes someone properly human, how that would affect internal discrimination between people, as well as their hierarchy over other living beings. As the douen disapprovingly observes to a scornful Antonio in *Midnight Robber,* "Oonuh tallpeople quick to name what is people and what is beast."[111]

But satisfying as these revelations are, utopian desire is ultimately not merely personal but "historical and collective wish fulfillment."[112] The mystifying interruptions of the present in Calamity's first-person voice by a third-person narration of a Middle Passage is clarified (only to the readers) in the end. The account of the oceanic metamorphosis is what Harris would call an epic moment, and by epic he means "an eruptive phenomenon of both science and the novelistic imagination": in other words, quantum fiction with a sense of time, place, and subjectivity not shared by conventional linear fiction. "We arrive backwards even as we voyage forwards" is how Harris expresses this simultaneous sense of time.[113] Sharing a "plural mask" partially with Calamity and Agway, a "dada-hair lady" (dada meaning "curly" in Yoruba) and a young boy, along with other slaves, metamorphose into seal-like creatures when a slave ship goes down and everyone else drowns. Utopias are not only wish fulfillment; they may be "hallucinatory visions in desperate times."[114] The prayers of the "dada-hair lady," probably associated with magic and medicine in the village from where she was kidnapped, are answered but not quite in the way she anticipates. Here menstruation, likened to the flow of mother's milk, rather than menopause, is the suggestive "gift" that gives, the flow of taboo blood (also from a gunshot wound) to the sea a heretical and feminist sacrificial offering that enables the metamorphoses, in a kind of reverse evolution, and saves many slaves.[115] "*The people's arms flattened out into flexible flippers. The shackles slipped off their wrists. . . . The people's bodies grew thick and fat. Legs melted together. . . . The people's faces swelled and transformed: round heads with snouts. Big, liquid eyes.*"[116]

Unlike Makandal's solitary metamorphosis, Hopkinson's insistence on the collective and on female agency and biology is deliberate, if controversial. The presence of the fish people is attributed to folklore, myth, and even island rumor, none of which turns out to be unfeasible. The way Edwidge Danticat's short story "Children of the Sea" pictures it, an entire province of Africans bound for transatlantic slavery exists leagues below the surface of the ocean,[117] an uncanny literal embodiment of Kamau Brathwaite's claims of a submerged Africa on Caribbean shores.[118] As in Walcott's poetry, the vestiges of human remains in the sea transform into "something rich and strange," a creatively grotesque recycling of waste into abundance, death into revivification, catastrophe into mystery.[119] The magical realist elements in the novel present this event and Chastity's encounters with the fish people, from her childhood to when she returns Agway to the sea, as if they were a commonplace.

Despite various attempts to stifle the "truth" of their existence, many people on the island seem to have seen the fish people at some point. When eventually caught on a spy-camera, these beings are presented as inexplicable fantasy by the mainstream media: "*One question remains:*

is this photograph of the women swimming nude finally proof of the existence of fish people? Or is it just an example of the types of hijinks performed by some of the more boisterous visitors to Cayaba? We may never know."[120] The readers know, whatever they make of it. It is ironic that the media speculation turns the magical fish people into a possible scam pulled off by rowdy tourists through techno wizardry, because the novel concludes with the island community's protests against exploitative tourism. Chastity is inspired to join the demonstrations to which she contributes the shrimp apparently left as a gift by the fish people. As in Melville's short story "Erzulie" in *The Migration of Ghosts* and her novel *The Ventriloquist's Tale,* the legacies of slavery, multinational capitalism, illegal dumping of toxins, excessive touristification, and the lack of local autonomy are the real historical conditions exposed and critiqued through folk beliefs and magical realist depictions.[121]

While the liveliness of Hopkinson's novel does indeed suggest a play on the fishy, the tall tale of the trickster, the inkling that someone's leg—most likely the reader's—is being pulled, there is also something deadly serious at work here, an antinomy characteristic of the best in magical realism and apparent in Hopkinson's speculative fiction. She reminds us that literature, with all its intuitive and imaginative capabilities, is allied with speculative philosophy whose promise lies in not forcefully seeking absolute answers to the big questions in life through logical reasoning or empirical evidence. Speculation here avoids both the dogma of science and the blind faith of orthodox religion in order to focus more on the conjectural possibilities in ethics, aesthetics, and metaphysics.

The Magic of Words and the Literary Imagination

The material power of words is repeatedly asserted in Hopkinson's fiction. The subaltern not only speaks but does so in a bravura fashion that overwhelms her tormentor. In "Ganger (Ball Lightning)" and "Precious," the women in each story talk their way out of mortal danger. While Issy rescues herself and her lover from an animated wet suit that tries to electrify them by distracting it with seductive conversation, Precious begins her tactical attack on her abusive husband by first disarming him. "I had to placate him. I kept talking." Precious's mouth spews jewels every time she opens it, one of the reasons her husband holds her captive in Hopkinson's more skeptical reading of this folktale. But as Precious goes on to vent her rage, the gemstones become "flying" weapons. "All those years of resentment gouted forth: emeralds green with jealousy; seething red garnets, cold blue chunks of lapis. . . . I ejected them from my mouth with the force of thrown rocks."[122] After she verbally denounces her father, her stepmother, and her husband, she finds that jewels no longer drop from her mouth, leaving her free of her husband's custody. She bursts into joyous laughter at this realization.

Malinowski's "ethnographic theory of the magical word" provides an intriguing explanation for the chatty skeletal lexicon in *The Ventriloquist's Tale,* Hopkinson's account of jeweled weapons, Brathwaite's insistence on the "sound elements" of Creoles, and the power associated with mantras, chants, and incantations in many religious and magical rituals.[123] Stanley Tambiah explains that the belief in "magical speech, man-made, existed from the very beginning as primeval text coeval with reality, and could be launched as 'breath' and transformed into magical missiles by accredited magicians."[124] The writer, the priest, and the magician all wield the power of the word that can be appropriated as a weapon of the weak as well as exploited as a means of dominance.

The "sonic text" is not simply magical or religious. It bears repeating that nonwhite and more specifically black communities are not merely on the receiving end of technology. They have long influenced or participated in the conventions of science and technology, particularly in expressive cultures. Greg Tate draws a connection from Egyptian civilization to the contributions of Afrofuturism and interest in the latest gizmos in black and Latino communities.[125] We see it replayed in fiction from the presence of the Book of the Dead in Danticat's *The Dew Breaker* to the "GhettoNerd" Oscar and his science fiction/fantasy comic books and characters in Díaz's novel.[126] Such a tradition is not without its dark side, since "Borged" hybrid identity is not always enabling, implying instead the evil power of the alien and also signifying the victimization of perceived alien others.[127] Like Hopkinson, Tate has a more critical sense of familiar science fiction paradigms. Discussing Ralph Ellison's *Invisible Man* as a modern precursor to contemporary Afrofuturism, Tate insists that the novel "deals with the condition of being alien and alienated [and] speaks . . . to the way in which being black in America is a science fiction experience."[128] Although not written as science fiction, Danticat's accounts of various characters deprived of human rights prove that the experience of alienation is shared across the black diaspora.

Danticat's memoir *Brother, I'm Dying* ironically signifies on the notion of universal brotherhood through broken familial and national filiation in medical and political crisis, presenting Joseph Dantica, her uncle and sometime foster parent, as the undesirable "invisible man" killed through neglect and coldblooded immigration procedures in Miami while fleeing

Haiti. The dreaded detention center, Krome, a name that conjures up the metallic, aloof, high-security repressive apparatus of a science-fiction penal complex, confirms its chilly legality in the incapacity to see Dantica as anything but a serial number, "Alien 27041999." A series of mistranslations, misdiagnoses, and cultural misunderstandings—even virulent stereotypes—leads to his tragic death when he is refused the emergency medical assistance he desperately needs. His herbal medicines, referred to as "a voodoolike potion," are taken away, and while that may not have immediately caused the death of an elderly man in ill health, Dantica is puzzled and disturbed by it as much as by the loss of his journals and notebooks in which he had been recording his troubles in Haiti. (He tells his niece that the US immigration authorities had burned them.)

This invisibility and erasure, coupled with the destruction of his artificial "voice box" that he uses after his radical laryngectomy (paid for by American missionaries but adding to his cyborg untranslatability for the suspicious officials), link his history to his physiology. The machine is ruined when he vomits on it in his dying throes, which the medical officer skeptically interprets as Dantica faking it. Caught between the internecine violence of a postcolonial Haiti and the inflexible U.S. border, the phrase from which the memoir takes its title—"Brother, I'm Dying"—addresses more than a biological sibling in its plea for transnational human rights.

As in Amabelle's inability to pronounce *perejil,* which marks her for genocide in *The Farming of Bones,* Dantica's voice is doubly distorted for the immigration authorities, both for his accent and through the voice box. The frigidly impersonal immigration records and interviews minimize Danticat's warm, caring uncle to nothing more than an illegal, unintelligible cipher, an errant alien seeking superior human civilization. When confronted with the loss of his larynx due to a tumor, he muses on the significance of voices and reflects on the importance of communication technology: "the telephone, the radio, microphones, megaphones, amplifiers."[129] But eventually it is through print, her imaginative record of the life and death of her uncle, that Danticat determinedly reproduces her uncle's lost voice and represents him in the fullness of his being, not as an abject alien number.

Subaltern speech is an admittedly risky enterprise. Faris may be going too far in arguing that it "is almost always ventriloquized" since the terrorized are usually silenced.[130] But Hopkinson seems to agree in the way she describes how Tan-Tan's "Robber Talk" bursts forth: "She was, *somebody* was speaking out loud. Words welled up in the somebody's mouth like water. Somebody spoke her words the way the Carnival Robber Kings wove their tales, talking as much nonsense as sense, fancy words spinning out from their mouths like thread from a spider's behind: silken shit as strong as story."[131] The Granny in "Riding the Red" counsels against old wives' tales being dismissed as so much superstitious drivel: the old wives were the ones who had lived through them and remembered them best, she pointedly adds.[132] Magical thinking in psychology is similarly considered to be a "primitive" mental activity prevalent in young children, an illogical expectation that reality can be transformed in desirable ways through certain irrational measures. It is even tied to severe mental derangement such as schizophrenia.[133]

But as Martin Grotjahn reminds us, children and schizophrenics are creatively alike in being able "to ventilate their unconscious without [always] getting into trouble."[134] In an analysis that shares much in common with Harris's theory of the literate imagination, Grotjahn distinguishes technical invention from the inventions of the imagination, which demand a different range of skills and produce a different kind of gratification. He goes on to state rather generally that in times of doubt the American mother tends to turn "to the expert or to a book" for advice, while the European mother turns "to Grandmother. So far as the relationship to the unconscious of the child is concerned, Grandmother probably knows the answer."[135] Turning to Grandmother is, if anything, even more common in the Caribbean. As Nalo Hopkinson's speculative fiction reveals, children and old wives—new moons in the old moons' arms—reveal to us the magical power of storytelling. The web of stories these Scheherazades spin links memories and narratives together in an inventive chain, and the very act of narrating them underlines not just the pleasure of storytelling but also the defiant fight for survival in a threatening world.

5 Medusa's Laugh

Carnivalesque Comedy and the Caribbean Grotesque

> The social comedies I write can be fully appreciated only by someone who knows the region I write about. Without that knowledge it is easy for my books to be dismissed as farces and my characters as eccentrics.
>
> —V. S. Naipaul, "London"

> The Caribbean sensibility is not marinated in the past. It is not exhausted. It is new. . . . It will survive the malaria of nostalgia and the delirium of revenge, just as it survived its self-contempt.
>
> —Derek Walcott, "The Muse of History"

> You don't have to be funny to live here, but it helps.
>
> —Zadie Smith, "Dead Man Laughing"

REVOLUTION IS a serious business. This may be why one does not automatically reach for anti-slavery, anticolonial, and postcolonial literature when in the mood for a hearty laugh. Even if the outcome is not always revolutionary, the suffering of those concerned and their bitter struggle for full human status and civil rights constitute significant themes of these literatures, topics hardly conducive to unrestrained merriment. Aside from the unsettling insurgency of violent revolution, the troubled relationship between laughter and power struggle offers another reason for the uncommonness of postcolonial humor as a topic. The safety-valve theory suggests that laughter dispels or diffuses what Frantz Fanon via Jean Paul Sartre would call the "nervous condition" of the natives whose explosive tension provides the momentum of radical transformation in the status quo. In other words, the boiling-over point can be reached only if the intense heat of justified anger is not allowed to let off steam. Humor and its corollaries offer coping mechanisms that may have an anticlimactic cooling-down effect, making it an "uneasy bedfellow" of postcolonial (and, one may add, Marxist and feminist) studies.[1]

This less heated reaction is certainly possible and surprisingly not undesirable to some writers who, like Derek Walcott, implicitly or explicitly worry that the grim history of slavery and colonialism and the graveness of revolution can too easily lead to an unreflective nostalgia for a precolonial past, an abiding melancholy in the present, and a "delirium of revenge" that will poison the future of multiethnic, postcolonial populations who have to create a new state and live together with once inimical adversaries. At the same time, neither anger nor activism is necessarily foreclosed in comedy, as several texts discussed in this chapter reveal. Although one may insist "the empire laughs back," any essentialist argument for a generalized postcolonial laughter is difficult, given the range of cultural contexts and political realities of this diverse geographical spread.[2] Interpreting humor as a specific cultural attribute and providing unitary readings on the nature of laughter with any one easily predictable effect may run aground, but nevertheless we can attempt some coherent, if provisional, framework.

While I am not unilaterally asserting any national or racial style of humor and its particular effects, there are certain conditions of possibility that shape a sense of humor in particular ways, leaving aside the personal and the idiosyncratic. At the same time humor is, dare one say, a universal attribute; and as with magical realism and fantasy, what seem to be culture-specific comic modes can travel across countries to be appreciated by an international audience.[3] The very compilation of volumes on such topics, scarce though they may be, suggests that some generalizations can indeed be drawn, and that something holds this admittedly tenuous center together.

Roydon Salick, for instance, far from excising humor in the modern Caribbean with its brutal past of settlement, slavery, and colonization, claims that "comedy roots and sprouts everywhere" in the region and argues for a distinct brand of anglophone "West Indian" humor, characteristic of a people he claims are "loud, expressively vocal," with an "endless fascination for wordplay." The latter he then identifies as a particularly Trinidadian pastime: "Trinidad is the home of 'mauvaise langue,' of 'picong,' of 'mamaguy,' of 'ole-talk,' of 'shit-talk,' of 'fatigue,' of 'giving tone,' of 'grand charge,' . . . of the carnivalesque 'pierrot grenade.'"[4] To this list we can add the calypso.

While the range of terms for linguistic play is indeed an indication of its pervasiveness in Trinidadian culture, Mervyn Morris and Carolyn

Cooper may not exactly agree with Salick that Trini Creole is "the richest dialect in the English-speaking Caribbean."[5] Their analyses of Louise Bennett's poetry have not only drawn attention to her rollicking sense of humor, they have also celebrated the performative inventiveness of "Jamaican," a Creole so vital it attains the status of what Kamau Brathwaite would call a nation language rather than a "dialect."[6] Without the ubiquitous presence of Carnival as in Trinidad, the performative aspects of Bennett's Jamaican Creole are not tied to the specific event, but nevertheless demonstrate various qualities of the carnivalesque, as I will discuss later.

The Jamaican axiom "Tek bad tings mek laugh" could arguably formulate a "comic vision": the national equivalent of making lemonade when life hands one lemons. While it is true that humor from any country can often travel well, there is no doubt that some familiarity with the language and the context helps a great deal in catching the joke as I found on one occasion when members of a Kingston audience laughed helplessly over fast-paced Creole dialogues in a play riffing on local events, while those of us less familiar with them missed the cues altogether. But even as national humor is specific in its richness, it does have some impact even in contexts not attuned to its local resonance.

"Don't Worry, Be Happy" or "Don't Happy, Be Worry"? Between Elation and Elegy

The often-deadly seriousness of postcolonial issues seems to belie pleasure, including for some critics the aesthetic fulfillment one demands from "good" literature. But the Caribbean has had to suffer from a reverse stereotype, which this book claims throughout, of being the carefree scene of a hedonistic paradise, geographically and culturally constructed for tourist enjoyment. Even the justly famed exuberantly expressive cultures of the Afro-Caribbean have a shadowy side, which Fanon ambivalently tags as a "muscular orgy,"[7] and Walcott forebodingly perceives as "the emphatic gaiety of that dance at the edge of the abyss."[8]

Fanon at least grants the ecstatic dances and other signs of "hampered aggressivity" in the black colonial subject some physiological and emotional, if temporary, release: "The evil humours are undammed, and flow away with a din as of molten lava."[9] But Walcott understands high spirits in the Caribbean to be coerced by factors other than colonialism. He warns against the seduction of the modern version of touristified minstrelsy, the shallow "commercial elation"[10] bound to the "music of Happy Hour and the rictus of a smile."[11] Much of Walcott's critique echoes V. S. Naipaul's critical assessment of Trinidad in the sixties, when the latter bemoans the "ebullience and irresponsibility" of the "Land of the Calypso," and in a particularly striking choice of words, speaks of the "gaiety . . . assault[ing him]."[12]

Occasionally, when students fresh from a Caribbean cruise take my class in the amiable expectation of unalloyed enjoyment, I find myself focusing not so much on the cultural topics of dance, music, and the pleasant memories of vacation that drew them to the course but rather on the issues dominant in Caribbean literature: genocide, slavery, indentured servitude, racial and class injustice, ethnonational conflict, labor riots, social—specifically gendered—violence, and so on. This tends to swing the class reeling to an opposing and, to my mind, equally undesirable sense of crushing Sisyphean trauma. Walcott is aware of these risky extremes and complains simultaneously of the morbidity in the region's literature and "history, that Medusa of the New World," to use his eloquent phrase.[13]

In a common climatological stereotype, Walcott on the one hand aligns the tropics with a "brilliant vacuity," with mindless ease, while the somber winters and four seasons of European climates add "depth and darkness to life as well as to literature."[14] On the other, he is stuck with the paradox of the overwhelming pathos in Caribbean history set in a natural landscape of great beauty but scarred by colonial anguish and postcolonial angst. The landscape itself is not always bright but tends to reflect trauma in brooding literary depictions, where the tropical environment seems just as capable of "depth and darkness" as presumably any gloomy English winter. But this elegiac mode then seems overdone, and Walcott perversely switches to the desirability of a "political philosophy rooted in elation."[15]

In his Nobel lecture, Walcott opens deliberately with the performance of the *Ramleela* in a village named Felicity, addressing a number of tensions and debates with this choice. Rather than set the Indian population apart in Trinidad as irrevocably other, he brings them center-stage through this religious festival. Unlike Naipaul's more negative sense of British colonial mimicry and Indian authenticity woefully reproduced in the elsewhere of the Caribbean, nothing about this Hindu celebration in a contemporary Trinidadian village with a "gentle Anglo-Saxon" name thousands of miles from India or England ultimately seems inauthentic. Walcott explains, "I was polluting the afternoon with doubt and with the patronage of admiration. I misread the event through a visual echo of History—the cane fields, indenture, the evocation of vanished armies, temples, and trumpeting elephants—when all around me there was quite the opposite: elation, delight in the boys' screams, in the sweet-stalls, in more and more costumed characters appearing; a delight of conviction, not loss. The name Felicity made sense."[16] The faith of the East Indians and an ongoing sense of history not immobilized by its past bestow meaningful dignity on the cane effigies of their gods and demons.

Echoing Wilson Harris's evocation of carnival masks as symbolic of life's ceaseless potential, the reanimation of ancient ritual prevails over the nagging ache of the phantom limb and the suggestive parallel with the ruins of Percy Shelley's Ozymandias, both of which occur to Walcott in the elegiac interpretation of the religious festival. He quotes James Anthony Froude immediately after the above remarks in a satirical echo of *The Middle Passage,* which is peppered with what J. J. Thomas would call froudacities.[17] The not so muted reference to Naipaul is a calculated challenge, since few writers are accused of reinforcing a message of dereliction and a wrecked history in the Caribbean more than Naipaul, to whom I will return later. But here in the village's organic, seasonal rituals, away from the forced "commercial elation" of the nightclub, the bar and beach scene, is Kamau Brathwaite and Wilson Harris's recuperative sense of limbo, a more spontaneous "delight," one that embraces both the pain and the promise of New World identities.

Walcott struggles between wanting the compulsorily enacted effervescent qualities of the Caribbean to rise (or more precisely fall) to the poignant note of elegy, if not the imposing genre of tragedy, while simultaneously eschewing a petrifying backward glance into its tragic history. Meanwhile, David Scott reminds us that another Caribbean intellectual, C. L. R. James, thought and wrote a great deal more about tragedy than has been noted. In Scott's view, the politics of revolution seems more aptly plotted in a contemporary frame through the poetics of tragedy, not because he believes that the Caribbean is incapable of comedy (which is not really his focus), but because, as he sees it, the postcolonial "problem-space" misguidedly follows its anticolonial antecedent in its emphasis on Revolution as Romance. Walcott is impatient with "sighing" over the inert rubble of the past or, worse, being transfixed by its Gorgon's glare, and denies the symbolic echo of the fallen statue of Ozymandias in favor of the ongoing revelry in Felicity. But Scott redirects our attention to "the tangible ruins of our present, the congealing context of our postcolonial time."[18] He returns to the iconic hero of the Haitian Revolution, Toussaint L'Overture, in the revised (1963) edition of James's *The Black Jacobins* through the mythos of tragedy rather than the romance narrative, which he claims structured the first (1938) edition of this magisterial study.[19]

Scott's invitation to reread James, interrogate not just colonial but anticolonial versions of history, and reframe postcolonial futures is not interested in a strictly formalist debate about proper genres and narrative theory. Nor is he trying to dismiss the import of anticolonial revolutions and pose James (and by implication Toussaint) as defeated figures "sighing" over the tragic flaws of individual character and regional history. Even if he begins with the sweeping claim that "the anticolonial utopias have gradually withered into postcolonial nightmares," he insists that his elicitation of the tragic does not imply doom and futility.[20] Rather, although anticolonial romance was self-assured in a manner unnervingly similar to its adversary, colonial Enlightenment, it has been superseded by the tragic hubris of rationality exposed in postcolonial dystopias. In contrast, "tragedy sets before us the image of a man or woman obliged to act in a world in which values are unstable and ambiguous. And consequently, for tragedy the relation between past, present, and future is never a Romantic one in which history rides a triumphant and seamlessly progressive rhythm, but a broken series of paradoxes and reversals in which human action is ever open to unaccountable contingencies—and luck."[21]

Since it is not my intent here to unpack the provocative challenges of Scott's argument, I want to continue my discussion of Caribbean comedy and humor by following a road not taken in his choice of tragedy over romance in our admittedly volatile and arguably underachieving postcolonial era. Scott's reliance on the categories rather neatly laid out by Northrop Frye and Hayden White may have limited the modes of emplotment and the range of possibilities for how the story gets told, since tragedy, comedy, and satire—the other available choices after romance—are presented as what one might call the primary colors of the narrative spectrum.

But narratives can range across the spectrum, and tragedy, comedy, and satire are often boon companions in the most unexpected ways. In fact, such an "unstable and ambiguous" mixture, to borrow Scott's phrase, is perhaps even more evocative and expressive of our unhinged times. Even if we accept his sense of an iconic shift from Caliban to Hamlet (or, to translate freely these characters from Shakespeare's drama to a Caribbean context: from the anticolonial romantic revolutionary to the postcolonial melancholic intellectual), we might remember that Shakespeare's plays often shifted from one mood, if not mode, to another within the same text. A similar ambivalence and complexity more attuned to Caribbean realities may be what Walcott desired when he expresses his hope for a new West Indian drama in a pair of oxymorons: "a stronger, exhilarating despair; not a despair that belongs to others but a truly tragic joy."[22] Walcott's resolution of his dilemma over opting for comedy or tragedy, elation or melancholy, dismisses the relevance of Carnival in the particular passage from where this quotation is drawn.

It is, however, the Carnival as enacted in its seasonal and quotidian cycles that Mikhail Bakhtin credits with the ambivalence of the grotesque mode, which I argue encapsulates Walcott's contradiction. While Bakhtin focuses on the medieval and Renaissance carnivals and carnivalesque elements in Europe, I want to draw some connections across cultural and temporal contexts but with an eye on the differences in the anglophone Caribbean. For instance, Harris's references to carnival masking with which I will conclude this chapter avoid both the minstrel masking that Naipaul and Walcott critique and the excessively optimistic emphasis of Bakhtin's sense of the carnivalesque, emanating from his more unruly sense of carnival forms. Both the grotesque and the carnivalesque will obviously engage a wide range of implications, positive, negative, and moving in between. My point is that such complex terms cannot be fixed into any determinate or singular meaning and they demand a flexible interpretation. Likewise, the modes or emplotments by which we read Caribbean (fictional or historiographic) narrative often refuse to be curbed and slip into each other like grotesque art forms.

The Grotesque as a General Mode

The etymology of the English term "grotesque" has been traced to the Italian *la grottesca* and *grottesco* from *grotta* or cave (not meant, however, as a literal designation of the art form as a cave painting). In the late fifteenth century, a series of excavations of ancient palatial ruins in Italy unearthed art and architecture demonstrating the ornamental style that imaginatively intermingled various animate and inanimate, animal, plant, and human forms. In one example of the grotesque, Wolfgang Kayser describes the Renaissance Italian master Raphael's (Raffaelo Sanzio da Urbino) work as follows: "curled and involuted shoots, from whose foliage animals emerge and cause the difference between animal and vegetable forms to be eliminated; slender vertical lines on the lateral walls, which are made to support either masks or candelabra or temples, thereby negating the law of statics."[23] Kayser adds that Raphael's art in this mode was moderate compared to the more fantastic excesses of some of his contemporaries. The grotesque was extended from hybrid art and architectural forms to literature as early as the sixteenth century in France and a couple of centuries later in England.

Despite his comments on the playfulness and the topsy-turvy nature of this style, Kayser goes on to dwell on the unsettling aspects of the grotesque in its more contemporary usage—as infernal, ugly, bizarre, and ominous. Bakhtin's subsequent analysis of carnivalesque folk humor notes that Kayser ignores the "true nature" of the grotesque, which is ambivalent: a complex mixture intertwining diverse forms. But the former's own emphasis on the other extreme from Kayser, on comedy and laughter, on parody and diablerie, on the Rabelaisian carnivalesque excesses of eating, drinking, defecation, sexual activities, and other forms of debauch results from his attention to the bawdier medieval and Renaissance periods he claims Kayser overlooks in favor of the later, darker periods of Romantic and modernist grotesque.

The temporal shifts are important for Bakhtin, who believes that the separation of modes into genres was a modern phenomenon. "In world literature there are certain works in which the two aspects, seriousness and laughter, coexist and reflect each other, and are indeed whole aspects, not separate serious and comic images as in the usual modern drama."[24] He claims that far from deserving its inferior status in comparison to the noble grandeur of tragedy, laughter "has a deep philosophical meaning" and offers insights not available to tragedy even as it complements the latter.[25] However, Bakhtin is so invested in elevating laughter and comic elements from their low status into an eminent level that he forgets, it seems, his initial stress on the ambivalence of the grotesque and veers toward their rather unitary role as redemptive, festive, and revitalizing. While comedy and laughter are usually more tied to such positive attributes, humor, James Wood notes, is more ambivalent, particularly in Sigmund Freud's conception of "broken humor," which Wood characterizes as "the comedy of irresponsibility" or "the mingling of emotions that Gogol famously called 'laughter through tears.'"[26] But my reading of the grotesque assumes that comedy, laughter, and humor are all ambivalent, unstable forms and are not singularly affirmative and joyous, particularly in the context of Caribbean literature. It must be added that tragedy is never simply about tears and sorrow either and may exist in close proximity to the comic.

I read the Caribbean in a larger context here, since the amalgam I am describing is very familiar to the culture of New Orleans. In 2006, the decision to go ahead with Mardi Gras festivities despite Katrina's devastation of the city generated much controversy, with critics bemoaning the irresponsibility of a culture that celebrated in the midst of disaster. Carnival, after all, was about pleasure, masquerade, wantonness, and so on, and to engage in such decadence when collective tears had not been dried seemed in very bad taste. It also betrayed to the censorious a childish failure to behave decorously given the scale of the catastrophe. Local journalist Jarvis DeBerry, whose home had flooded, expressed some irritation over the national media coverage that claimed to know how things really were in the traumatized city. "Especially annoying was a *Washington Post* story which gave the impression that each of an estimated 10,000 people spending Mardi Gras 'under the bridge' at Orleans and Claiborne avenues was wallowing in sadness. They were all assumed to be despondent because they're black New Orleanians and so many black New Orleanians had their neighborhoods destroyed. Not even their apparent joy mattered because, as the headline helpfully explained, 'Under the Bridge Joy Masks Despair.'"

DeBerry disagrees roundly with this reading. He continues, "New Orleanians never feel compelled to mask despair to exhibit joy. Think all those dancers at a jazz funeral are happy? That they're subverting one emotion in favor of another? No. They're feeling two things simultaneously. That's a perfectly natural state of being—unless, of course, one lives outside of New Orleans."[27] Although Bakhtin considered the separation of genres with the underlying distinction between emotions to be a modern phenomenon, and DeBerry claims that this particular state of simultaneity is specifically black and generally New Orleanian, the intermixture is not exclusively ethnic, regional, or temporal but is cross-cultural and transhistorical, even if it erupts in particular collectivities and certain periods of history more than in others. Why it emerges when it does varies in its particulars but also shares some causal similarities across contexts.

If Kayser seems to turn to the darker aspect as Bakhtin accuses him of doing, it is because he believes that what he calls a comedy of the grotesque or tragicomedy, which in turn implies mirthless laughter, strangled laughter, and black humor, has more "affinity" with our "epoch," unlike Scott's sense of the conventional tragic as the mood of the times.[28] However, Kayser briefly comes close to Bakhtin's more frequent stress on the ambivalent in his description of an uncertain state of affairs in which any reaction—laughter, tears, etc.—seems a little off, and the reaction can only be an "embarrassed smile" when we are continually met with a situation or character that "forbids the use of such conceptual categories" as tragedy, comedy, and satire.[29]

"It is no accident that the grotesque mode in art and literature tends to be prevalent in societies and eras marked by strife, radical change or disorientation," Philip Thomson reminds us.[30] The conventional interpretation of the grotesque as one thing or another—either the burlesque, comic, riotous Rabelaisian sense made famous by Bakhtin's celebration of the carnivalesque or the uncanny, terrible, disgusting connotation emphasized by Kayser—is rather misleading, as Thomson and like-minded theorists of the grotesque have pointed out. The frisson in the grotesque lies in it not being simply one thing or another, but in its traditional sense of intermingling, in the oscillation between these and other possibilities, in the lack of resolution of exactly what it is to the reader or viewer: ludicrous and funny or horrifying and scary and perhaps all at the same time. In such an interpretation, Thomson concludes, what "is perhaps the most profound meaning of the grotesque" is its revelation that "life is alternately tragic and comic, the world is now a vale of tears, now a circus."[31]

While I agree with Thomson's insistence on uncertainty as a significant characteristic of the grotesque, what I want to stress here is the difficulty of charting a binary vertical structure of inversion or alternation of clearly identifiable categories, since not only is it unclear where the borders are transgressed, but what constitutes the border between comedy, tragedy, and satire remains just as hazy in this theorization of the grotesque. In other words, all conventional expectations of generic characteristics (which Bakhtin claims is a modern trend) will have to be put on hold.

In the sense of the grotesque I am using here, comedy is not an automatic stimulant of laughter any more than laughter itself is necessarily indicative of blissfully uncomplicated well-being and therapeutic release of aggression. But then neither is tragedy suggestive only of death, darkness, and doom. Instead, all these components circulate, merge, or intertwine in ways difficult to separate into neat individual classifications and typologies. The thetic conception of high rationalism is overturned in this complex alloy and, as we will see, associates the grotesque not just with emotional and intellectual muddles regarding literary genres and aesthetic regulations in art and architecture, but also with gendered and racial anxieties. Such anxieties may explain why hybrid forms may not simply be welcomed in their imaginative intermixtures, and when it comes to race in particular, these anxieties play into the darker, grosser sense of the grotesque. Those who would want tragedy and comedy to keep to their respective corners frown upon genre confusion.[32] But such confusion is a powerful emotive reaction to extreme stress, demonstrating the complexity of the human mind in traumatic situations.

Black Humor, Slavery, and the Racial Grotesque

The refusal to treat the tragic as properly tragic is not simply a Nietzschean or Bakhtinian imperative. Ralph Ellison argues that black experiences in the pre–civil rights era of North American history should not be seen "as existing sheerly through terror; they are a result of a tragicomic confrontation with life."[33] Although one would not want to flatten different historical and geographical specificities both within the United States and between its hemispheric neighbors, Black Atlantic fiction following colonialism and slavery probably offers some of the most productive examples of this sense of the "tragicomic," which I am reading as a form of the grotesque. As elucidated in Ellison's essay "An Extravagance of Laughter," a dramatic performance on Broadway inspires his discussion of the complexity of black life not just in the overtly racist South of that period, but in the unacknowledged subtle racism of the North where black people have to be more sophisticated readers of what is hidden beneath a mantle of liberal tolerance. He calls his peregrinations in New York the "equivalent of one-winged flying" as he gingerly negotiates the tricky terrain hampered by the handicap of invisible racism.[34]

And yet it is precisely Ellison's reflections on everyday racism in the United States that rouse his irrepressible laughter. He explains how the seeming madness of laughing at such an appalling state of affairs enables him to get a handle on an intolerable situation: "During such moments the world of appearances is turned upside down, and in my case Caldwell's comedy plunged me quite unexpectedly into the deepest levels of a most American realm of the absurd while providing me with the magical wings with which to ascend back to a world which, for all his having knocked it quite out of kilter, I then found more rational."[35] The point Ellison is making is powerfully illustrated by an allegorical anecdote about the confounded legacy of naming in post-slavery societies. Ellison recalls the story of a young black man named Whyte being harassed by a pair of policemen in Alabama who object to his last name, " 'cause it stands to reason that there's no way in the *world* for a nigra as black as that to pretend that his name is 'White.' Not unless he's blind-staggers drunk or else plum out of his nappy-headed, cotton-pickin' mind!"[36] The unfortunate Whyte is forced to defend the correctness of his proper name in the bewildering nominations of a miscegenated South, where even if literal white paternity did not make itself visible in one's pigmentation, a less tangible paternalism often induced the inheritance of the master's name: blacks were indeed white in that sense.

This unpleasant confrontation is then circulated, embellished, and retold in "an extravagance of laughter" by other black students at Tuskegee. They claim that the apparently clueless policemen compel Whyte to recite his biographical antecedents until "the poor cat sounded like a country preacher scatting out the 'begats' from the Book of Genesis!"[37] Ellison quotes one of the storytellers: "They went after Whyte like he had insulted their mammas! And when he still wouldn't deny his name, they came down on him like he was responsible for all the fuckup [meaning the genetic untidiness and confusion of black and white nomenclature] of Southern history!"[38] The seemingly hilarious episode abruptly concludes as racial harassment often does: Whyte is knocked senseless by the unamused cops.

While acknowledging the violence, Ellison chooses to emphasize the way this anecdote provides the opportunity for the inventiveness of the tall tale, a hallmark of black oral culture. "Thus was violence transcended with cruel but homeopathic laughter, and racial cruelty transformed by a traditional form of folk art," he concludes.[39] He admits that the drive through the area continued to be harrowing, since the Phenix City police remained oblivious to civil rights, leading black motorists who drove through unimpeded to feel like the mythical phoenix emerging from the ashes.

The satirical pun on Phenix City in its echo of the ceaselessly regenerating bird is not flippant, since Ellison is insisting on creative survival amid the flames of brutal racism in a somewhat different way from Makandal's miraculous escape from immolation discussed in the previous chapter. But survival, whether through the trickster-storyteller's magical manipulation of harsh reality or the chancy avoidance of state control, cannot be unduly romanticized. If there is a touch of hysteria to all this "extravagance," then the symbolic reference to flight and escape, however temporary, is not a coincidental link to magical realism and its response to terror through narrative excess, a carnival of representation, which exaggerates and distorts reality in fantastic ways until it can provide dazzling new perspectives or make life imaginatively endurable. The grotesque quality of the *jouissance* is evident in the necessary "cruelty" of the linguistic representation as well as the troubled nature of the laughter this funny/horrifying story calls up, although this is not to assume that all readers will crack a smile. Here it is the contagious laughter from the black students to Ellison that calls for analysis, and if it is absurd, so much more the ridiculous racial classifications that justified centuries of abuse and discrimination.

Black humor, then, operates through a double consciousness as well as a double entendre. Fanon states that "the black soul is a white man's artifact,"[40] but the struggle to break through this imposed construction is not always rendered tragic. Black humor in the Atlantic diaspora is both a racial and a literary marker, a laughter that expresses not merely the European modernist characteristics of the Absurd but also the specific experience of being black in slavery and post-slavery contexts.

Like Ellison, Jamaicans also find buoyant but satirical humor in racial realities and deceptions, if Louise Bennett's poem "Pass Fe White" and others of its ilk are any indication. Using her characteristic tone of neighborly gossip and conversational exchange of stories between people, Bennett skewers the snobbery and stupidity of racism both in the United States and in Jamaica:

Miss Jane jus hear from 'Merica,
Her daughta proudly write
Fe sey she fail her exam, but
She passin' dere fe wite!

She say fe tell de truth she know
Her brain part not so bright,
She couldn' pass tru college
So she try fe pass fe wite.[41]

Bennett exposes a number of double standards and enjoys revealing the blind spots of those supposedly in control of racial and class stereotypes. Thus Miss Jane's daughter is assumed to have a good pedigree by those in the United States and a good degree by those in Jamaica ("Some people tink she pass B.A./Some tink she pass D.R."). She passes for both bright and white but is "not quite" either, to use Homi Bhabha's succinct qualifier in his discussion of colonial mimicry.[42] As Bennett reveals, one cannot automatically assume intellectual superiority or its reverse in an entire race. Whites are the dupes of the academically challenged girl who is nevertheless smart enough to know exactly what it takes to get ahead in "'Merica." The appearance is all.

In another poem, "Colour-Bar," Bennett wickedly lampoons the convoluted color variations and corresponding terminology of Jamaican society even as racism continues to be crude and binary. The West Indies had what Naipaul at first delicately calls a "nice eye for shades of black" and color differentiations, which he parodies later as an intricate spectrum of "white, fusty, musty, dusty, tea, coffee, cocoa, light black, black, dark black."[43] Ironically, as characters in George Lamming's emigrant novels are shocked to realize in England, and many others found in an even more racially polarized United States, all the painstaking internal distinctions between the size of the islands and the shade of colors come to naught in the flat monochromatic palette of the "mother country" where everyone from the archipelago is West Indian and those who cannot "pass fe white" are simply black. Mixed race, high colored, "yaller" or "red" Jamaicans (to add to Naipaul's range) are in a particularly vulnerable position since they don't fit any of the schematically rigid distinctions by which race and skin color are defined and experienced in everyday life despite the hypersensitive variants professed in a racial, color-coded genealogy. Their attempts to associate themselves with white people are rejected and their anxious disclaimers about being black are matched by the antagonism from the latter community:

What a debil of a mix-up!
Wat a dickans of a plight!
Dem say dat dem noh nayga,
Nayga sey dat dem noh w'ite.[44]

In "White Pickney," Bennett attacks the chaos caused by mixed-race antecedents to familial cohesion and societal belonging, as infants with a white mother and a black father or vice versa now need to find a society that will accept them wholly as they are. In white-majority countries such as England and the United States, they would be denied white status, but in black-majority countries such as Jamaica they would be not be accepted as black depending on their complexion and other physical and cultural attributes. So, in a Swiftian move, Bennett advises shipping them off to their "pupa's" countries by exercising a choice that in reality is severely limited:

Dem half o' dis an half o' dat
Dem neida dose nor dese—
So since dem half-an half, dem chice
Watever side dem please.[45]

The perplexing effects of race mixing is mischievously targeted by Bennett as an unexpected consequence of the Second World War, where black soldiers stationed in England and white soldiers in Jamaica (or Trinidad) leave their "souveneer[s]" behind.[46] To thus conflate soldiers who abandon their offspring with absent-minded tourists who forget their cheap keepsakes discloses the momentous effects of these casual liaisons even as it spoofs them. Paternal inheritance and all the rights that come with it are denied these children in a different context from slavery but with some unnerving echoes of it.

Bennett's preference for Creole is integral to her use of humor, not because of the general assumption that "dialect" is automatically comic or inevitably more farcical. Rather, as demonstrated in Bakhtin's analysis, the *jouissance* facilitated by the mixed cultures and "interorientation of dialects" cracks open the elitist and insular dogmas of purity, erudition, decorum, and segregation. The "linguistic clownery" and mischievous larks of the Rabelaisian imaginary were made possible, Bakhtin argues, by the mingling of French with Italian, influenced by Greek-Oscan-Latin mixtures, with classical and vernacular roots.[47]

Édouard Glissant uses the word "explosion" in a similar way to indicate the dynamic creativity of Creoles, the extinction of which he portentously links to the depletion of hybrid cultures and all that is unique about the Caribbean.[48] He laments the fact that a Creole is devalued as a conveyor of abstract expression or intellectual depth, implying that unlike a standard Western language such as French in Guadeloupe, it is not considered "knowledge . . . (an exclusive privilege of *superior* languages)."[49] English and French, for example, which come with a wide range of scientific and technological vocabulary (English more than French, which puts it at the top of this hierarchy), are associated with the "world of the serious, of work" and Creoles, which the children use "at play," are assumed to belong to the recreational realm, the domain of "irresponsibility."[50]

But play is not simply about freedom and lack of restraint, as child psychology will tell us. Nor is a Creole merely an undisciplined, unruly offshoot of the more proper parental stem. Supposedly jocular "dialects" are also capable of doing significant intellectual work attributed solely to serious languages. The childlike intonation, alliteration, and nursery rhyme rhythm to Bennett's poetry ("dem neida dose nor dese," "dat dem noh . . . dat dem noh") may invoke the playful, but it does not necessarily trivialize the unfortunate predicament of mixed-race subjects in racially uncompromising situations. The taunts are directed at several subjects, including the white people who consider themselves superior as well as black and colored people who buy into that conflation of whiteness with worth.

Class and cultural inequalities also dictate why dialects, regional varieties, slang, and cant fall into low language and are stigmatized, while the standard version is elevated. Given that tragedy is regarded as a high genre and comedy is held in less esteem, nonstandard linguistic variants are considered incapable of delivering serious messages and are correspondingly associated with a farcical and infantile type of comedy. Naipaul was well aware of this, which is why, as quoted in one of the epigraphs to this chapter, he worries that his early work, much of which was written in Creole and dealt with quotidian street and village life in Trinidad, would be dismissed as farce. It also explains his gradual move away from what he once referred to as a "lively and inventive Trinidad dialect" into the proper, dry Victorian prose of his later writings.[51] While Naipaul's move away from Creole paralleled his infrequent turn to the comic in his later work, he clearly thought more highly of comedy at one point. He makes the extraordinary claim in the early sixties that "the West Indian writer [was] incapable of comedy," because racial and nationalist loyalties made it difficult to sustain the ironic distance necessary for a comic vision.[52] Irony and satire are avoided because their deflationary tactics make it difficult for the "insecure [who] wish to be heroically portrayed."[53]

An anticolonial politics and its allegiances, in other words, would reject a more self-critical comedy for the warmer afterglow of romance and tragedy, both of which cater to the heroic, albeit in different ways. Were Naipaul to include himself in the incapacity for comedy, it would be an odd indictment of his early work, which he specifically referred to as "social comedies." His anxiety that they would be dismissed as farcical proves that he was conscious of their actual potential. I want to pause briefly to consider this assumption on his part that one mentions farce only to dismiss it as such. If comedy is considered a lower genre, farce occupies an even more disreputable position in that chain of being. But there are several instances of farce in Caribbean theater, performance, and fiction (including in Naipaul) that, far from being enjoyable but ultimately inconsequential high jinks, draw out its potential for theoretical complexity and political critique.

If there is any doubt about the comedic possibilities of colonial narratives, one only needs to watch or even read Walcott's *Pantomime,* which exploits the parodic potential of the eighteenth-century classic and prototype of colonial settlement, Daniel Defoe's *Robinson Crusoe.* By converting the popular, long-lived adventure tale into its dramatic possibilities, Walcott engages in an aggressive dialogue not only with the British canon but also with its popular culture variants such as pantomimes and music hall comedies. In drawing attention to the performative aspects of identity formation and subversive mimicry through such intertextuality, the play is a case not so much of the empire writing back as the empire laughing back. I emphasize the distinction because in the latter case there is no doubt that, far from reproducing the "apemanship and parrotry" of colonial education, as Ngũgĩ wa Thiong'o warned, this use of the canon argues that it *takes* the master's tools to dismantle the master's house.[54]

Harry Trewe, the white, middle-aged, failed actor from England and not exactly a roaring success in his new profession in Tobago, as his decrepit hotel proves, tries to reenact Crusoe's story in pantomime, a common English practice in earlier centuries. His general factotum—cook, butler, handyman, reluctant co-actor in Trewe's Christmas panto, and recalcitrant black "man Friday"—the retired calypsonian Jackson Phillip, sharpens his tongue on an increasingly frustrated Trewe. Constantly inverting and reversing the paternalistic relationship that Trewe tries to duplicate from the original version, Phillip renders the colonial fantasy absurd and incomplete by refusing to follow his scripted role and by exaggerating the serious elements of the plot, such as the shipwreck, to the point of ridiculous, overacted melodrama.

At first desiring a light skit appropriate to the nature of Christmas entertainment, Trewe is offended by Phillip's palpable lack of respect for the entire enterprise, by which I mean more than just Trewe's playacting. Phillip's talking back to his boss and to colonial smugness, his easy code-switching from Creole to standard English, his sarcastic, *knowing* observations on the original tale and Trewe's adaptation, his *excess* of representation that is the hallmark of parody, all unnerve Trewe, who finally orders him back to his tasks: "Now, I'm very serious, I've had enough of this farce. I would like to stop."[55] Walcott manages a sly dig at local audiences as well, alluding to the common complaint that there was little encouragement for writers in that period. Trewe cautions, "We're trying to do something light, just a little pantomime, a little satire, a little picong. But if you take this thing seriously, we might commit Art, which is a kind of crime in this society."[56]

But if serious Art alone makes people "think too much," the seemingly "light" farce does not seem to prevent audiences from understanding Phillip's relentless exposure of all that is taken for granted in Crusoe's narrative, including the presumption of his civilized superiority over Friday, who, unlike Phillip, is a docile subject manipulated easily both by Crusoe and his original creator. The repartee between Trewe and Phillip about "tradegy. With one joke," and "codemy, with none," emphasizes the generic grotesque that I have been discussing as well as grotesque humor that is not only playful.[57] Trewe recognizes that Phillip's role playing is all part of a threatening "game" in which the former can no longer assume control. Trewe says, "You're playing the stage nigger with me. . . . It's a smile in front and a dagger behind your back, right? Or the smile itself is the bloody dagger."[58] As Bhabha says of such mimicry, "History turns to farce and presence to 'a part,'" while "the twin figures of narcissism and paranoia . . . repeat furiously, uncontrollably."[59]

The project of stripping bare the colonial facade to reveal an insecure, bombastic master (narrative) precedes and perhaps encourages the final act of physical violence in the play. Phillip strangles Trewe's pet parrot that has been insulting Phillip with derisory calls of "Heinneger, Heinegger." Even before this attack against Crusoe and Trewe's prop, Phillip's noisy and disruptive hammer blows against Trewe's property as he repairs the failing structure are as metaphorical and menacing as the candle that Antoinette carries before she presumably burns the Rochester figure's house down in Jean Rhys's *Wide Sargasso Sea.* Colonial violence thus crosses borders and inflames the British canon and the English landscape. So do colonial subjects.

In Andrea Levy's *Small Island,* Airman Gilbert Joseph, who dreams of proving his technical expertise in the war against Germany, finds himself stationed in England in an unskilled position, fighting a war on another front. He drolly describes (often in Jamaican Creole) the distrust that he meets with from a population unused to black men in the public sphere, although occasional outbursts reveal that he is worn down by the constant slights. Even Queenie Bligh, the more progressive Englishwoman he befriends, has to be cajoled by his jokes; and when she wonders if these tactics are deliberate, he replies with perfect seriousness, "Laughter is part of my war effort."[60]

Here the affirmative qualities of humor are apparent, since they make Gilbert a likeable protagonist and endear him to initially hostile characters, including his finicky wife Hortense, who marries him to fulfill her dream of living in the "mother country" that she idealizes only to be sorely disappointed. His later altercation with visiting American GIs who are aghast by his hobnobbing with Queenie and who then incite a full-scale race riot in a theater is related in such a slapstick manner that there seems nothing irregular in Queenie's father-in-law, Arthur Bligh (already shell shocked in the earlier war with Germany), bemusedly gazing at the violence as "if he was still watching a film."[61] The fact that the trio had come to watch what some would call a farce in its own right, the pastoral fantasy in the film version of the plantation fiction *Gone with the Wind,* is appropriate.

As Ellison would note, the extravagance of laughter that provokes his fit on Broadway could well have struck a black man in this quiet English village, except that all black soldiers have their attention diverted by the battle raging between white American GIs and themselves with a hapless English public caught in between. As in Ellison's report of Whyte's injury at the hands of the Phenix City police, state intervention here institutionalizes and buttresses the racism Gilbert confronts in the private sphere in England and in this case has unintended consequences. Bligh is tragically shot to death by a jittery MP, and another one prevents Gilbert from approaching a distraught Queenie: "'Get away from her, nigger.' Only now did I experience the searing pain of this fight—and not from the grazing on my face or the wrench in my shoulder. Arthur Bligh had become another casualty of war—but come, tell me, someone . . . which war?"[62]

After the war (the one against Germany because, to answer Gilbert's question, the race war is still ongoing in the forties), when he is Queenie's tenant in London, she begs him and Hortense to take her newborn child (the offspring of a liaison with a black Jamaican soldier). She reminds him of the riot and of newspaper reports, which Bennett's poem "White Pickney" was also drawing upon, that "all the half-caste babies" of black Americans and white Englishwomen would be sent to their "colored" fathers in the United States. Not having that drastic recourse since the father is Jamaican, Queenie says, she will be forced to send her child to an orphanage rather than risk raising him with her white husband whose anger will inevitably hurt the child. A teary Queenie confesses, "I giggled, but God knows why."[63] Ellison would probably be able to explain her mirthless giggle, since he would understand her anguish about her son's fate in a racially polarized world.

Glenda Carpio's assertion that "black humor in the fictions of [U.S.] slavery" had multiple functions illuminates Levy's use of humor in her novel, set in Jamaica and England many years after the end of transatlantic slavery. Explaining why the sorrow and anger of experiencing racial injustice metastasize into humor, Carpio argues that black humor masked aggression and appeased the brutal master, exposed and critiqued racial prejudice, affirmed black humanity, sublimated murderous rage and tension, expressed grief and grievance not as traditional jeremiad but paradoxically through laughter, and defanged the venomous assault of racial hostility, among other things. But she also cautions against easy readings of such comic instances by noting the grotesque nature of laughter that seems to be deficient in wholehearted joy or amusement, and is more defined by the uneasiness that one is "laughing at a tragedy that is about to unfold."[64]

Minstrelsy and Cruel Humor: Maryse Condé, V. S. Naipaul, and the Mighty Sparrow

Even as he approved of their sublimating potential, Freud noted in the aggressive elements of laughter, and particularly of wit, the "work" they performed in reactivating infantile pleasures, lifting repressions, and releasing tensions. Henri Bergson assumed that one automatically found a black face funny in a theory of humor that combines superiority, incongruity, and nervous release.[65] Blackface minstrelsy plays a risky game with the supposedly predictable laughter it promotes, as the boisterous, merrymaking John Indian does in Maryse Condé's *I, Tituba, Black Witch of Salem.* His apparent willingness to don the smiling mask subversively juggles two stereotypes: the agelastic, arid Puritans who believe joy is sinful and the ludic slaves who, like children, find it difficult to suppress their playful tendencies even under traumatic conditions. John Indian confides to Tituba, "They expect niggers to get drunk and dance and make merry once their masters have turned their backs. Let's play at being perfect niggers."[66] However childish John Indian may seem to the hoodwinked masters, the child's world is not necessarily an immature or unhealthy one. In some ways the child's playfulness and unrestrained imagination is healthier than adult repression and conformity, as I discussed in the previous chapter.

The menacing nature of performance, masking, and the cruelty of childish play present a different aspect of the theatrical imagination and comic performance when the children and John Indian indulge in an orgy of accusations. The hostile element in black humor is also evident as John Indian's participation confers a disturbing aura on the mask of the playful, always performing slave who wants nothing more than to please his master. The bumbling, buffoonish servant suddenly seems capable of a great deal of harm precisely when he gives the master what he wants to hear. Although the figure in blackface and his trickster qualities have been ascribed to African influences, Ellison believes that the "darky entertainer" is very much a construct of the white American imagination. While the trickster can be a creative agent of chaos and disorder, the fear that in such performance the black man "is reduced to a negative sign that usually appears in a comedy of the grotesque and the unacceptable" never leaves Ellison.[67]

The fact that the etymology of Sambo probably derives from the Spanish "*zambo*," meaning "clumsy person whose bowlegged walk suggests a monkey's gait," implies a hemispheric and not just (North) American span to forms of minstrelsy.[68] The inveterate comic was perhaps largely a fantasy of the slave owner's making, particularly to justify slavery as a rational, benign system and soothe anxieties over slave rebellion. But the wide variety of verbal wit and word games in the repertoire of any culture is never free of a tinge or more of cruelty, sometimes self-directed, and in contexts of unequal power relations, they gain additional complexity.

Cruel humor is something that interests Naipaul. One of his interviewers describes an otherwise dour Naipaul rather pleased over the impending publication of his disturbing novel *Guerrillas*. When asked what it was about, "'Nasty, wicked people,' he says with relish. For the first time today he smiles," the interviewer observes.[69] In another exchange some years later with Bharati Mukherjee and Robert Boyers, where he admits the novel lost him a substantial readership, Naipaul discusses the comic potential of *Guerrillas* and *A Bend in the River,* both novels that readers could be forgiven for regarding as quite removed from comedy. Sensing the skepticism of his interviewers, he insists, "Do you know *Guerrillas* is full of jokes? If I had read *Guerrillas* aloud you would be roaring with laughter. Really." To which Boyers doubtfully replies, "*This is something I'll have to think about.*"[70] Clearly a number of readers would share this doubt, and I will discuss just what kind of comedy Naipaul is invoking when I turn to entropic comedy and the grotesque, here more along the lines of Kayser rather than Bakhtin.

In the several and what some readers might find offensively humorous anecdotes Naipaul provides in *The Middle Passage* of inter-island rivalry, ethnic prejudice between the Afro- and Indo-Caribbean populations, class snobbery and racial hypocrisy, not just Trinidad but many postcolonial societies seem culpable in the argument he makes. Laughter is not just about the weak attacking the strong and vice versa but also involves the weak attacking other weak people. Thus when not openly competing, black and Indian people in the region outdo each other in their eagerness to "tolerate" the other, since tolerance is a sign of superiority, and who gets to do the tolerating is a sign of how close they are to the dominant numerical minority, the whites. The superiority theory also works in the jokes they make about each other, seen in other societies where one minority attacks the other.[71]

And yet in a surprising about-face, Naipaul claims that it is precisely the picaroon spirit and "its ability to beguile and enchant" that defines the "natural eccentri[city]" of the Trinidadians and makes them adaptable, unconventional, and unsanctimonious. "He [the Trinidadian] can never achieve the society-approved nastiness of the London landlord, say, who turns a dwelling-house into a boarding-house, charges exorbitant rents, and is concerned lest his tenants live in sin. Everything that makes the Trinidadian an unreliable, exploitable citizen makes him a quick, civilized person whose values are always human ones, whose standards are only those of wit and style."[72] The episodic, picaresque fiction of Selvon, Naipaul father and son, and Willi Chen demonstrate these characteristics, suggesting a national style of humor attuned to local traditions, but also sharing a regional kinship. In some ways the picaroon of colonial society is also a word warrior, but a warrior who enjoys a good joke and is not averse to sharing it.

The diabolical laughter of Bennett is echoed more cuttingly in the Trinidad calypsos, many of which share some similarities with her performance poetry. Gordon Rohlehr draws connections between the "festive space" of the Carnival and the calypso tent where official, elite culture is derided and cut down to size, but he also qualifies that they are "contested social spaces," not always oppositional and progressive. Taking Walcott and other exiles to task for what he claims is their bourgeois disdain of calypsos, Rohlehr ultimately supports Bakhtin's assessment of the liberatory potential of carnivalesque lawlessness in his focus on calypsonian mirth, even as he concurs with Bakhtin on its ambivalence. What he calls "the truly grotesque, macabre laughter" of the "Congo Man," the calypso in which (like Bennett in recordings of her poem "Colonisation in Reverse") the Mighty Sparrow laughs, growls, and giggles his way through taboo subjects such as interracial desire, oral sex, and cannibalism, is an example of such deliberate provocation.[73] The fact that the elites are not without a sense of humor can be seen when Sparrow sings this calypso (once banned for its controversial lyrics) to appreciative middle-class audiences, including perceivably white people, who sing, sway along, and respond to his interactive calls and questions. However, the bizarre nature of the lyrics and their discomfiting allusions to news reports of Belgian nuns captured in the Congo and to black men's desire for white women suggest that some of the laughter, years after the song was composed and presumably after the ban is lifted, is embarrassed or strangled laughter. That Sparrow is aware of this awkwardness is apparent when he teasingly asks one of the audience members if he is "not trying to be politically correct."[74] Sparrow's raspy timbre and shrill cries (which one respondent on a YouTube viewing approvingly likens to a "cartoon voice"), his facial contortions, rolling eyes, and bodily gyrations display considerable enjoyment but also recall the routine antics of minstrelsy in somewhat uneasy ways, both for his live audience as well as those viewing his performance on the Internet. The performer and the live audience seem to be masking other emotions despite the seamless appearance of convivial banter.

Another YouTube video of the calypso does not show Sparrow but matches it with various film and cartoon depictions of cannibalism, including a clip of a Tom and Jerry cartoon in which a darkened Jerry (signifying a stereotyped African Friday) dressed in a straw skirt, a bone atop his head and wiggling a spear, guffaws and prances in tune to Sparrow's music while boiling Tom (the Crusoe figure) in a pot.[75] One of the final clips is taken from *The Pirates of the Caribbean* series and shows Jack Sparrow, fittingly enough, dandyishly sprinting on the beach after his fleeing crew, pursued by cannibals and the voiceover of Mighty Sparrow's irreverent laughter.[76] I emphasize the intertextual and interactive aspects of Sparrow's song through the years to argue for its long shelf life and its creative reinventions in popular culture across the Atlantic in ways that possibly Sparrow himself did not anticipate.

"Dead Man Laughing": Creole Comedy and Entropic Humor

The cartoonish quality of such performances needs further comment in the light of Bakhtin's observations on the ambivalence as well as the regenerating potential of laughter. In "Laugh Yourself to Death!" Slavoj Žižek discusses the controversial aspects of holocaust comedies and their particular characteristics. He aligns comedy with tragedy, not in their Apollonian and Dionysian affinities as Nietzsche saw it, but in their common commitment to immortality. However, the tragic hero affirms immortality by paradoxically dying in noble triumph, while the comic hero refuses to die, choosing instead "very vulgar, opportunistic, terrestrial life."[77]

Thus, the Jack-in-the-box popping up of cartoon figures after various episodes of explosions and mutilations, their continuous (re)animation, suggests the resourcefulness of the "small fellow," as we see not just in the cartoons Žižek mentions, but also in folktales, fables, and trickster tales. If Theodor Adorno could muse about the barbarism of poetry after Auschwitz, just as controversial is the possibility of the comic amid the harsh experiences and legacies of slavery, indenture, and colonialism. And yet death and laughter can go together in cartoonish doggedness in these painful contexts, although not always as literally as in Tom and

Jerry's frolic. It is perhaps no coincidence that Naipaul's *A House for Mr. Biswas* and Zadie Smith's *White Teeth* begin and end with death, actual in the former novel and attempted but foiled in the second.

Borrowing from thermodynamics, Patrick O'Neill offers a theory of the comedy of entropy that bears many of the characteristics of the grotesque I had discussed earlier in this chapter and which characterizes the world of Biswas. In a closed system, when the quantity of energy does not change and no external sources are provided, the available energy moves toward a condition of entropy, "complete inert uniformity and equilibrium."[78] An entropic universe challenges the Newtonian mechanized universe and proposes a more uncertain foundation to history and the laws of physics. The loss of faith in certainty drastically alters traditional expectations of tragedy and comedy that were based in a more stable sense of human significance and divine providence. Not only do we live in times where traditional tragedy "has beaten a retreat," we now have "varieties of comic writing whose affinity to tragic writing is so marked as to disorient completely our stock responses to traditional tragedy and comedy and disrupt totally the traditional cathartic reaffirmation of the norms of an ordered societal system."[79]

Entropic comedy has some family resemblance to similar theories of the grotesque, which encompasses black humor, tragedy, satire, parody, and the Absurd. There is no longer any Archimedean point of certainty from which one operates, since the Enlightenment truths and triumphs of the rational spirit that persisted until the mid-nineteenth century have given way to a more irresolute knowledge of the physical universe and its laws. When classical physics has been troubled by quantum theories, and science is full of inside jokes and mathematical conundrums such as Zeno's paradoxes, modern and postmodern literatures, argues O'Neill, inevitably reflect the continual breakdown of harmonious order and anticipated meaning into the random and the unexpected, accelerated by the turmoil of modern times.

Although the previous chapter opposed science and technology to the playful use of the imagination, here we have to acknowledge that the former domains are just as aware of uncertainty principles and nature's unpredictable gags. While the laughter is not simply ludic, there is nevertheless *jouissance* in the wry acknowledgment of breakdown, not just in Roland Barthes's celebration of the multiplicity of textual meaning, but in what is perhaps a desperate merriment. Just as Bakhtin claims of premodern genres, in modernist literature O'Neill concludes that "we are as apt to laugh at our tragedies as we are to weep at our comedies."[80]

If the modernist and postmodernist Western traditions of O'Neill's focus generate entropic comedy as a response to pervasive instability and rootlessness of that part of the world, we are likely to find the same in other literatures reacting to and reflecting their specific historical conditions of crisis and uncertainty. We thus have to keep in mind Naipaul's early sense of himself as a writer and of the society he grew up in, which is haunted by the particular ordeals of the first post-indenture generation as well as his specific family quarrels that inspired *A House for Mr. Biswas.*

Biswas's virtually fruitless and continuous struggle against the Hanuman House contingent embodies a collective agency and represents for Rohlehr the creolized individual wrestling with an intractable, even hostile, (post) colonial society. "It is therefore possible to see his rebellion, grotesque and strange as it is, as a paradigm of the perennial West Indian struggle for a more truly democratic society."[81] Rohlehr's nuanced critique of *House* expresses some of the ambivalence of the Caribbean grotesque, but ultimately insists on its affirmative quality. In a move that insists on reading both Naipaul and Biswas as creations of Trinidad, Rohlehr elsewhere "wonders whether the catharsis which Biswas seeks both in a real and a vicarious grotesqueness isn't a feature of Creole society in Trinidad. He [Biswas] seems to share with [it] a capacity to convert anxiety to absurdity, and to make a grasp of the absurd dimension a part of his total psychology of struggle."[82] The stress here is on the grotesque not as static feature of distortion and abnormality but as dynamic process, indeed as productive (joke) work, as artistic labor that "convert[s] anxiety [in]to absurdity."

The particular "pappyshow" that Trinidad history participates in renders it a daily (not always edifying) spectacle circumventing the ritual season of Carnival to display and parody itself unceasingly in Naipaul's presentation of it. History, to rephrase Marx's formulation, presents itself as comedy, tragedy, and farce simultaneously. Most often, however, Biswas is unable to pull off the conventional solemnity of tragedy since the squalid material of his life and the trivial characters that appear in it do not have the gravitas to be thus presented. But there is nevertheless a comic dignity to Biswas. Martin Grotjahn points out that wits, like clowns, are not always genial but often hostile and lonely figures who prove that it "is not funny to be funny."[83] At the same time, clownish figures such as Charlie Chaplin defy the pain of reality by refusing to be cowed by it. In what Žižek would call "the idiotic persistence" of Biswas's repeated attempts to transform his living conditions, we see the cartoonish defiance of the character who, to adapt Samuel Beckett's words, tries, fails, tries again, fails again, fails better.[84]

In one of his numerous reflections on writing and the conditions under which it came to be what it was, Naipaul describes at length a fictional encounter with an English writer he names Foster Morris, who had also written about Trinidad many years earlier. Although Naipaul's persona at first approaches him as a younger, less established writer seeking approval (which he does not get), he eventually rejects Morris's wounding criticism of his work. Objecting to what he considers Morris's uninformed portrayal of Trinidad in a book about the 1937 oil field strike, the writer accuses Morris of misrepresenting the Trinidadian context with the easy imposition of an English background, and of assuming that both countries share a similar sense of the past, of history, and of tradition.

At first Naipaul's persona believes that "the sense of the absurd, the idea of comedy" that Morris is oblivious to masks Trinidad's fretful, "floating" sense of uprootedness.[85] But later, discussing George Lamming's novel *In the Castle of My Skin* over tea in the BBC canteen, Naipaul notes a comic situation in the novel and comes to a new understanding.[86] "I learned as a new truth what I really had always known, and what so far in my writing (veering between farce and introversion) I had suppressed: that comedy, the preserver we in Trinidad had always known, was close to me, a double inheritance, from my story-telling Hindu family, and from the creole street life of Port of Spain." He continues, "The jokeyness that was my double inheritance from my Trinidad background, however good, however illuminating, was also a way of making peace with a hard world; was on the other side of hysteria. This was true of the colonial society I was writing about; it was also true of my own position in London, which was full of uncertainty."[87]

Naipaul's analysis of his turn toward comedy in his early writing, a comic sense that disappears in his later work, which is more precise but also more humorless, is consonant with Rohlehr's insight about Naipaul's creolization. The latter wryly seems to recognize his gradual distancing from his Creole gift of comedy—here meaning both Afro- and East Indian Caribbean—when he admits that "this anxiety or hysteria, the deeper root of comedy" gains precedence over the latter and "had become [his] subject."[88] But that there is hysteria, a Naipaul keyword usually applied to the objects of his censure, behind his comedy is a provocative admission. It explains the biting irony and satire that fuel his comic sense.

As in the case of Anand, these armed companions of the grotesque become an apotropaic weapon and a shield, a source of aggression and a coping mechanism, an indication of neurosis and the preservation of sanity. There are all too many occasions in Naipaul's work where culture is reduced to a cadaver and critique is performed as an autopsy. If the mark of a satirist is cool anger, then Naipaul's often icy verdict of human folly certainly provides the appearance of frigid detachment. But the revelation of the hysteria behind this pose unsettles the Olympian aura with which Naipaul renders critical judgment.

James Wood, however, reads Naipaul's pose of superiority and distance as just that, a pose, a "mask" that hides Naipaul's despair and insecurity in England when he was struggling to make it as a writer. Wood insists that the novel is a sympathetic comedy and offers it high praise, calling Biswas "one of the few enduring characters in postwar British fiction," the classification as British indicating the crossover potential of the Creole comedy.[89] Since Biswas is "nobly hysterical," he is still a "great comic character," the capacity to ennoble a nervous breakdown the mark of entropic comedy and no doubt a sign of the times.[90] Wood's reference to the work of Zadie Smith and Salman Rushdie as types of "hysterical realism" is less complimentary. Unlike John Barth who believes that postmodern fiction had "replenishing" potential, Wood views Smith's surfeit of improbable events, characters, and coincidences as indicating exhaustion and evading reality.

White Teeth, I want to argue, is another version of the grotesque, and while not quite conventional magical realism, it certainly toys with the terrors of reality in its own style. Smith's "hysterical" narrative surplus avoids the bleak nihilism of Biswas's universe, although paradoxically this is not to counter Wood's claim that Naipaul delivers a compassionate comedy as well. Even as Smith's novel, which was published in 2000, has millenarial pretensions of apocalypse, it parodies and reduces those fears. On the sliding scale of the grotesque, *House* is closer to Kayser's darker sense while *White Teeth* has more affinity with Bakhtin's concept of "extraordinary realism."[91] In O'Neill's description of entropic comedy, nihilism is not irrevocably paralyzing or even gloomy: "Rather than being offered the stoic's dagger, we find ourselves invited to join in the game, to play, to laugh."[92]

White Teeth does just that far more flippantly than Naipaul when it begins with Alfred Archibald Jones, an inconsequential middle-aged man who could have been named J. Alfred Prufrock instead, trying to commit suicide in his car and being fortuitously saved by an impatient Muslim butcher whose storefront he chooses as the site for gassing himself to death. The comic spirit of the novel is affirmed in the very beginning with this opening scene of an unlikely hero who does not die, not through any kind of deus ex machina but in the impersonal language of chaos theory: "While he slipped in and out of consciousness, the position of the planets, the music of the spheres, the flap of a tiger moth's diaphanous wings in Central Africa, and a whole bunch of other stuff that Makes Shit Happen had decided it was second-chance time for Archie. Somewhere, somehow, by somebody, it had been decided that he would live."[93]

Even when death occurs in real life, it is not shattering but rather life's final joke in the literal image of entropy. Despite all her concern for his health and her anxious hospital visits, Smith is not around when her father dies and, she is told, his death was so sudden he was himself caught unaware: "From these facts I tried to extrapolate a story, as writers will, but found myself, instead, in a kind of stasis. A moment in which nothing happened and keeps not happening, forever."[94] While Biswas embodies Naipaul's tormented sense of Seepersad's "failed harder" life in Trinidad, Archie in her novel signifies Smith's more accommodating version of Harvey Smith's ordinariness and even triviality, each approach perhaps outlining differences not just between Black British and postcolonial/migrant generations, but also between the modernist and the postmodernist.

Unlike Naipaul's tortured verification of the Absurd which never gives up its unacknowledged longing for meaning and significance, Smith is more willing to accept the absurdity of the contemporary individual who can die randomly and unnoticed, not "neatly crafted like an American sitcom: 'The One in Which My Father Dies.'"[95] There is not only very little sense of conventional heroism here, even the expectation of it is foreclosed. Rather than the heroism of the anticolonial, as Scott charges, Smith's view of the postcolonial verges on the postmodern in its irreverence toward not just colonizers but all her subjects, as we see in the bumbling ineptness of the revolutionaries in her novel. At the same time, she also grants each of them a certain dignity.

When it comes to taking sides, children of mixed-race descent such as Smith, whose mother was Jamaican just like Irie in the novel, may have a harder time of demonizing the other, particularly when biological bonds are involved. In her essay "Dead Man Laughing," Smith reveals her white, English father's love of a joke, which she shared, and their mutual enjoyment of various English comedies: "The sadder and more desolate the comedy, the better Harvey liked it."[96] Her reflections after his death suggest that Harvey Smith has some kinship with Mohun Biswas: she refers to her father as "a creative man whose frequent attempts at advancement were forever thwarted, or so he felt, by his accent and his background, his lack of education, connections, luck."[97] We cannot get too carried away by this potential fraternity given the brutal history of colonialism, mutated into the racist attacks on migrants in London suburbs and the hostility they face described in Smith and Levy's novels. But such convoluted kinship across battle lines is nevertheless sketched throughout the novel and is epitomized in Irie's complex genealogy. If one were to translate the intertwined animate and inanimate "bodies" of grotesque art into a family tree, then Samad's involved South Asian connections (India, East Bengal, East Pakistan, Bangladesh, a Hindu forbear, Muslim background) and Irie's mixed heritage across Africa, the Caribbean, and Britain demonstrated in her amusing map and key parody the solemn correctness of pedigreed lineage and regulated alliance.

The Laughing Medusa

For those who may think that colonial history, with its devastating consequences of genocide, slavery, indenture, enforced migration, looting of colonies, racism, and unimaginable violence, is not a subject for comedy, "it may very well be that such violence could be translated into comedy precisely because the *game* of Empire was finally up," as Phyllis Lassner suggests.[98] Wilson Harris, like Smith, prefers not to view the Caribbean through a framework of tragedy, "upon which had been subtly inscribed a perspective of the Gorgon, Gorgon of post-war years, Gorgon of colonialism, Gorgon of bankruptcy, frustration, slump."[99] As I have discussed in other chapters, his multiple references to both metaphorical and literal masks in his fiction and nonfiction present a unique theory of the relevance of Carnival in the Caribbean with some similarities to Bakhtin, who highlights the seasonal, life-giving, and fertility rituals regularly performed in Carnival. Faces, masks, figures (such as jesters and harlequins), ghosts, voices, shadows, sounds, vibrations, all converge in a universal theater in which the victor and the vanquished rarely occupy fixed positions. However controversial this may seem in an anticolonial and revolutionary politics that demands clear battle lines and identifiable antagonists, Harris's perspective is particularly significant to Guyana, where Indigenous and other minority concerns continue to be overshadowed in the electoral rivalry between the two dominant postcolonial groups, the Afro- and Indo-Guyanese who were once subject to slavery and indenture.

Harris is conscious of empires and bloodletting that preceded the conquistadorial and colonial eras as well. Thus, even as he portrays Pizarro's hubris and Cortez's megalomania in *The Dark Jester* as a contrast to a more enigmatic and Christ-like Atahualpa, the first-person narrator who has a vision of Cortez in the twentieth century and fires at him ultimately misses.[100] He comes to the realization that killing Cortez even in a fantasy would only reply in a "one-fisted" language and endlessly repeat a cycle of violence.[101] Similarly, in *White Teeth,* Archie takes a bullet (twice) rather than kill, and both times he also survives. While death is not in itself devastating when it occurs in comedy, the refusal to die, as Žižek points out (and to kill, Harris and Smith would add) is a particularly noteworthy feature of the comic spirit.

We can be tempted to slip on the classical tragic mask frozen into a mournful expression and mimic the static hubris of centuries of conquest, according to Harris, different sides exchanging the part of victor and vanquished, but unable to cross the chasm between them since they are bound to repeat classical tragedy. "What is Jest," demands the Dreamer in the first line of *The Dark Jester,* and immediately answers, "Jest is an attempt to bridge the apparently unbridgeable."[102] The Jester is a sphinx-like figure that guides the Dreamer through the history of conquest in the Americas. Both Jester and Dreamer assume different quantum personalities through the ages, as is typical of Harris's fiction where one character is never singular or whole but fragmented into puzzling pieces of different beings, sometimes "particles" (or waves, Harris would say) of animal, bird, human, spirit, and thing.

But Harris's sense of the abysmal also incorporates the regenerative potential of the grotesque. His characters often find themselves gazing into the void and seeing different visions and possibilities depending on their attributes and what they signify for the author. In *The Dark Jester,* the void offers "bridges" into the creative grotto: "On those bridges we come upon caves in which are works of art. Forbidding works they seem to tell us of our deepest selves. And through those selves that may seem alien we touch the frontiers of regeneration."[103] The literal sense of the grotesque as a bridge, a Jest "blown by art across ages, across centuries,"[104] offers tremendous potential for reclassifying the antagonists and aliens as part of us, as "hidden or unacknowledged kith and kin."[105]

The Dreamer queries in *The Dark Jester,* "How can Captain and Bishop stir in each other? How can Man stir in Beast and Bird?"[106] Once we consider these intermixtures, Harris suggests, we can overcome the petrifying effect of the "classical grotesque,"[107] and Medusa's frozen visage of horror and tragedy will break into a smile just as the Gorgon rock does in the conclusion to *Tumatumari* (which means sleeping rock). Harris would agree with Bakhtin, then, that the "last thing one can say of the real grotesque is that it is static; on the contrary it seeks to grasp in its imagery the very act of becoming and growth, the eternal incomplete unfinished nature of being."[108] Neither the abyss nor the apocalypse holds any fears for Harris, since human history, art, and the imagination are still in "unfinished genesis."

If Medusa has so far been read as the appalling prospect of the Caribbean colonial past, I conclude with her not just smiling but laughing defiantly. Following the invitation of Hélène Cixous, we can acknowledge that even the most terrifying image holds within it apotropaic and recuperative potential: "You only have to look at the Medusa straight on to see her. And she's not deadly. She's beautiful and she's laughing."[109]

Lest we fear that laughter may distract from the urgent task of taking the enemy seriously enough to engage in necessary combat—not the mindless violence that Harris fears but the inevitable confrontation when one fights for social justice—we may console ourselves with the realization that she who laughs last, laughs best. It is not insignificant that Ti-Jeanne routs her malevolent grandfather in the conclusion to Nalo Hopkinson's *Brown Girl in the Ring* with the help of Jab-Jab, her syncretic ghoulish guide and divine jokesmith, proving that the comic is imbued with a fighting spirit. In the aftermath of her successful battle, Ti-Jeanne learns something not just about herself but of the staying power of the Caribbean mythos, the perpetual memory in the dismembered limbs of its ancestral tribes and various diasporas which keep coming back to prolific, insurrectionary life even if in skeletal forms:

> She understood then. She knew why the Jab-Jab was always grinning. She laughed, starting deep in her belly. . . . She laughed at the sorry man who had thought he could hold death forever in a calabash. She laughed, because now she knew who the Jab-Jab was.
>
> The elevator dinged. The door opened, and there he was, tophatted, skull-faced, impossibly tall. He held a pretty nightshade coyly in front of his mouth and giggled along with her. Papa Legbara, Prince of Cemetery. Her Eshu. The Jab-Jab.[110]

Ti-Jeanne discovers the indispensability of the grotesque.

The range of writers this chapter has surveyed and their multiple concerns emphasize the vital powers of comedy and laughter even in the bleakest of conditions. But this is not to say that these perspectives are without risks. Naipaul's withering irony and dry wit, for instance, have won him many enemies and could be considered enervating by those who have no taste for it. His categorization of laughter as hysterical in the Caribbean and in postcolonial contexts may also pathologize them. At the other extreme, Smith's lively but buffoonish characters in her novel run the risk of diminishing the fallout of empire. But despite these hazards, the varieties of comic approaches, their intermixtures, and the motley emotions they evoke endow Caribbean humor with a profoundly philosophical and political character that cannot be taken lightly.

Epilogue

What is important is that we start retracing the path for ourselves.
—Édouard Glissant, *Poetics of Relation*

Genealogy is history in the form of a concerted carnival.
—Michel Foucault, "Nietzsche, Genealogy, History"

IN A SHORT story with the heavily freighted title "There Are a Lot of Ways to Die," Neil Bissoondath, like his uncles V. S. and Shiva Naipaul and many other writers, assaults the plastic image of the Caribbean. The central character, Joseph Heaven, returns from Toronto in the fond hopes of reconnecting with his native Eden, but following the formula of most return plots, he faces demoralizing failure. He comes across a travel poster in a restaurant that "showed an interminable stretch of bleached beach overhung with languid coconut-tree branches. Large, cursive letters read: Welcome to the Sunny Caribbean. The words were like a blow to the nerves. Joseph felt like ripping the poster up."[1] While neither Bissoondath nor the other writers discussed in this book literally do so, the sentiment underlies the metaphorical violence of their response to the picturesque "framing" of the region and the commercialization of its great natural beauty and vibrant expressive cultures.[2]

At the same time, paradise is also haunted by pathology, in sensationalized U.S. media reports and pop culture images, for instance, of crime, poverty, drug lords, natural disasters, voodoo, zombies, riots, and political dysfunction. Even as the pathological narrative militantly exposes social problems that run deep and long in the history, it can be as reified as the paradisiacal stereotype that it attempts to demolish. One of the tasks in this book is to make these distinctions clear as it presents the complex array of literary engagements with this double bind.

As I explained in my introduction, this book is not simply about paradise or pathology, although both are present in colonial discourses and also in the works of Caribbean writers. However, in pursuing the mobile strategies of indirection and unsettlement recommended by Earl Lovelace and Édouard Glissant, the subtitle to this book, *Caribbean Detours*, is perhaps more significant than the main title, *Pathologies of Paradise,* and should operate as its dangerous supplement. The topics this book charts cannot evade the paradise or pathology of Caribbean geopolitics, but its lay of the land also presents what lies betwixt and between, and seeks less well trodden routes, pathways that take one deeper into the "interior," opening up different perspectives of familiar terrain.

While the literature unapologetically refuses to be isolated from the social contexts that influence it, the writers are not invested in articulating clear social policies or providing historically accurate documents. Instead, what Wilson Harris calls the theatre of the arts enacts, or in his case reenacts, the cultural and social history of the Caribbean onto a literary canvas, and, in doing so, establishes the "sovereignty of the imagination," to use George Lamming's formulation.[3] In his 2003 address at the Mona campus of the University of the West Indies, Lamming, whose fiction was inspired by anticolonial revolts, speaks soberly of the contemporary Caribbean: "The temptation to find the shortest route possible to wealth has increased. And so has the frustration of an idle and disenchanted youth. The rural population continues its decline; the cities grow more crowded and dangerous. From Kingston to Port-of-Spain, the story is much the same. And immigration is a rescue which is only available to those who have had extensive training and whose skill ensures their survival elsewhere."[4] Although Harris and Lamming have different uses for the imagination (Harris, for example, being less interested in an overtly political agenda), they both emphasize the piloting role of literature that rejects "the shortest route possible." Their deliberative ethics were not without blind spots of their own—as women writers, for instance, would contend—but the literary imagination struggles against the bleak sociological realities of the terrain and offers their particular understanding of how they, along with their compatriots, have arrived there. This sense of self-understanding and collective knowledge in order to imagine a new future seems not just an intellectual enterprise but also a salvific one, as Jamaica Kincaid maintains when she insists that her writing had the power to save her.

There is some pathos in the sovereignty that Lamming attributes to the imagination, because the alternative futures limned by the writers sometimes seem frustratingly out of reach in the stagnant or, worse, recidivist politics of the postcolonial. But the imagination must persist, it cannot but do so, and it surfaces again and again in the literature: it is, after all, a poet who leads Dante out of the circles of Hell. When the signposts to the future are not always forthcoming, readers are rerouted through the past in another direction from colonial accounts. Glissant identifies *détournement* as a key aspect of the poetics of relation, "in which each and every identity is extended through a relationship with the Other."[5] Just how critical this return to the past is as a necessary detour is emphasized in Kevin Baldeosingh's *The Ten Incarnations of Adam Avatar.*

The Adamic trope is an inevitable accessory of paradise discourse, Derek Walcott, in particular, using it to revise imperial accounts even as he rehearses the classics, and reorienting colonialist portrayals of the landscape, history, memory, and identity. The fusion of the Hindu belief in rebirth with the Christian story of genesis in Baldeosingh's novel allows him both to engage paradise discourse critically and to insist on a redemptive future so favored by Harris. Indeed, much in the novel recalls Harris's concepts of the phantom limb, infinite rehearsal, and unfinished genesis even as it bears the individual stamp of the younger author with the specific Hindu belief in transmigration. Baldeosingh's wistful hope for "the plurality of global culture" in Trinidad is signified in his evocation of Carnival, once again indicating Harris's conceptual influence on the novel.[6] The felicitous link between the migration of souls across centuries and the migration of bodies in transoceanic passages enables an epic genealogy to unfold as various historic episodes are presented through ten different avatars of the Caribbean subject. In addition to the relentless undermining of the colonial version, there are at least two extensions of Harris's and Walcott's adamic counter-narrative: the identity of the transcriber as Indo-Caribbean and the inclusion of female avatars. Baldeosingh also presents the ethnic, racial, and cultural mixtures of the Caribbean in all their variety.

The novel begins with "Amerindian," which takes us back to the time before Columbus, although it somewhat problematically situates Guaikan's narrative in a preconquest chronology. This tends to schematize Amerindian presence as a coming into history with colonization, while writing it out of the postcolonial through a comprehensive genocide. However, because his avatar is invoked by other incarnations, Guaikan does not quite disappear in the novel as his people would in most anglophone Caribbean literary history. The fictional text is itself a migrant discourse, moving between ethnography, history, anthropology, psychoanalysis, philosophy, and, of course, literature. Baldeosingh criticizes disciplinary and continental regimentation when Adam Avatar, the final incarnation, who quotes Eastern and Western authors, says he teaches a course in "Syncretic Thinking 101—a combination of philosophy, psychology, literature, history, biology and physics," and claims that the university he works at would never have allowed this course if it were not for external funding.[7]

In emphasizing the genocide of the Tainos, however, Guaikan, who belongs to the Ciguayao people, shatters the nostalgia of the Adamic trope in Columbus's arrival and the myth of the New World. Other avatars follow, each one traversing different periods in Caribbean history through different embodiments whose accounts open up multiple entries into regional formation. The settings vary from Haiti, Jamaica, Barbados, Guyana, and Trinidad (neglecting smaller islands, however), and the avatars include a Spanish Creole colonist who renounces the Conquest; a Portuguese slaver who becomes captive in a mutiny; a white indentured servant who turns brothel keeper; a Jamaican planter's cross-dressed daughter who has a brief fling with piracy and returns to it in earnest when her mulatto ancestry is revealed; a female slave who travels to different islands to incite revolt; a mixed-race slave owner with Sadeian drives; a Trinidadian stick fighter; an East Indian from Guyana; and, finally, the academic Adam Avatar, although his mysterious disappearance at the end of the novel does not foreclose other lives in a continuing future. Different literary types and modes (romance, pornography, journal writing, magical realism) are promiscuously mixed, as are the characters.

Adam himself, the focalized protagonist who reveals these pasts to an earnest psychiatrist, Dr. Surendra Sankar, changes in complexion like some of the other characters whose past ancestry lightens or darkens their skin and alters the texture and color of their hair. Each avatar remembers the past, even if in flashes, so it is never lost either in their memories or in the buried documents disinterred from time to time and handed over to Sankar. Despite the authenticity of these documents, Sankar diagnoses Adam's revelations as "textbook hebephrenic schizophrenia" and treats the multiple personalities as aberrant symptoms of mental illness.[8] But Adam's concluding reflections portray the vast array of characters and mixtures as unique to the Americas, and specifically to the Caribbean. "I am, genetically and otherwise, a 'true Trini.' My *café-au-lait* complexion, my tight cap of curly hair, my slanted green eyes mark a mixed ancestry that fits me into any company."[9] Rather than depict Trinidad and, by implication, the rest of the archipelago as an insular "small place," Baldeosingh makes it a global capsule that tows, in the vicissitudes of history, various continents and cultures that are then embodied in the people. Adam thus presents Trinidad as a cultural laboratory and believes that "with the several diverse cultures pressed into this island space, we can more readily discover what the essence of humanity is."[10]

The creolized ideal is not nostalgic or uncritical, however, since the hypocrisy of colonial ideology and the physical violence that led to creolization are both confronted and denounced, not just by the conventional victims, but also by the conquistador and slave owner who, as insiders, are even more brutal in their disclosures. All the narratives, even by those who parrot the racist rhetoric of their types and their time, are ultimately critical of the devastating enterprise of empire. We are not allowed to forget that what brought these mixtures in place was hardly the utopian vision of "One Love" or of a brave new world of gloriously hybrid subjects, but rather rape and pillage. Nor are we encouraged to believe that postindependence societies are more enlightened, as the account of interethnic riots in Guyana makes clear. Instead, the genealogies of Adam Avatar are meant literally to bring home the diverse strands in each Caribbean individual. I say literally because Caribbean literature as marketed is largely from the diaspora, and as time goes on, diasporic authors will likely focus their content outside the region as well. Without making any nativist argument for authenticity and silencing the diversity of voices, one has to wonder what it means when Caribbean literature is profoundly mapped by writers outside the geographical Caribbean, rhizomic and errant as its contours may be.

Earlier I had suggested that the formula for the return narrative ends in predictable failure. Works by Caryl Phillips and Joan Riley are examples of this trajectory, which refuses to romanticize homecoming.[11] But not all stories lead to dead ends. Velma Pollard's *Homestretch* tracks the resettlement of a retired couple who return to Jamaica after thirty years of working in England.[12] As the title signifies, though, this is the final lap of their life and they are happy to be back in a community they embrace, despite some snags and adjustments. In conjunction with David and Edith, the older couple, the younger Brenda discovers her "birthright" in the course of her visit and brings schoolchildren of Jamaican descent from England to learn about their heritage. Like Faith Jackson in Andrea Levy's *Fruit of the Lemon,* she will not stay, but returns to England reconciled with her Jamaican heritage and family history.[13] Pollard dedicates the novel to Riley and includes an epigraph from Dennis Scott's poem "Homecoming" from *Uncle Time:* "It is time to plant/feet in our earth. The heart's metronome/insists on this arc of islands/as home." While this organic, biological sense of rootedness may seem sentimental, Pollard also raises conflicts and tensions in national identity and does not denounce Brenda for returning to England. At the same time, the novel refuses to play into lyrical celebrations of homelessness and roving cosmopolitanism, and insists on groundedness as a longed-for, if difficult to maintain, ideal.

While Baldeosingh, who lives and writes in Trinidad, acknowledges the paradox that the lack of strong regional publishing is one reason "why anyone who wants to be a Caribbean writer has to leave the Caribbean," he insists he will nevertheless continue to write from Trinidad.[14] Thus, the characters in *Ten Incarnations* travel across the Caribbean and even into Europe and India, but ultimately the novel ends with Adam Avatar returning to Trinidad. Like Alford George in Lovelace's novel *Salt,*[15] Adam finds the world not elsewhere but in his island: "Ancient Africa and India and China, old Europe, new America."[16] The penultimate chapter, "Human," emphasizes the inception of the modern Caribbean in a cultural mixture that encapsulated and embraced the world, which, as Glissant might note, was transplanted from the closed prison of the plantation to the open space of a poetics of relation. The genealogies that the avatars present are ultimately united as part of the same family tree growing in and through the Caribbean. To quote Glissant, "The always multilingual and frequently multiracial tangle created inextricable knots within the web of filiations, thereby breaking the clear, linear order to which Western thought had imparted such brilliance. So Alejo Carpentier and Faulkner are of the same mind, Edward Kamau Brathwaite and Lezama Lima go together, I recognize myself in Derek Walcott, we take delight in the coils of time in García Márquez's century of solitude. The ruins of the Plantation have affected American cultures all around."[17] Glissant's genealogy of the Americas rehabilitates the static "ruins of the Plantation" into rhizomic, creative foliage, drawing a manifold extended family rather than a rigidly linear root tree of pure racial and cultural descent.

A number of novels and memoirs reproduce innovative and even parodic family trees to emphasize the peculiarity of Caribbean genealogies. In the first chapter I mentioned Harold Sonny Ladoo's spatial and familial map, and in the previous chapter, I discussed Zadie Smith's hilarious parody of Irie's family tree in *White Teeth* (tellingly planted midway in her novel and not at the beginning, as is the convention). Despite Smith's irreverence, increasingly the trend to document family history may express the need to move beyond the rootlessness of untraceable diasporic origins and, as in Lorna Goodison's *From Harvey River: A Memoir of My Mother and Her People,* to assert generational continuity *within* the Caribbean.[18] Goodison also foregrounds the mother's lineage rather than the traditional patrimonial inheritance.

In Dionne Brand's *At the Full and Change of the Moon,* somewhat like the circular, similarly named clan of García Márquez's *One Hundred Years of Solitude,* the family chart, mapped very differently from the linear units of a family tree, descends from Bola of 1821 to Bola of 1982. But unlike the grand ambitions of the search for antecedents, this repetition is not dynastic, but highlights, as does Ladoo, powerlessness, loss, and even namelessness: "The one who was taken in a hurricane"; "The girl who was flooded in everything"; "The sisters who went to England." The founding mother is a slave whose name, "Marie Ursule," reveals nothing of her origins beyond the period of being owned by the Ursuline nuns. Similarly, in Lawrence Scott's *Witchbroom,* the family tree is spotted with question marks and missing data, rather than an impeccable display of names and dates. The tree is not only sparse and cryptic, it is split twice horizontally with these two statements: "Records lost due to shortage of paper and ink"; "Records lost in the Diaspora." The very title of Scott's novel defaces the "original" family tree and deforms its perfection to portray multiple outgrowths as a result of plantation histories. The fibrils and rhizomes of Glissant's preference, the gossamer web of Anancy's weave, the pumpkin vine of the nonbiological kinship networks, and the multiracial family in Margaret Cezair-Thompson's *The True History of Paradise,* where family members have European, African, Indian, and Chinese names—all these "glue" the "shards" of continents together, to borrow Walcott's famous image of the broken vase.[19]

Baldeosingh's novel expands the family tree into the Hindu notion of avatars, recapitulating the mixed descent of Caribbean subjects in a series of rebirths. However, the abrupt disappearance of Adam is a telling sign that the past may be recounted in great detail, but the future remains to be seen. The lack of closure seems to support David Scott's contention that "postcoloniality has been concerned principally with the decolonization of representation."[20] Baldeosingh thoroughly demystifies colonial versions of the region's history but is unable to conceive of a lived future well into postcoloniality. However, if his project partly obeys the Fanonian dictum to provide "that space in which the ex-colonized are restored to their own history, and their humanity,"[21] it also exceeds Fanon's sense of the human (or the Adamic) by portraying a multiplicity of subjects and stories. There are a number of unanswered questions in the massive novel, including the mysterious figure of the Shadowman, sometimes represented as a black man, at other times as human incarnations of Ogun, Kali, and Shiva; sometimes a menacing nemesis, at other times a protective guardian spirit.

Perhaps the lengthy novel ends inconclusively because, despite having led the reader through a thorough reorientation of the past, it cannot see its way too clearly beyond the present. Although many of the writers I have examined here are still close to the history of colonialism, the topsy-turvy world of current capital flows suggests that another prospect lies ahead, a perhaps radically different sense of the postcolonial. The formerly wealthy countries of the world are in financial crisis, their "former vassals"[22] are seeing rising fortunes, the Arab Spring has brought internal conflicts within nations rather than a war against the West to the fore, and global power dynamics seem to have shifted to another hemisphere from the one Columbus propelled into a new world. All these seismic shifts do not mean that Caribbean problems have disappeared—after all, Europe's debt crisis has not mitigated Jamaica's continuing debt problems. However, the changing of the old order seems to indicate not just a new script but also an entirely fresh cast of actors, heroes, and villains. So it is not surprising that Baldeosingh's novel ends with Adam Avatar's abrupt disappearance. What the future holds remains to be seen, and what we are left with to guide us are the signposts from the past revisited by Adam.

Notes

Introduction

1. Benjamin, "Theses," 255.

2. Not all students have the same experience, of course. Some already know the Caribbean in more serious and scholarly contexts; others have direct knowledge, having lived there or because of heritage connections. But I dwell on the most striking contrast in order to emphasize the opposing poles of paradise and pathology.

3. There is significant output on the paradise motif not just in the Caribbean but also drawing on the original myth of Genesis and on poets such as Milton and Dante. Some of it is connected to the concept of the garden, but its idyll and that of the pastoral are complicated by the agricultural plantations of colonial enterprise. See John Armstrong, *Paradise Myth*; Albert Balink, *My Paradise is Hell* (New York: Vista, 1948); Sharae Deckard, *Paradise Discourse, Imperialism, and Globalization: Exploiting Eden* (New York: Routledge, 2010); Melanie A. Murray, *Island Paradise: The Myth* (Amsterdam: Rodopi, 2009); John Prest, *The Garden of Eden: The Botanic Garden and the Re-creation of Paradise* (New Haven, CT: Yale University Press, 1981); Sale, *Conquest of Paradise*; Ian Gregory Strachan, *Paradise and Plantation: Tourism and Culture in the Anglophone Caribbean* (Charlottesville: University of Virginia Press, 2002); and Frank Fonda Taylor, *To Hell with Paradise: A History of the Jamaican Tourist Industry* (Pittsburgh: University of Pittsburgh Press, 1993). I list only a brief selection here. But unlike many of these texts, my discussion here of paradise and anti-paradise discourse is only a launch pad for other important issues and modes that constitute this book, topics that range from gardens to the grotesque. Critiques of tourism or paradise myths are therefore only incidental to my detours.

4. Walcott, "The Antilles," *Twilight,* 81.

5. Brathwaite, *Arrivants,* 274.

6. Walcott, "The Antilles," *Twilight,* 83.

7. Lovelace, *While Gods Are Falling,* 8.

8. Giorgio Agamben, *Homo Sacer: Sovereign Power and Bare Life,* trans. Daniel Heller-Roazen (Stanford: Stanford University Press, 1998). For a provocative analysis of "bare life" as not simply restricted to the concentration camp, see Nadi Edwards, "Notes on the Age of Dis: Reading Kingston through Agamben" in *Small Axe* 25 (Feb. 2008): 1–15. Discussing, among other texts, Brathwaite's threnodic *Trench Town Rock* (New York: Lost Roads Publishers, 1996), Edwards draws links between Brathwaite's mournful invocation of Dis, the underworld deity and Dante's city in Hell, and the devolution of Kingston into another kind of dystopic camp.

9. Glissant, *Caribbean Discourse,* 5.

10. Ibid., 25.

11. J. Michael Dash, introduction to Glissant, *Carribbean Discourse,* xli.

12. Lovelace, *While Gods Are Falling,* 9.

13. Culler, *Framing the Sign,* 156.

14. Melville, *Ventriloquist's Tale.*

15. Milton, *Paradise Lost,* ed. Scott Elledge (New York: Norton, 1993), 9.1115–17, 1114.

16. Taussig, *Shamanism,* 289.

17. Cassid, *Sowing Empire,* 12.

18. Senior, *Gardening,* 14.

19. Sheller, *Consuming the Caribbean.*

20. Senior, *Gardening,* 16.

21. Ibid., 15.

22. Bobby McFerrin's 1988 hit song has reappeared in multiple contexts, some of the more famous being a slighting reference to it by the hip-hop group Public Enemy in "Fight the Power"; the musician Rambo Amadeus's parody "Don't Happy, Be Worry"; and its appropriation by George H. W. Bush's presidential campaign in 1988 (dropped after the singer protested). McFerrin's apparent inspiration for the phrase was the Indian mystic Meher Baba, who used it as a marketing ploy in reaching out to his followers.

23. García Márquez, *Autumn of the Patriarch,* 242.

24. Ibid., 198.

25. Ibid., 199.

26. Sangari, "Politics of the Possible," 227. Emphasis in text. See chapter 4 for a longer analysis of magical realism.

27. John Armstrong, *Paradise Myth,* 1.

28. Lamming, *Castle of My Skin,* 71.

29. Gillis, "Taking History Offshore," 25.

30. Carew, *Rape of Paradise,* 13.

31. See, for instance, various travel logs in *The Islands and the Sea: Five Centuries of Nature Writing from the Caribbean,* ed. John A. Murray (New York: Oxford University Press, 1991).

32. James L. Larson's *Interpreting Nature: The Science of Living from Linnaeus to Kant* (Baltimore: Johns Hopkins University Press, 1994) outlines some of the internal controversies and differences between naturalists.

33. See, for instance, Richard Grove's essay "The British Empire and the Origins of Forest Conservation in the Eastern Caribbean, 1700–1800," in *Islands, Forests, and Gardens in the Caribbean: Conservation and Conflict in Environmental History,* ed. Robert S. Anderson, Richard Grove, and Karis Hiebert (Oxford: Macmillan Caribbean, 2006), 132–73.

34. Foucault, *Order of Things.*

35. Carew, *Rape of Paradise,* 175.

36. Paul Lawrence Farber, *Finding Order in Nature: The Naturalist Tradition from Linnaeus to E. O. Wilson* (Baltimore: Johns Hopkins University Press, 2000), 12.

37. Walcott, "The Caribbean: Culture or Mimicry," 9.

38. Lévi-Strauss, *Tristes Tropiques,* 80, 81.

39. As Foucault puts it, the studied attentiveness of natural history led not so much to expansions as to "exclusions," a paring down to essentials as compared to the earlier overcrowding and confusion of characteristics. See the chapter "Classifying" in *The Order of Things,* 125–65.

40. Crosby, *Columbian Exchange,* 75. However, the longhorn and the horse brought by the Spanish were immensely productive migrants, and the natives of North America welcomed the horse, along with other livestock. Not so the rats and rabbits, which were pretty much an ecological disaster on the archipelagos.

41. D. Arnold, *Problem of Nature,* 88–89.

42. Crosby, *Ecological Imperialism,* 2–3.

43. Crosby, *Columbian Exchange,* 40.

44. Crosby, *Ecological Imperialism,* 92.

45. Lucile H. Brockway, *Science and Colonial Expansion: The Role of the British Royal Botanic Gardens* (New York: Academic Press, 1979), 57.

46. Kincaid, *My Garden (Book),* 103.

47. For connections between colonialism, culture, and plantations, see Joan Pong Linton, *The Romance of the New World: Gender and the Literary Formations of English Colonialism* (Cambridge: Cambridge University Press, 1998), 156. Linton reminds us of the masculinist emphasis on plantation (as against the more feminized garden) in terms such as "husbandry," which emphasized men in planting activities, albeit more commandingly.

48. Raymond Williams, "Culture," *Keywords,* rev. ed. (New York: Oxford University Press, 1983), 87–88.

49. Cliff, "Contagious Melancholia," 222.

50. Kincaid, *My Brother,* 19–20.

51. Ibid., 83.

52. Sale, *Conquest of Paradise,* 28.

53. Drayton, *Nature's Government,* 68.

54. Sheller, *Consuming the Caribbean,* 19–20. See Susan Scott Parrish's *American Curiosity: Cultures of Natural History in the Colonial British Atlantic World* (Chapel Hill: University of North Carolina Press, 2006), and Judith A. Carney and Richard Nicholas Rosomoff's *In the Shadow of Slavery: Africa's Botanical Legacy in the Atlantic World* (Berkeley: University of California Press, 2009) for similar arguments.

55. Cliff, "Caliban's Daughter," 47.

56. Benjamin, "Theses," 262.

57. Butler, *Precarious Life,* 134. See also Emmanuel Levinas, *Totality and Infinity: An Essay on Exteriority,* trans. Alphonso Lingis (Pittsburgh: Duquesne University Press, 1969).

58. Cixous, "Laugh of the Medusa."

59. Walcott, "The Muse of History," *Twilight,* 36.

60. Glissant, *Poetics of Relation,* 6.

61. Kincaid, *My Brother,* 195–96.

62. Morrison, *Beloved,* 275.

63. Alison Donnell, *Twentieth-Century Caribbean Literature: Critical Moments in Anglophone Literary History* (London: Routledge, 2006), 135.

64. Elizabeth M. DeLoughrey, *Routes and Roots: Navigating Caribbean and Pacific Island Literatures* (Honolulu: University of Hawai`i Press, 2007).

65. Danticat, *Krik? Krak!,* 220.

66. Díaz, *Oscar Wao,* 7.

1. The Empire and the Garden

1. I am repeating on Paul Gilroy's argument in *The Black Atlantic* that European modernity, usually trumpeted as a sign of Europe's advanced march distinguished from other lagging cultures, would not have been possible had it not been for transatlantic slavery. I expand that to include other exploits of European imperialism and point toward terrestrial and oceanic spaces beyond the Black Atlantic and its Western orientation.

2. See Braziel, "'Caribbean Genesis'"; Handley, *New World Poetics.* Handley's "lowercase model, *a*damic" is a tarter, less facile, postcolonial version of the prelapsarian, territorial Adam (2; emphasis in text). While Handley's project productively fords hemispheric waters, my chapter will critique the (con)scripted, gendered discourse of the Adamic in both biblical and literary perspectives.

3. Lamming, *Castle of My Skin,* 71. See also the discussion of this passage by Lamming and Anthony Bogues in *The George Lamming Reader,* 216–17. Lamming identifies the demystifying satire in this passage as an example of the decolonizing imagination.

4. For a literary reading of a similar phenomenon—the manipulation of the New World settlers' "garden of the covenant" into the slaveholders' "garden of the chattel"—and its inevitable split at the seams, see Lewis P. Simpson, *The*

Dispossessed Garden: Pastoral and History in Southern Literature (Athens: University of Georgia Press, 1975).

5. I borrow the phrase "slave sublime" from Gilroy, who uses it to indicate the wrenching struggle to represent, to embody in art and music and performance, the unspeakable horrors of slavery. But my use of it is inflected by his final chapter in *The Black Atlantic,* which, ironically, finds a convenient forgetting of the history of slavery not just in Eurocentric versions, but in what Gilroy idiosyncratically calls "Africentricity" (187–223).

6. Walcott, "The Antilles," *What the Twilight Says,* 81.

7. Bridges, *Child of the Tropics,* 54.

8. Ibid.

9. Ibid., 81.

10. Ibid., 202.

11. Persaud, *Butterfly in the Wind,* 87. I read *Butterfly* as an anomaly in the dominant tradition of Indo-Caribbean fiction, which (with few exceptions like Samuel Selvon) so far has been haunted by a sense of malaise.

12. Persaud, *Butterfly,* 113.

13. Ibid., 108.

14. Brontë, *Jane Eyre,* 304.

15. Allfrey, *Orchid House,* 168.

16. Ibid., 59.

17. Ibid., 99.

18. Rhys, *Wide Sargasso Sea,* 41.

19. Ibid., 88.

20. Walcott, *Remembrance and Pantomime* (1.5), 44.

21. Rhys, *Wide Sargasso Sea,* 77.

22. Naipaul, *Enigma of Arrival,* 7.

23. Ibid., 52.

24. Ibid., 172–73.

25. Ibid., 227.

26. Ibid., 224.

27. Ibid., 227.

28. Ibid., 238.

29. Ibid., 226.

30. Ibid., 160.

31. Rhys, *Wide Sargasso Sea,* 17.

32. Ibid., 11. Emphasis in text.

33. Rodríguez, *House/Garden/Nation,* 128.

34. For a discussion of this term, see Sarah Phillips Casteel, *Second Arrivals: Landscape and Belonging in Contemporary Writing of the Americas* (Charlottesville: University of Virginia Press, 2007).

35. Kincaid, *My Garden (Book),* 152.

36. Ibid., 37.

37. Ibid., 143.
38. Ibid., 66.
39. Ibid., 151.
40. Ibid., 122.
41. Foucault, *Order of Things,* 135.
42. Sedgwick, *Epistemology of the Closet,* 39.
43. Warren, *Ecological Feminist Philosophies,* xiii. Emphasis in text.
44. Coulthard, *Race and Colour,* 89, 90. See also Audre Lorde's expression of her black and lesbian identity in the (both literal and metaphorical) erotic use of fruits used to describe her lovemaking with Afrekete in *Zami,* 249–51. Compare this perspective with the lyrics to Lewis Allan's powerful "Strange Fruit," in which the "Black body swinging in the Southern breeze,/Strange fruit hanging from the poplar trees" defamiliarizes the tropes of fecundity and pleasure into the senseless wastefulness of death in the lynching of black men. Lewis Allan was a pseudonym for the Jewish schoolteacher from New York, Abel Meeropol, who penned the words sung so memorably by Billie Holiday that she claimed the song as her own. For its history, see *Strange Fruit: Billie Holiday, Café Society, and an Early Cry for Civil Rights* by David Margolick (Philadelphia: Running Press, 2000).
45. Naipaul, "Jasmine," *Literary Occasions,* 45.
46. Boose, "Father's House," 64.
47. Mootoo, *Cereus Blooms at Night,* 220.
48. Ibid., 195.
49. Ibid., 109.
50. Ibid., 47.
51. Ibid., 48.
52. In *An Archive of Feelings,* Ann Cvetkovich meticulously alludes to Sarah's "sapphic connection" with Lavinia, "because the women never overtly identify as lesbians in the novel" (142). She insists that "their relationship . . . remains unclassifiable within the categories of Western homosexuality" (144). See also Omise'eke Natasha Tinsley's discussion of why she uses the phrase "women who love women" rather than specific labels in the introduction to her book *Thiefing Sugar,* 1–28.
53. Mootoo, *Cereus,* 77.
54. Ibid., 128.
55. Ibid., 71. Emphasis added. Vinay Lal describes the *napumsaka* as "a neutered transvestite of ambiguous sex" (125). While Tyler is not a hijra or a *napumsaka* in the conventional sense of the term, Lal's titular negation—not this, not that—drawn from a Sanskrit chant, reminds us of the inadequacy of definitive categorizations in a complex system of signification and lived experience. See Lal, "Not This, Not That: The Hijras of India and the Cultural Politics of Sexuality," *Social Text* 17, no. 4 (Winter 1999): 119–40.
56. Mootoo, *Cereus,* 128.

57. Sedgwick, *Epistemology,* 26.

58. On homophobia in the Caribbean, see Jacqui Alexander, "Not Just (Any) Body Can be a Citizen: The Politics of Law, Sexuality and Postcoloniality in Trinidad and Tobago and the Bahamas," *Feminist Review* 48, no. 1 (Autumn 1994): 5–23; Jamaica Kincaid, *My Brother;* Lawson Williams, "Homophobia and Gay Rights Activism in Jamaica," *Small Axe* 7 (March 2000): 106–111.

59. See Melba Wilson, *Crossing the Boundary: Black Women Survive Incest* (London: Virago, 1993). The burdensome, consuming secret that cannot be revealed without convulsing the family is a recurrent motif in such texts. Since the twentieth century, however, one can speak of an "incest boom," where different fields have explored the significance and occurrence of incest from anthropological, psychoanalytic, and other angles, including as an experience of trauma. In the context of literature, see Elizabeth Barnes, ed., *Incest and the Literary Imagination* (Gainesville: University Press of Florida, 2002). I do not consider consensual incest here, which carries a different weight from the rape and abuse described in Mootoo's novel.

60. Mootoo, *Cereus,* 30.

61. Ibid., 215. Emphasis in text.

62. Rodríguez, *House/Garden/Nation,* 13.

63. Kutzinski, "Violence and Sexual Others," 45. Emphasis in text.

64. Mootoo, *Cereus,* 237–38.

65. Cliff, "Caliban's Daughter," 37.

66. Senior, "The Immovable Tenant," *Gardening,* 104.

67. Cliff, "Caliban's Daughter," 40. See also *No Telephone to Heaven,* which opens with a definition of the term in an epigraph.

68. McCracken, *Gardens of Empire,* 131.

69. Cliff, "Caliban's Daughter," 45.

70. Alaimo, *Undomesticated Ground,* 16.

71. Mootoo, *Cereus,* 127.

72. Foucault, *Order of Things,* xviii. Emphasis in text.

73. Mootoo, *Cereus,* 126.

74. Spivak, *Critique of Postcolonial Reason,* 257.

75. Ibid., 207.

76. Marlene NourbeSe Philip equates the "father tongue" (and the English language) with the penis, fellatio, and the overseer's whip in her collection of poems *She Tries Her Tongue, Her Silence Softly Breaks,* 33. Mootoo similarly interprets the woman's silence as induced by force, no longer the overseer's but of Mala's father's tyranny within the family circle.

77. Froula, "Daughter's Seduction," 132n32.

78. Alice Walker, *The Color Purple* (New York: Harcourt, Brace, 1982).

79. Walker, *Our Mothers' Gardens,* 240.

80. Sidney Mintz, *Sweetness and Power: The Place of Sugar in Modern History* (New York: Penguin, 1985).

81. Kincaid, "On Gardening," 793.

82. Foucault, "Neitzsche, Genealogy, History," *Language, Counter-memory, Practice,* 147.

2. Toxic Domesticity, Curative Kinship

1. Freud, "The Uncanny" [Das Unheimliche, 1919].

2. Powell, *Fullness of Everything,* 23.

3. Pollard, "Out of Joint," *Leaving Traces,* 85.

4. Ibid.

5. Naipaul, *India,* 178.

6. Romero, *Home Fronts,* 11.

7. Amy Kaplan, "Manifest Domesticity," *No More Separate Spheres!*

8. Domestic fiction is a specific category of nineteenth-century women's writing in England and the United States. The theory and criticism now cover a wide range that can only be mentioned here. For instance, Nina Baym notes that antebellum women writers did not suffer from the "anxiety of authorship" discussed by Sandra Gilbert and Susan Gubar and wrote on a prolific range of genres and topics. See Nina Baym, *Woman's Fiction: A Guide to Novels by and about Women in America, 1820–70,* 2nd ed. (Urbana: University of Illinois Press, 1993). See also Nancy Armstrong, *Desire and Domestic Fiction: A Political History of the Novel* (Oxford: Oxford University Press, 1987), and Ann Douglas, *The Feminization of American Culture,* 2nd ed. (New York: Noonday, 1988).

9. Alvarez, *Time of the Butterflies,* 96.

10. Danticat, *Farming of Bones,* 203.

11. Lee, "At the New Year," *Behind the Counter,* 38. I thank Timothy Chin for drawing my attention to the Chinese store as a space of cultural identity.

12. Lee, "Friday," *Behind the Counter,* 2.

13. Lee, "Funnels," *Behind the Counter,* 42.

14. Lee, "My Mother Is a People," *Behind the Counter,* 17.

15. See a *Time* magazine piece by Michael Scherer on how female federal regulators are "cleaning up the mess" left by investment banks and Fortune 500 companies that employ a miniscule percentage of women. While the influence these officials wield is gratifying, one cannot but note the conventional implications of women cleaning up after men. Scherer, "The New Sheriffs of Wall Street," *Time,* May 24, 2010, 22–27.

16. Lee, "Advice," *Behind the Counter,* 135.

17. Significantly in Patricia Powell's *The Pagoda* (New York: Knopf, 1998), the burning down of the Chinese shop is compensated by the fantasy of building a pagoda where Jamaican-Chinese subjects can reconnect with a lost heritage and sustain a threatened existence amid interracial strife and economic rivalry. The yearning for a stable, physical dwelling, as with Naipaul's Mr. Biswas, also expresses the desire for some form of rootedness in unstable, insecure conditions.

18. Lee-Loy, *Searching for Mr. Chin,* 106.

19. Ibid., 113.

20. See Elizabeth Nunez, *Bruised Hibiscus* (New York: Ballantine, 2000), for an account that Orientalizes the "Chinaman," but ties his rape and abuse of women in the home to economic injustice and social upheaval in China.

21. Michael Rothberg, "Decolonizing Trauma Studies: A Response," *Studies in the Novel* 40, nos. 1 and 2 (Spring and Summer 2008): 224–34. DOI: 10.1353/sdn.0.0005. The volumes are part of a special issue that aims to enlarge the field of trauma studies from its Eurocentric focus.

22. E. Ann Kaplan, *Trauma Culture,* 19. Kaplan borrows some of these terms from other scholars.

23. Judith Lewis Herman categorizes domestic violence under human rights violations and as political crimes that serve to perpetuate an unjust social order. She unapologetically compares the "casualties of sexual and domestic oppression: rape victims, battered women, and abused children" to the posttraumatic stress disorders of "combat veterans, political prisoners, and concentration camp survivors" ("Crime and Memory," 129).

24. E. Ann Kaplan, *Trauma Culture,* 93.

25. Ibid., 127.

26. Gilbert and Gubar, *Madwoman in the Attic,* 51. One has to be careful about playing into the tropical stereotype of Caribbean dementia in the invocation of Bertha Mason, but it is hard to avoid the trope in Caribbean fiction, even if writers also critique it. As Gilbert and Gubar find, women's writing often challenges the easy association between the domestic space and feminine fulfillment. Although they locate men and in particular male writers as the legators of the poisoned apple, women also play a significant role in infecting each other.

27. The lines that influence the title of chapter 2 in Gilbert and Gubar are from Emily Dickinson: "Infection in the sentence breeds/We may inhale Despair/At distances of Centuries/From the Malaria" (45). See poem #1261, *Complete Poems of Emily Dickinson,* 553.

28. Dabydeen and Samaroo, *Across the Dark Waters,* 10. In their introduction, the editors confess that their own volume reflects the domination of the historiography by men who are more focused at this point on ethnicity to the exclusion of gender issues.

29. Espinet, "Invisible Woman."

30. Brand, "No Language Is Neutral," 133.

31. Guha, "Historiography of Colonial India," 44. Emphasis in text.

32. See Patricia Mohammed, "Reflections on the Women's Movement in Trinidad: Calypsos, Changes and Sexual Violence," *Feminist Review* 38 (Summer 1991): 33–47. See also Tracy S. Robinson, "Fictions of Citizenship, Bodies without Sex: The Production and Effacement of Gender in Law," *Small Axe* 7 (March 2000): 1–27.

33. In traditional contexts where the father expects service from the woman in the house, including sexual relations, he exerts his fundamental right to such

service over his duty as a parent when he turns to incest against his daughter. In their essay "Father-Daughter Incest," Judith Herman and Lisa Hirschman provocatively claim that such a situation must be read not as rape, but as seduction, since the latter word more accurately emphasizes the complexity of the daughter's feelings and the father's exploitation of his daughter's love and sense of duty (270).

34. Kanhai, "Masala Stone Sings," 209–37.

35. Mootoo, *Cereus,* 133.

36. Spivak, *Critique of Postcolonial Reason,* 257.

37. While collective trauma may be more visible, I am drawing attention here to individual trauma in domestic situations that find clear expression in what Anne Whitehead calls "trauma fiction," specific and admittedly varying narrative strategies of articulating trauma that is not always in the public eye. See Anne Whitehead, *Trauma Fiction* (Edinburgh: Edinburgh University Press, 2004).

38. S. Bloom, "Elephant in the Room," 146.

39. Ibid., 159.

40. Lorde, *Zami,* 74–75. Emphasis in text.

41. Danticat, *Breath, Eyes, Memory,* 88.

42. Ibid., 203.

43. Ibid., 170.

44. Gilbert and Gubar, *Madwoman in the Attic,* 34. See also Brenda O. Daly and Maureen T. Reddy's introduction to their coedited volume, *Narrating Mothers,* 3, 11.

45. This does not mean that connections with other writers cannot be made. Laura Niesen de Abruna traces the hostile mother-daughter relationships in Rhys's and Kincaid's novels, and is probably among the first to claim that they allegorically signify unresolved tensions with the mother country, England. See de Abruna, "Family Connections."

46. Kincaid, *My Brother,* 162.

47. Ibid., 68–69.

48. Suleiman, "Writing and Motherhood," 356. Emphasis in text.

49. Kincaid, *Mr. Potter.*

50. Hirsch, *Mother/Daughter Plot,* 67.

51. Judith Fetterley defines immasculated women as those who are given male attributes. See *The Resisting Reader: A Feminist Approach to American Fiction* (Bloomington and London: Indiana University Press, 1978), xx.

52. See Brown-Guillory, "Disrupted Motherlines."

53. Antonia MacDonald-Smythe's suggestion that the other arm tucked into the skirt is engaging in self-pleasuring is a compelling one, as is her sense that for Kincaid, the mother here represents the repression of libidinal subjectivity that, upon the mother's death, is developed in Xuela's onanism. Unlike MacDonald-Smythe, I am reading the portrait as a picture of the mother, not the daughter,

although both could be implied. See MacDonald-Smythe, "Self-Fashioning and the Libidinal Subject," 338.

54. Ferguson, *Jamaica Kincaid,* 1. Along with some of the essays in Nasta's *Motherlands* that similarly equate mother and land, this collapse of the mother into the colonizer seems to be a fairly accepted reading of Kincaid's biographical context.

55. Alexander, *Mother Imagery,* 19.

56. Kincaid, "Jamaica Kincaid and the Modernist Project," 222.

57. See Kim McLarin, "*Mr. Potter* (Book)," review of *Mr. Potter, Black Issues Book Review* 4 (July/August 2002): 34.

58. Kincaid, *Mr. Potter,* 100–101.

59. Ibid., 130.

60. Ibid., 77.

61. Ibid., 188.

62. Kincaid, interview with Patricia O'Conner, "My Mother Wrote My Life," *New York Times Book Review*, April 7, 1985: 6.

63. "Momism" was a term coined by Philip Wylie in his book *Generation of Vipers*, 2nd ed. (Urbana-Champaign: Dalkey Archive Press, 2007). Among other attacks, he assailed the American cult of motherhood and the excessive nurture of strong mothers, resulting, he claimed, in sappy males.

64. Kincaid, *My Brother,* 27.

65. Paravisini-Gebert, *Jamaica Kincaid,* 16. Kincaid also speaks of her breakdown in *My Brother* (28) and elsewhere.

66. Hilton Als, "Don't Worry, Be Happy," review of *Lucy* by Jamaica Kincaid, *Nation,* December 18, 1991, 208.

67. Sandhya Shetty, "(Dis)figuring the Nation: Mother, Metaphor, Metonymy," *Difference: A Journal of Feminist Cultural Studies* 7, no. 3 (Fall 1995): 58.

68. Goodison, *I Am Becoming My Mother.*

69. Gilbert and Gubar, *Madwoman in the Attic,* 51. See in particular chapter 2, "Infection in the Sentence: The Woman Writer and the Anxiety of Authorship." They challenge the Bloomian model of father-son rivalry by introducing the woman writer and where she fits (or does not fit) this paradigm. Pursuing Frantz Fanon's rejection of a straightforward Oedipal narrative for black men, I am cautious about conferring full patriarchal power on Caribbean male writers or colonial subjects who tended to embody phallic impotence against the power of the metropolis, tellingly figured as the mother country. I am arguing for a more careful calibration of gender dynamics in contexts not considered by Gilbert and Gubar.

70. Lamming, *Pleasures of Exile,* 23–50.

71. Naipaul, "Prologue to an Autobiography," *Literary Occasions,* 70. Subsequent references to Naipaul's father will use his first name to distinguish him from his son.

72. Naipaul, "Two Worlds: The Nobel Lecture," *Literary Occasions,* 187.

73. Naipaul, "Foreword to *The Adventures of Gurudeva,*" *Literary Occasions,* 116. Naipaul fittingly extends his father's dedication of the short stories to him to include MacGowan and Henry Swanzy, forming a literary circle of influence (127).

74. Harold Bloom, *The Anxiety of Influence: A Theory of Poetry* (New York: Oxford University Press, 1973). Bloom presents male poets as engaging in an Oedipal struggle for individuation with their literary forefathers, the distinguished predecessors against whom they have to make their own mark. Conversely, Naipaul's "anxiety" is not so much about not being able *to live up to* his father's literary output, but that he would *be limited* to it.

75. Naipaul, *Between Father and Son,* 269.

76. Naipaul, "Foreword to *A House for Mr. Biswas,*" *Literary Occasions,* 130.

77. Naipaul, *Biswas,* 465.

78. Ibid., 540.

79. Naipaul, "Unsparing Vision," 128.

80. Naipaul's mother was a small businesswoman who by all accounts was competent and even well liked, but Naipaul claimed to hate her. See Diana Athill's discussion of his mother in *Stet,* 217–19. As Athill perceptively puts it, "Anyway, dislike of a mother usually indicates damaged love" (219).

81. I am obviously riffing on Jacques Lacan's theories but am unable to stay within their framework. Lacan's mirror stage and his notion of the Symbolic (the realm of language, culture, and the Name-of-the-Father) are inclusive concepts of child development. In contrast, the misrecognition that Naipaul wants to emphasize is not a universal phase of childhood nor is it idealized, but emphasizes the particular angst of a colonial subject that Naipaul worries is an inescapable postcolonial inheritance. What seems to be at stake here in the challenge to predictable paradigms of patriarchy, both in the Indo- and Afro-Caribbean histories of indenture and slavery, is the seriously unstable condition of the father, the specular disintegration pointed out by Fanon in the experience of racism.

82. Naipaul, "Prologue," *Literary Occasions,* 109.

83. Ibid., 111.

84. Naipaul, *A Writer's People,* no pag. Emphasis in text.

85. Walcott, "The Antilles," *Twilight,* 69.

86. Goodison, *From Harvey River,* 209. The subtitle of the later London editions was changed to *A Memoir of My Mother and Her Island.*

87. Ibid., 274.

88. See Samuel Cohen, "The Novel in a Time of Terror: *Middlesex,* History, and Contemporary American Fiction," *Twentieth-Century Literature* 53, no. 3 (Fall 2007): 371–93. In agreement with scholars like James Berger and Dominick LaCapra, Cohen resists the temptation to heal wounds and seek happy closure in trauma narratives.

3. "Disasters in the Sun"

1. Shiva Naipaul, *Black and White,* 3. Cheddi Jagan reports a similar ignorance about Guyana during his student days in the United States. When he identifies himself as Guyanese, Americans ask him, "What part of Africa is that?"—presumably confusing it with Guinea, he says. See Jagan, *West on Trial,* 57. Since I will be discussing V. S. Naipaul as well, all further references to Shiva Naipaul, with due respect, will use his first name to distinguish between the brothers.

2. Shakespeare, *Hamlet,* 1.1.118. Horatio refers to similar ill omens before the murder of Julius Caesar.

3. Ibid., 1.2.135–37.

4. Buck-Morrs, *Dreamworld and Catastrophe,* 188.

5. *Witness to Jonestown,* accessed April 9, 2011, http://www.msnbc.msn.com/id/30645716/vp/27187801#27187807. There are now several video clips of the tragedy, some of them quite graphic.

6. D'Aguiar, *Bill of Rights,* 74.

7. Ibid.

8. Ibid., 71.

9. Benjamin, "Theses," 263.

10. For an account of the popular culture reactions to the brazen Musilmeen coup, see Kevin K. Birth, "Bakrnal: Coup, Carnival and Calypso in Trinidad," *Ethnology* 33, no. 2 (Spring 1994): 165–77. Explaining the various performative incorporations of the coup in calypso lyrics, dance movements at the 1991 Carnival, and in youth culture, Birth concludes, "The coup became a comedy in which the country was given reason to laugh at Abu Bakr, and even more so at the government" (175).

11. Since "jungly" is not of common usage, Shiva Naipaul is probably alluding to the Hindi word usually transcribed in English as "junglee," which means wild, savage, uncivilized, "hirsute and unkempt," as Roydon Salick notes, tracing the etymology of the English "jungle" from the Hindi word (204). See Salick, "The Bittersweet Comedy of Sonny Ladoo," *Comic Vision.*

12. Shiva Naipaul, *Black and White,* 87.

13. Ibid., 91.

14. Ibid., 24.

15. As Harry Trewe says in Walcott's *Pantomime,* "Attempted suicide in a Third World country. You can't leave a note because the pencils break, you can't cut your wrist with the local blades" (97). This ineptness is opposed by Junot Díaz's portrayal in *The Brief Wondrous Life of Oscar Wao* of superefficient massacres and death squads as a particularly Third World skill (see my introduction).

16. In her magisterial study, Hena Maes-Jelinek challenges Shiva's allegations of Guyanese peculiarity by pointing to a series of killings and suicides in other parts of the world. See her chapter on Harris's novel and D'Aguiar's poetic version in *Labyrinth of Universality,* 419–37.

17. Shiva Naipaul, *Black and White,* 117.

18. Ibid., 9.

19. Benjamin, "Theses," 257.

20. Shiva Naipaul, *Black and White,* 9.

21. Lewis, *"Gather with the Saints."*

22. V. S. Naipaul clearly shared his brother's views. Says Patrick French of the former in *The World Is What It Is,* "He detested hippies, yippies, beatniks, free schools, flower power, Black Power, flag burning, hair growing, sit-ins, be-ins, teach-ins and love-ins" (266).

23. Shiva Naipaul, *Black and White,* 170.

24. D'Aguiar, *Bill of Rights,* 30.

25. Shiva Naipaul, *Black and White,* 175.

26. Buck-Morrs, *Dreamworld,* 188.

27. Henry David Thoreau, *Walden and Civil Disobedience* (Middlesex, UK: Penguin, 1986), 50.

28. See Melvin Dixon, *Ride Out the Wilderness: Geography and Identity in Afro-American Literature* (Urbana: University of Illinois Press, 1987), for a more detailed reading of how the wilderness figures in slave songs and writings as site of deliverance and trial. For both Shiva and V. S. Naipaul, the jungles of Guyana function as the hideout of criminals, the natural lair of wanted men such as Michael X, not as the site of mystic revelations as it does for Harris.

29. Lewis, *"Gather with the Saints,"* 13.

30. Voltaire, *Candide,* 120.

31. Marx, "Economic and Philosophical Manuscripts," 328.

32. Shiva Naipaul, *Black and White,* 132.

33. For an interesting account of the gender politics in the Jonestown leadership hierarchy, see Mary McCormick Maaga's sympathetic *Hearing the Voices of Jonestown.* Contradicting Maaga's account are allegations of rape, abuse, and torture by an increasingly out-of-control Jones.

34. Harris, *Jonestown,* 14.

35. See Harris, *Radical Imagination,* 55. The interview by Alan Riach and Harris's lectures are useful in decoding the latter's obscure and mystical fiction. There is now a growing body of excellent literary criticism focused on this author.

36. See Harris's interview in 1986, reprinted as "Wilson Harris with Fred D'Aguiar," in *Writing Across Worlds.*

37. Harris, *Radical Imagination,* 23.

38. Ibid., 22.

39. Alvin O. Thompson views violence as the "red thread . . . that runs throughout the region," a color he insists is not just symbolic but literal. Harris, on the other hand, sees a "therapeutic thread" that overrides the good-evil binaries. See Thompson, *Haunting Past,* 15; Harris, *Radical Imagination,* 58.

40. Harris, *Jonestown,* 30.

41. Ibid., 159.

42. Voltaire, *Candide,* 18.

43. Harris, "History, Fable and Myth," 25, 26.

44. Brathwaite, "Caliban," *Arrivants,* 195.

45. Harris, "History, Fable and Myth," 27.

46. Henry, *Caliban's Reason,* 103, 106.

47. Harris, *Jonestown,* 233.

48. Ibid., 71.

49. D'Aguiar, *Bill of Rights,* 73.

50. Layton, *Seductive Poison,* 260. The book, published twenty years after Layton's defection and flight, has a foreword by Charles Krause, one of the journalists shot in the melee at the landing strip near Jonestown. He speaks highly of Shiva Naipaul's analysis and also ties the utopian commune to the cultish aura and idealism of the sixties (xii, xv).

51. Gerard Aching cautions against conflating various traditions of Carnival and the carnivalesque as universal, and against reading them as always subversive and populist. In Persaud's novel, masking traditions confer a dangerous anonymity on the thugs of the dominant regime who collude with the repressive state apparatus and prey on unarmed citizens with impunity. See Aching, *Masking and Power: Carnival and Popular Culture in the Caribbean* (Minneapolis: University of Minnesota Press, 2002).

52. Persaud, *For the Love of My Name,* 38.

53. Ibid., 43.

54. Ibid., 170.

55. Ibid., 15. Emphasis in text.

56. Henry, *Caliban's Reason,* 102.

57. V. S. Naipaul, *The Suffrage of Elvira* (London: André Deutsch, 1958).

58. V. S. Naipaul, "A Handful of Dust," *Writer and the World,* 485–502.

59. Ibid., 488. Buck-Morss notes that a Moscow laboratory mummified Forbes Burnham's body in 1985. By 1991, embalmed figures and monuments of Soviet regimes had become national embarrassments to the Russians (79).

60. "Conversation with V. S. Naipaul," 86.

61. Bhabha, "The World and the Home," 152.

62. Ibid., 150.

63. Ibid.

64. Ibid., 152.

65. Sharp, *Life and Death of Michael X,* 3. Sharp's account (heavily sprinkled with quotations from Shakespeare's historical plays), while critical of Michael X, is not entirely condemnatory.

66. V. S. Naipaul, "Power?," *Writer,* 137.

67. Meeks, *Radical Caribbean,* 3.

68. Meeks provides a chronology of the revolution in *Radical Caribbean,* 8–35. See also Ivar Oxaal, *Race and Revolutionary Consciousness: A Documentary*

Interpretation of the 1970 Black Power Revolt in Trinidad (Cambridge, MA: Schenkman, 1971).

69. See, for instance, the collection of essays in *The Black Power Revolution, 1970: A Retrospective* for a sense of the internal rivalries, conflicts, and debates more than twenty years later by many of the actors on the scene.

70. Samuel Selvon, *Moses Ascending* (London: Heinemann, 1984). The fact that the novel was first published in 1975 suggests interesting intersections (and perhaps an ethnic solidarity, given the slighting references to Lamming in the novel) with Naipaul's sense of the seventies, much of which is presented in the ribald, politically incorrect humor of Selvon. The section "Cargo Rap" in Caryl Phillips's *Higher Ground* (New York: Vintage, 1989), often spoofs the sixties radical and is based on *Soledad Brother: The Prison Letters of George Jackson* (New York: Coward-McCann, 1970).

71. See Earl Lovelace, *The Dragon Can't Dance* (London: André Deutsch, 1979) and *Is Just a Movie* (London: Faber and Faber, 2011).

72. Malik, *From Michael de Freitas to Michael X,* 10. The autobiography was ghostwritten by John Stevenson.

73. Sharp, *Life and Death,* 51.

74. Ibid., 90–91.

75. Naipaul, *Guerrillas,* 186.

76. Benjamin, "Theses," 253.

77. Naipaul, *Guerrillas,* 203.

78. Joan Didion, "Without Regret or Hope," review of V. S. Naipaul's *The Return of Eva Perón with the Killings of Trinidad,* in *New York Review of Books,* accessed February 19, 2012, http://www.nybooks.com/articles/archives/1980/jun/12/without-regret-or-hope/.

79. Jamal, *From the Dead Level,* 42. Hakim left Trinidad abruptly soon after Gale's "disappearance," and was shot dead in 1973 by members of De Mau Mau (who alternated between being community police and vigilantes in the Roxbury neighborhood to which he returned). The deaths of several figures in the Michael X circle and his own hasty hanging in 1975 have encouraged conspiracy theories, with the Nation of Islam, the British government, and even the FBI as rumored agents.

80. Athill, *Make Believe,* 51, 75.

81. Athill is mistaken here, since Naipaul's first wife, Pat, linked Peter Roche to a lecturer Naipaul had met at Makerere. See Patrick French's biography, *The World Is What It Is,* 261.

82. Athill, *Stet,* 228.

83. *The Bank Job,* directed by Roger Donaldson (Lionsgate, 2008), DVD. I thank my students for drawing this film to my attention.

84. Athill, *Make Believe,* 5.

85. Dilip Hiro and Stephen Fay, "Race Relations: Man, It's Beautiful—But Does It Work?," *Sunday Times,* October 29, 1967, 8. John L. Williams notes that the *Sunday Times* was fined for flagrant contempt of court, since this char-

acterization, it was claimed, prejudiced the trial. See Williams, *Michael X,* 163. Various articles in the *Times* in September and November 1967 track Michael's self-dramatizing court appearances on the charges of stirring up race hatred.

86. V. S. Naipaul, *Enigma of Arrival,* 101–2.

87. V. S. Naipaul, *A Bend in the River* (London: Knopf, 1979).

88. French reveals in his biography that Naipaul's affair with Margaret progressed while Pat was assiduously taking notes on the murder trial in Trinidad. Margaret and Naipaul arranged later to meet there while Naipaul was going to write about the trial (313, 328).

89. V. S. Naipaul, *Guerrillas,* 78.

90. V. S. Naipaul, *Guerrillas,* 12.

91. Freud, "Medusa's Head," 212.

92. V. S. Naipaul, *Guerrillas,* 8.

93. For a discussion of various uses of the English canon in the novel, see John Thieme, "Apparitions of Disaster: Brontean Parallels in *Wide Sargasso Sea* and *Guerrillas,*" *Journal of Commonwealth Literature* 14, no. 1 (1979): 116–32; Johannes Riis, "Naipaul's *Woodlanders,*" *Journal of Commonwealth Literature* 14, no. 1 (1979): 109–15; Anne R. Zahlan, "Literary Murder: V. S. Naipaul's *Guerrillas,*" *South Atlantic Review* 59, no. 4 (1994): 89–106.

94. V. S. Naipaul, *Guerrillas,* 107.

95. Dance, "Matriarchs, Doves, and Nymphos," 26.

96. Parry, "Between Creole and Cambridge English," 5.

97. V. S. Naipaul, "Michael X," *Writer,* 157, 179, 190.

98. V. S. Naipaul, *Guerrillas,* 247.

99. Ibid., 60.

100. Suleri, *Rhetoric of English India,* 17, 77.

101. V. S. Naipaul, *Guerrillas,* 21.

102. V. S. Naipaul, "Michael X," *Writer,* 155.

103. Ibid., 161–62.

104. Walcott, *Remembrance and Pantomime,* 113.

105. Although Carnival is distinct from the carnivalesque, like David Danow I read the latter as embodying the "spirit" of the former, particularly in the more rebellious, impious sense. See Danow, *The Spirit of Carnival.*

106. Robertson, *Justice Game.*

4. Magic, Science, Fantasy, and Religion

1. Harris, "Merlin and Parsifal," *Unfinished Genesis,* 64. While Harris is engaging in polemic for a reason here, the idea that science is absolutist in its claims is not quite fair. Many in the scientific community would acknowledge uncertainty and limited knowledge.

2. Harris, "Theatre of the Arts."

3. Keats, "Letter to George and Tom Keats, December 1817," *John Keats: The Major Works,* ed. Elizabeth Cook (Oxford: Oxford University Press, 2001),

369–70. Keats's famous definition of Negative Capability, "when man is capable of being in uncertainties, mysteries, doubts," is something Harris would find very much to his taste.

4. Harris, "Merlin and Parsifal," *Unfinished Genesis,* 58.

5. The phrase is peculiarly apposite to Harris's critique of a paradoxically blind Reason. Although he uses it to stand for the arrogant power of the Father, the ship named *Titanic* would also signify for Harris the ultimate disaster of technological hubris. The enigmatic first-person narrator of *The Ghost of Memory* refers to Columbus as "blind," as against the belief that he "saw his way clearly." Columbus's complacent sense of being in the area we know as Japan when he was actually in the Americas represents for Harris the "blunder" and "catastrophe" of such Titanic Reason. See Harris, *Ghost of Memory,* 6, 94.

6. Tambiah, *Magic, Science, Religion,* 85.

7. Malinowski, *Magic, Science and Religion,* 18, 17.

8. Ibid., 19.

9. Not just nonwhite but even white communities in the Caribbean operated within this magical realist framework where magic and folklore exist within the realm of the ordinary. Jane C. Beck draws connections between Anglo-Irish and Afro-Caribbean folklore and beliefs: the blond mermaid (sometimes identified as a seal-woman in mermaid lore) with Mamajo (Mama d'eau, similar to the Yoruba Yemoja); *ligaroo* or *loup garou* (Fr.) and *sucoyan* (which links to the succubus) with the witches and hags of Britain and Ireland; *La jablesse, la diablesse* (Fr.) with the jack o' lantern who leads people astray, and so on. See Beck, "The West Indian Supernatural World: Belief Integration in a Pluralistic Society," *Journal of American Folklore* 88, no. 349 (July–September 1975): 235–44.

10. See, for instance, the various essays in *Sacred Possessions,* ed. Margarite Fernández Olmos and Lizabeth Paravisini-Gebert.

11. Melville, "The Parrot and Descartes," *Migration of Ghosts,* 109, 111.

12. Hawkes, "Swisser-Swatter," 27. The specific lines in Shakespeare's *The Tempest* are as follows: "A strange fish! Were/I in England now (as once I was) and had but this fish/painted, not a holiday fool there but would give a piece of/silver. There would this monster make a man; any strange beast there makes a man" (2.2.26–30). Peter Hulme has explored the colonial significance of Shakespeare's play with great depth and acuity in more than one work. See, for example, his *Colonial Encounters: Europe and the Native Caribbean, 1492–1797* (London: Methuen, 1986).

13. Hawkes, "Swisser-Swatter," 26.

14. Julian Barnes, *Flaubert's Parrot* (London: Jonathan Cape, 1984).

15. Parkinson Zamora and Faris, "Introduction: Daiquiri Birds and Flaubertian Parrot(ie)s," *Magical Realism,* 2. Barnes is not alone in his distaste for magical realism. See other complaints against the commercialization of the mode in "Magical Unrealism" by Kevin Baldeosingh (http://caribscape.com/baldeosingh/literature/sober/1999/magical.html); Alberto Fuguet and Sergio Gomez, eds.,

McOndo, Barcelona: Mondadori, 1996; Fuguet, "I Am Not a Magical Realist!" (http://www.salon.com/june1997/magical970611.html). Rhonda Cobham points out that magical realism is not exactly dominant in anglophone Caribbean writing and cautions against the reified flattening of the folk into the orality and magic common to this mode. See Cobham, "Of Boloms, Mirrors and Monkeymen," 25–56.

16. Faris, *Ordinary Enchantments,* 3, 167.

17. Barth, "The Literature of Exhaustion," *Friday Book,* 64. "The Literature of Replenishment: Postmodernist Fiction" is included in the volume (193–206). In response to the ensuing controversy over the claim in the first essay, Barth notes that he was not implying the death of literature or language, but "of the aesthetic of high modernism" (206).

18. Melville, *Ventriloquist's Tale,* 7.

19. Taussig, *Shamanism, Colonialism, and the Wild Man,* 97.

20. Marío de Andrade, *Macunaíma,* trans. E. A. Goodland (New York: Random, 1984).

21. Melville, *Ventriloquist's Tale,* 5.

22. Sangari, "Politics of the Possible," 227.

23. Taussig, *Shamanism,* 31

24. Ibid., 37.

25. Ibid., 121.

26. Melville, "The President's Exile," *Migration of Ghosts,* 7.

27. Ibid., 11.

28. Harris, "Merlin and Parsifal," *Unfinished Genesis,* 65. Emphasis in text. Harris points out that he uses the phrase in his novel *Jonestown* (see chapter 3) and among its meanings, I find the notion of the old and new supporting each other useful to my discussion of *New Moon's Arms* later in this chapter.

29. Harris, "The Music of Living Landscapes," *Unfinished Genesis,* 46.

30. Ibid., 40.

31. Harris, "Literacy and the Imagination," *Unfinished Genesis,* 75–89.

32. Malinowski, *Magic, Science and Religion,* 50.

33. Ibid., 43.

34. Harris, "New Preface to *Palace of the Peacock,*" *Unfinished Genesis,* 54.

35. Ibid., 54.

36. Harris, "Quetzalcoatl and the Smoking Mirror: (Reflections on Originality and Tradition)," *Sisyphus and El Dorado,* 6, 7. It seems appropriate to include not just the talking parrot but also the trickster spider and the signifying monkey as black diasporic challenges to the notion of dumb brutes.

37. Jefferson-Miles, "Quantum Value," 181. See also Vera Kutzinski, "Wilson Harris's Phantom Bodies: Re-Reading the Subject," *Theatre of the Arts,* 139–52; and Harris's discussion of limbo and the phantom limb in "History, Fable and Myth."

38. Harris, "Quetzalcoatl," *Sisyphus and El Dorado,* 2.

39. Cixous, "Laugh of the Medusa," 290.

40. Harris, "The Unfinished Genesis of the Imagination," *Unfinished Genesis,* 257.

41. I use the more common spelling of "Ogun," but Hopkinson uses "Ogu." It must be said that Makandal is not presented entirely unsympathetically and is even heroic in the novel despite his rivalry with Mer (represented by an elemental battle between Erzulie and Ogun, water and fire, in which the latter wins).

42. Dayan, "Vodoun," 17.

43. See also my epilogue, where I discuss another version of such time travel in reincarnation. I argue that such "avatars" delineate a broad family tree representative of the various branches of Caribbean migration and mixture.

44. Glissant, *Poetics of Relation,* 12.

45. Hopkinson, *Salt Roads,* 42. Although I focus largely on her novels here, Web blogs, online science fiction journals and magazines, and community websites such as SFNovelists.com (in which Hopkinson participates along with Tobias Buckell, another Caribbean science fiction writer) are also important sources to consider.

46. Barth, "Tales within Tales within Tales," *Friday Book,* 218–38. Hopkinson explains that this bricolage allows her to reassemble the master's house rather than wholly dismantle it. See her introduction to *So Long Been Dreaming: Postcolonial Science Fiction and Fantasy,* ed. Nalo Hopkinson and Uppinder Mehan (Vancouver: Arsenal Press, 2004), 7–9.

47. Hopkinson, *Midnight Robber,* 48.

48. Not all manifestations of the Midnight Robber are radical or political in the conventional sense. Some of them are also manipulative, hustling appearances.

49. However, Pamela R. Franco argues that the Midnight Robber and the Jab Jab are among traditional, oppositional, black male figures of the preindependence period that were elevated against the unmasked, lightly clad female participants of the eighties in carnival parades. These women preferred to "wine" rather than costume and role play, and were then attacked for their "inauthentic," lascivious behavior. See Franco, "Invention of Traditional Mas."

50. Hopkinson, *Midnight Robber,* 326.

51. Philip, "Discourse on the Logic of Language" and other poems in *She Tries Her Tongue, Her Silence Softly Breaks.* Philip dedicates the collection to "all the mothers."

52. Hopkinson, *Midnight Robber,* 320.

53. Ibid., 320.

54. Ibid., 327.

55. Ibid., 328.

56. Ibid., 329.

57. I place "black witch" in quotation marks to underline the controversy over Tituba's precise ancestry and ethnic background, Native American or black Bajan.

58. Hopkinson, *Brown Girl,* 52.

59. Hopkinson is clearly borrowing from the Anancy stories of African and Caribbean provenance as well as from other folktales. Hopkinson's Dry Bone, on the other hand, seems to have more in common with the "Old Man of the Sea" in the Sindbad tales narrated by Scheherazade in *Tales from the Arabian Nights.*

60. Gender issues may have something to do with Rudy's malevolent use of Vodoun. Paula Morgan notes that a "predominantly negative portrayal of men and male-female relationships" is shared by African, African American, and Afro-Caribbean women writers. See Morgan, "Under Women's Eyes," 290. Historical male figures have exploited Vodoun as referenced in the note below.

61. Hopkinson, *Brown Girl,* 225.

62. Dayan sees Atibon Legba or Alegba in Haiti not as the canny trickster of Dahomey but as "'Papa Legba of the Old Bones.' Very old, he lives out the loss suffered by his people" (25). Francois Duvalier's adoption of Baron Samedi's attire and role as god of the cemeteries embodies the state's co-optation of Vodoun.

63. Walcott, "Ti-Jean and His Brothers," *Dream on Monkey Mountain and Other Plays* (New York: Farrar, Straus and Giroux, 1970), 81–166. In her acknowledgments for *Brown Girl,* Hopkinson calls Walcott's play "one of the first examples of Caribbean magic realism" she read (249).

64. Hopkinson, *Brown Girl,* 31.

65. V. S. Naipaul, *A Turn in the South* (New York: Alfred Knopf, 1989), 162.

66. Hopkinson, *Brown Girl,* 43.

67. Faris, *Ordinary Enchantments,* 181. Faris contrasts here the witch and the gingerbread house to the shaman's presumably cosmic powers.

68. Hopkinson, "Under Glass" (inspired by Hans Christian Anderson's "The Snow Queen"), *Skin Folk,* 63–82. Cristina Bacchilega tracks some of the other folk and fairy tale sources of Hopkinson's stories: "Riding the Red" from "Little Red Riding Hood"; "The Glass Bottle Trick" from "Maiden Killer" and "Bluebeard"; "Precious" from "The Kind and Unkind Girls"; and so on. See Bacchilega, "Reflections," 201–10.

69. Atwood, "*Handmaid's Tale* and *Oryx and Crake,*" 513.

70. Hayles and Gessler, "Slipstream of Mixed Reality," 483.

71. However, it must be borne in mind that neither scientific and technological wizardry nor science fiction is as commonplace in the rest of the world as it is in the United States, for instance.

72. The other problem in attributing magic, faith, and religion stereotypically to the non-West is to ignore the fact that scientific thinking is by no means absent in these parts, particularly Asian countries where science, technology, and engineering are prestigious disciplines to the detriment of the humanities. Conversely, magical thinking and collective faith are not absent in the overdeveloped areas, regardless of Carpentier's ontological arguments for the marvelous in Latin America and the Caribbean. See Amy Schindler, "Angels and the AIDS Epidemic:

The Resurgent Popularity of Angel Imagery in the United States of America," *Journal of American Culture* 22, no. 3 (Fall 1999): 49–61.

73. Marleen Barr, *Feminist Fabulation: Space/Postmodern Fiction* (Iowa City: University of Iowa Press, 1992). Barr's concept is a feminist take on male-dominated science fiction.

74. Hopkinson, introduction to *So Long,* 7 (see note 47 above).

75. Sheree Thomas, "Introduction: Looking for the Invisible," *Dark Matter: A Century of Speculative Fiction from the African Diaspora,* ed. Sheree R. Thomas (New York: Warner, 2000), x, xiii.

76. Hopkinson, "'Making the Impossible Possible,'" 101.

77. Hopkinson, "Ganger (Ball Lightning)," *Skin Folk,* 221–245.

78. Jameson, *Archaeologies of the Future,* xiii.

79. Ibid., 170.

80. I invoke one of several possible definitions of critical dystopia, which indicates a utopian enclave in a generally dystopian situation, holding on to the hope of change (unlike anti-utopia), but warning against the possibility of continued repression.

81. See, for various accounts and analysis, Monica Schuler, *"Alas, Alas Kongo": A Social History of Indentured African Immigration into Jamaica, 1841–1865* (Baltimore: Johns Hopkins University Press, 1980); Gay Wilentz, "If You Surrender to the Air: Folk Legends of Flight and Resistance in African American Literature," *MELUS* 16, no. 1 (Spring 1989–90): 21–32; Wendy Walters, "'One of Dese Mornings Bright and Fair,/Take My Wings and Cleave de Air': The Legend of the Flying Africans and Diasporic Consciousness," *MELUS* 22, no. 3 (Fall 1997): 3–29; Lovalerie King, "Resistance, Reappropriation, and Reconciliation: The Blues and Flying Africans in Gayl Jones's *Song for Anninho,*" *Callaloo* 27, no. 3 (Summer 2004): 755–67; Olivia Smith Storey, "Flying Words: Contests of Orality and Literacy in the Trope of the Flying Africans," *Journal of Colonialism and Colonial History* 5, no. 3 (Winter 2004), DOI: 10.1353/cch.2004.0090. Storey prefers trope to legend, emphasizing a move from folklore to literature. In the Caribbean literary context, see Wilson C. Chen, "Figures of Flight and Entrapment in Edwidge Danticat's *Krik? Krak!,*" *Rocky Mountain Review* 65.1 (2011): 36–55.

82. Piero Boitani, *Winged Words: Flight in Poetry and History* (Chicago: Chicago University Press, 2007), ix.

83. See the exquisite short story by Gabriel García Márquez, "A Very Old Man with Enormous Wings: A Tale for Children," in *Leaf Storm and Other Stories* by Gabriel García Márquez, trans. Gregory Rabassa (London: Pan Books, 1979), 105–12. Vera Kutzinski ties the story to the African American legend in her article "The Logic of Wings: Gabriel García Márquez and Afro-American Literature," *Latin American Literary Review* 13, no. 25 (January–June 1985): 133–46. The fact that García Márquez calls it a children's tale continues the close association between magical realism and the youthful imagination. Virginia

Hamilton has in fact written a beautifully illustrated children's book inspired by the legend and Faith Ringgold has incorporated it into her famous story quilts. See Hamilton, *The People Could Fly* (New York: Alfred Knopf, 2004); Ringgold, *We Flew Over the Bridge: The Memoirs of Faith Ringgold* (Boston: Little, Brown, 1995).

84. Works Project Administration, *Drums and Shadows.*

85. Ibid., 18.

86. Brodber, "Beyond a Boundary," 20–21. Interestingly, Brodber claims to have been unaware of the legend until later in her life.

87. Morrison, *Song of Solomon,* 322–23. Byrd then rubbishes the possibility of human flight. Despite Alejo Carpentier's assertion of "collective faith," one cannot rule out doubt even among the believers.

88. Carpentier, "On the Marvelous Real in America," in *Magical Realism,* 87. Makandal's name is variously spelled in different sources. In the essay, Carpentier spells the name "Mackandal," which diverges from Hopkinson's spelling in *The Salt Roads* and his spelling in *The Kingdom of This World.*

89. Ibid., 86. While Shannin Schroeder is right that every account of magic does not qualify as magical realism (a notoriously difficult to define term), and that Carpentier's argument for a marvelous real cannot be conflated with a definition of magical realism, there is a family resemblance. See Shannin Schroeder, *Rediscovering Magical Realism in the Americas* (Westport, Connecticut: Praeger, 2004).

90. Carpentier, *Kingdom of This World,* 44–47. The passages in question have been studied in numerous sources and I will not go into another reading here. See Chanady, *Magical Realism,* 158; Faris, *Ordinary Enchantments,* 50–55; Aching, "Beyond Sites of Execution," 115–21; Hart and Ouyang, "Globalization of Magical Realism: New Politics of Aesthetics," the introduction to their coedited volume (2–3). What is clear from the Carpentier readings is that critics diverge on how they read his presentation of Makandal's flight, suggesting that what counts as magical realist varies.

91. Carpentier, *Kingdom of This World,* 44.

92. Ibid., 45.

93. See, for instance, Peter Geschière's *The Modernity of Witchcraft: Politics and the Occult in Postcolonial Africa,* trans. Peter Geschière and Janet Roitman (Charlottesville: University of Virginia Press, 1997), for the political role of witchcraft in modern Cameroon. Geschière refuses an esoteric reading of witchcraft, arguing instead that it circulates as public knowledge, even if discreetly.

94. Gabriel García Márquez, *One Hundred Years of Solitude,* trans. Gregory Rabassa (New York: Harper and Row, 1970); Salman Rushdie, *Midnight's Children* (New York: Alfred Knopf, 1981).

95. Kundera, *Unbearable Lightness of Being,* 63.

96. See Hovet and Lounsberry, "Flying as Symbol and Legend." They argue that Morrison (like Earl Lovelace in *Salt*) wants flight to be viewed from the perspective of those left behind, usually the women and children.

97. For a critique of the male-centered, revolutionary Maroon ideology, see A. James Arnold, "Problematic Maroon."

98. Hopkinson, *Salt Roads,* 349.

99. Ibid., 377.

100. Hopkinson, *Brown Girl,* 211.

101. Ibid., 212. Emphasis in text.

102. Ibid., 215. Emphasis in text.

103. My reading differs here from that of Giselle Anatol, who reads the soucouyant as "a valuable model" for feminist readings of mobility (52). While this is certainly an enabling analysis, my focus is on the point Anatol concludes with, which is that the soucouyant has limitations as a model of flight. See Anatol, "Transforming the Skin-Shedding Soucouyant: Using Folklore to Reclaim Female Agency in Caribbean Literature," *Small Axe* 7 (March 2000): 44–59.

104. Kundera, *Unbearable Lightness,* 5.

105. Sangari, "Politics of the Possible," 235. Emphasis in text.

106. Chanady, *Magical Realism,* 24–26. Chanady prefers resolved antinomy to "hesitation," which marks what Jameson in *Archaeologies* calls "Todorov's rather pedestrian theory of the fantastic" (69). In fantasy, the supernatural is not accepted either by the author or by the reader, according to Chanady. Chanady's is one of the more painstaking attempts to define magical realism as a specific mode rather than as a catchall category. See also Warnes, *Magical Realism,* for a clear, detailed discussion of the term and why it matters as a distinct category.

107. Hélène Cixous, *White Ink: Interviews on Sex, Text and Politics,* ed. Susan Sellers (Stocksfield, UK: Acumen, 2008), 76. It should be noted that white ink is not restricted to white women, since Cixous appropriates the Freudian conflation of the Dark Continent with women and links feminism with antiracism. Cixous's complex sense of sexual difference and feminine creativity demand more detail than they can get here.

108. Gilroy, "Re-consideration of 'Breast Swingers,'" 10–11.

109. It bears repeating that the novel does not, however, fit into any neat slot as science fiction, fantasy, or magical realism, and Hopkinson herself seems not to care about tidy classification.

110. Benjamin, "Theses," 255.

111. Hopkinson, *Midnight Robber,* 92.

112. Jameson, *Archaeologies of the Future,* xii.

113. Harris, "Quetzalcoatl and the Smoking Mirror," *Sisyphus and El Dorado,* 5.

114. Jameson, *Archaeologies of the Future,* 233.

115. Hopkinson, *New Moon's Arms,* 315.

116. Ibid., 316. Emphasis in text.

117. Danticat, "Children of the Sea," *Krik? Krak!,* 3–29.

118. Brathwaite, "The African Presence in Caribbean Literature," *Roots,* 190–258.

119. Shakespeare, *The Tempest,* 1.2.400. Walcott's poetic images of the sea follow the transformation described in Ariel's beautiful lines: "Full fathom five thy father lies,/Of his bones are coral made;/Those are pearls that were his eyes;/Nothing of him that doth fade,/But doth suffer a sea-change/Into something rich and strange" (lines 395–400). I thank Philip Crispin for reminding me of this passage. For Harris, such survival is traced through the geological fossil sublimated in human memory and embedded in the landscape.

120. Hopkinson, *New Moon's Arms,* 291. Emphasis in text.

121. Melville, "Erzulie," *Migration of Ghosts,* 135–67.

122. Hopkinson, "Precious," *Skin Folk,* 253, 254.

123. Tambiah, *Magic,* 74. See also Brathwaite, "History of the Voice," in *Roots,* 259–304.

124. Tambiah, *Magic,* 74.

125. Greg Tate in an interview with Mark Dery, "Black to the Future: Interviews with Samuel R. Delany, Greg Tate, and Tricia Rose," *SAQ* 92, no. 4 (Fall 1993): 764. The special issue, edited by Mark Dery, is titled "Flame Wars: The Discourse of Cyberculture." For the work of Afrofuturism in music, see George E. Lewis, "After Afrofuturism: Another Dimension in Music" *Journal of the Society for American Music* 2, no. 2 (May 2008): 139–53. For other connections to literary and cultural studies and the cybersphere, see the special issue on Afrofuturism edited by Alondra Nelson, in *Social Text* 20, no. 2 (Summer 2002).

126. Edwidge Danticat, *The Dew Breaker* (New York: Vintage, 2004); Díaz, *Oscar Wao.*

127. Mark Dery, "Flame Wars," *SAQ* 92, no. 4 (Fall 1993): 564.

128. Tate, "Black to the Future," 766. See also Ralph Waldo Ellison, *Invisible Man* (New York: Random, 1952).

129. Danticat, *Brother, I'm Dying,* 39.

130. Faris, *Ordinary Enchantments,* 147.

131. Hopkinson, *Midnight Robber,* 245. Emphasis in text.

132. Hopkinson, "Riding the Red," *Skin Folk,* 2.

133. See Wilfrid L. Pilette, "Magical Thinking by Inpatient Staff Members," *Psychiatric Quarterly* 55, no. 4 (Winter 1983): 272. Joan Didion's account deals with this "illogical" process as it relates to grief and mourning. See Didion, *The Year of Magical Thinking* (New York: Alfred Knopf, 2005).

134. Grotjahn, *Beyond Laughter,* 240.

135. Ibid., 238.

5. Medusa's Laugh

1. Reichl and Stein, introduction to *Cheeky Fictions,* 2.

2. Ibid., 8.

3. See, for instance, Harper, *Comedy, Fantasy, and Colonialism.*

4. Salick, introduction to *Comic Vision,* v. Salick emphasizes, however, as several Caribbean writers do, that far from being simply a physical reaction to

the conventional sense of the comic, laughter is a complex, defiant, and survivalist tactic in these contexts.

5. Ibid., vi.

6. On Bennett and Jamaican Creole, see Cooper, *Noises in the Blood,* and Morris, "*Is English We Speaking.*"

7. Fanon, *Wretched,* 44.

8. Walcott, "What the Twilight Says," *What the Twilight Says,* 22.

9. Fanon, *Wretched,* 45. Fanon's use of "humour" recalls Luigi Pirandello's distinction between comedy, which is closer to laughter, and humor, a more conflicted state of mind related to the bodily fluids. *Umore,* in the medieval and Renaissance connotation, is related to the four humors (blood, bile, phlegm, and melancholy). Fanon's physiological allusion refers to the belief that bad humors can be drained from the body. See Pirandello, *On Humor,* trans. Antonio Illiano and Daniel P. Testa (Chapel Hill: University of North Carolina Press, 1960).

10. Walcott, "What the Twilight Says," *Twilight,* 24.

11. Walcott, "The Antilles," *Twilight,* 81.

12. V. S. Naipaul, *Middle Passage,* 54.

13. Walcott, "The Muse of History," *Twilight,* 36.

14. Walcott, "The Antilles," *Twilight,* 72.

15. Walcott, "The Muse of History," *Twilight,* 40.

16. Walcott, "The Antilles," *Twilight,* 67.

17. J. J. Thomas, *Froudacity: West Indian Fables by James Anthony Froude* (Philadelphia: Gebbie, 1890).

18. Scott, *Conscripts of Modernity,* 29.

19. C. L. R. James, *The Black Jacobins: Toussaint L'Ouverture and the San Domingo Revolution* (New York: Random, 1963).

20. Scott, *Conscripts,* 2.

21. Ibid., 13.

22. Walcott, "What the Twilight Says," *Twilight,* 22–23.

23. Kayser, *Grotesque in Art,* 20–21.

24. Bakhtin, *Rabelais and His World,* 122.

25. Ibid., 66.

26. Wood, *Irresponsible Self,* 15.

27. Jarvis DeBerry, "National Press Is All Over Us, All Wrong," *Times Picayune,* Sunday, March 4, 2006, B-7.

28. Kayser, *Grotesque in Art,* 11.

29. Ibid., 16.

30. Thomson, *Grotesque,* 11. As Thomson explains, the grotesque is tied to other forms that appear with it such as the absurd, the burlesque, the macabre, caricature, parody, satire, irony, and so on.

31. Thomson, *Grotesque,* 63.

32. Patrick O'Neill credits Nietzsche with a "complete re-evaulation" of the characteristics and function of these categories, leading ultimately not just to

Dionysian tragic impulses but to the association of comedy with the Apollonian intellectual ethos, where they had hitherto been used to distinguish one from the other. See O'Neill, *Comedy of Entropy,* 55.

33. Ellison, interview with Richard G. Stern, "That Same Pain, That Same Pleasure," *Collected Essays of Ralph Ellison,* 80.

34. Ellison, "An Extravagance of Laughter," *Collected Essays,* 616. Ellison's catalyst is Jack Kirkland's successful dramatization of Erskine Caldwell's novel *Tobacco Road,* which he saw on Broadway in 1936 as a guest of Langston Hughes.

35. Ibid., 614.

36. Ibid., 633. Emphasis in text.

37. Ibid., 635.

38. Ibid., 634.

39. Ibid., 635.

40. Fanon, *Black Skin, White Masks,* 14.

41. Bennett, "Pass Fe White," *Jamaica Labrish,* 212.

42. Bhabha, "Of Mimicry and Man," *Location of Culture,* 92.

43. Naipaul, *Middle Passage,* 15, 68.

44. Bennett, "Colour-Bar," *Jamaica Labrish,* 211.

45. Bennett, "White Pickney," *Jamaica Labrish,* 111.

46. Bennett, "Solja Work," *Jamaica Labrish,* 98. While Bennett parodies the "solja work" of producing mixed-race progeny and then leaving, calypsos such as "Jean and Dinah" and "Rum and Coca Cola" have targeted the sex work organized around American bases in Trinidad.

47. Bakhtin, *Rabelais,* 468, 472.

48. Glissant, *Caribbean Discourse,* 12.

49. Ibid., 182. Emphasis in text.

50. Ibid., 187.

51. Naipaul, *Middle Passage,* 69. Several critics have explored the serious dimension of Creole, including Mervyn Morris, "On Reading Louise Bennett, Seriously," *"Is English We Speaking"*; Carolyn Cooper, following Honor Ford Smith and Victor Chang's challenges, in *Noises in the Blood,* 90; Katherine Wiggan, "Comedy and Creole in Selvon's London Stories," in *Comic Vision,* 19–30. Sarah Lawson Welsh repeats Dabydeen's interesting point that Creole is tragic because it represents the brokenness of its users. See Welsh, "Experiments in Brokenness."

52. Naipaul, *Middle Passage,* 70.

53. Ibid., 68.

54. Ngũgĩ, *Decolonising the Mind,* 2.

55. Walcott, *Pantomime,* 124.

56. Ibid., 125.

57. Ibid., 139.

58. Ibid., 140.

59. Bhabha, "Of Mimicry and Man," *Location of Culture,* 91.

60. Levy, *Small Island,* 171.

61. Ibid., 188.

62. Ibid., 193.

63. Ibid., 522.

64. Carpio, *Laughing Fit to Kill,* 36. Carpio points out that American discourses of race focus on melodrama, sentimentalism, and seriousness but only reluctantly deal with humor, which is just as viable (27).

65. Bergson, *Laughter,* 41. Bergson believes that one laughs "at a negro" because there is something inherently funny about black skin, since it may be seen as "a white man in disguise." The extraordinary assumption about the authenticity of whiteness against which the "black mask" is measured as a funny copy is poignantly addressed in Fanon's *Black Skin, White Masks.* The superiority, incongruity, and psychic release theories are the most common explanations for the comic mode.

66. Condé, *I, Tituba,* 32.

67. Ellison, "Change the Joke and Slip the Yoke," *Collected Essays,* 103.

68. Cassuto, *Inhuman Race,* 154. Sambo also referred to a mix of native American and African American, another group that was discriminated against.

69. Naipaul, "Man in a Glass Box," Interview by Linda Blandford, *Conversations,* 54.

70. Interview by Mukherjee and Boyers, "A Conversation with V. S. Naipaul," *Conversations,* 87. Emphasis in text.

71. Naipaul mentions cruelty in another interview where he claims that black audiences laughed at Jewish concentration camps and Trinidadians at large laughed at people with disabilities. See Scott Winokur, "The Unsparing Vision of V. S. Naipaul," *Conversations,* 120. Lawrence Levine suggests that the target group functioned as a surrogate for the attacking group, as in anti-Irish jokes among African Americans, who also saw some kinship with the latter as a stereotyped and exploited minority. See Levine's superb chapter "Black Laughter" in *Black Culture and Black Consciousness.*

72. Naipaul, *Middle Passage,* 76, 77.

73. Rohlehr, "Calypsonian as Artist," 1–26.

74. www.youtube.com/watch?v=iocPpL_5q7Y posted by mack 8710 on January 22, 2007. Accessed May 1, 2010. This video is no longer available.

75. From "His Mouse Friday," the fifty-ninth episode of the Tom and Jerry cartoons, directed by William Hanna and Joseph Barbera (Metro Goldwyn, 1951). This short film was also banned for its invocation of cannibal stereotypes of Africa.

76. www.youtube.com/watch?v=tUvCEogdTIw posted by coolymic December 9, 2007. Accessed May 1, 2010. This video has since been taken down.

77. Slavoj Žižek, "Laugh Yourself to Death! The New Wave of Holocaust Comedies" (December 15, 1999), accessed April 24, 2011, http://www.lacan.com/zizekholocaust.htm.

78. O'Neill, *Comedy of Entropy,* 8.

79. Ibid., 20.

80. Ibid., 65.

81. Rohlehr, "Character and Rebellion," 91. However, feminist readings critique the sexist and heteronormative account of the maternal Tulsi unit in the novel that, according to Rohlehr, represents the allegorical struggle of Biswas against both home and nation. See, for instance, Rosemary Marangoly George, *The Politics of Home: Postcolonial Relocations and Twentieth-Century Fiction* (Cambridge: Cambridge University Press, 1996), and Gayatri Gopinath, *Impossible Desires: Queer Diasporas and South Asian Public Cultures* (Durham, NC: Duke University Press, 2005).

82. Rohlehr, "Character and Rebellion," 87. "Creole" has multiple connotations and contexts in the Caribbean, but it seems that the particular sense Rohlehr uses here indicates black culture, a perspective that Naipaul would accept.

83. Grotjahn, *Beyond Laughter,* 48.

84. Samuel Beckett, *Nohow On: Company, Ill Seen Ill Said, Worstward Ho* (London: John Calder, 1989), 101.

85. Naipaul, *Way in the World,* 79. According to Patrick French (*What It Is,* 465), Morris is based on Arthur Calder Marshall, a reviewer at BBC's *Caribbean Voices,* who rejected Naipaul's first book.

86. Naipaul's self-identified affiliation with a black Bajan writer, despite the later friction between the two, confirms Rohlehr's theory of a more general creolized sense of humor tied to the Caribbean at large.

87. Naipaul, *Way in the World,* 87, 95.

88. Naipaul, *Way in the World,* 96.

89. Wood, *Irresponsible Self,* 275.

90. Ibid.

91. Bakhtin, *Rabelais,* 309.

92. O'Neill, *Comedy of Entropy,* 22.

93. Smith, *White Teeth,* 4.

94. Smith, "Dead Man Laughing," *Changing My Mind,* 242.

95. Ibid., 241. Although Naipaul was not any great enthusiast of modernist literature in general and was a late admirer of Joseph Conrad, his affinity with the modernists cannot be denied.

96. Smith, "Dead Man Laughing," *Changing,* 238.

97. Ibid., 243.

98. Lassner, "Game is Up," 40. Emphasis in text.

99. Harris, *Tumatumari,* 129. At the same time, Smith seems to share Naipaul's anxieties about farce and refers self-consciously to her novel as "an idiotic comedy" ("Accidental Hero," *Changing,* 235).

100. Harris, *The Dark Jester,* 91.

101. Ibid., 92.

102. Ibid., vii.

103. Ibid., 51. Bakhtin tends to feminize Carnival, the lower body, and other forms of the grotesque as aspects of the maternal womb, a site of both life and death. While Mary Russo critiques his echoes of misogynistic representation, here Harris seems to share Bakhtin's more positive image of the womb as vertiginous and regenerative in his portrayal of the abyss and the grotto. See Russo, *Female Grotesque.*

104. Harris, *Dark Jester,* 60.

105. Harris, "Creoleness," *Unfinished Genesis,* 241.

106. Harris, *Dark Jester,* 60.

107. Harris, *Tumatumari,* 154.

108. Bakhtin, *Rabelais,* 52.

109. Cixous, "Laugh of the Medusa," 289. I am reading Medusa through Cixous's enabling feminist reversal and not in the conventional image of terrifying fear and magical authority as Maria Cristina Fumagalli does in *Caribbean Perspectives on Modernity: Returning Medusa's Gaze* (Charlottesville: University of Virginia Press, 2009). However, Cixous does tend to slip into an easy reading of laughter as rebellious and liberating, as Virginia Richter cautions. See Richter, "Laughter and Aggression."

110. Hopkinson, *Brown Girl,* 224–25.

Epilogue

1. Bissoondath, "There Are a Lot of Ways to Die," *Digging Up the Mountains,* 88.

2. See Ian Strachan's critique in *Paradise and Plantation* of colonial postcards, as well as of more contemporary mass-produced images by the Bahamian government intent on securing tourist dollars and ignoring the problematic ideologies embedded in these versions. See also Krista A. Thompson, *An Eye for the Tropics: Tourism, Photography, and Framing the Caribbean Picturesque* (Durham, NC: Duke University Press, 2006).

3. Lamming, *Sovereignty of the Imagination.* Like Ngũgĩ, Lamming conceives of the dependent colonial subject as engaged in "a daily exercise in self-mutilation," unable to break away from colonial ideologies even when physical violence is not enforced (7). The phrase, also used in the title of an interview by David Scott published in volume 12 of *Small Axe,* calls for self-reliance in economic and cultural matters.

4. Lamming, *Sovereignty,* 11.

5. Glissant, *Poetics of Relation,* 11.

6. Baldeosingh, *Ten Incarnations,* 444. Baldeosingh seems to have overcome his aversion to magical realism in this novel.

7. Ibid., 448.

8. Ibid., 202.

9. Ibid., 442.

10. Ibid., 443.

11. Caryl Phillips, *A State of Independence* (London: Faber and Faber, 1986); Joan Riley, *A Kindness to the Children* (London: Women's Press, 1992).

12. Velma Pollard, *Homestretch* (Essex: Longman Caribbean, 1994).

13. Andrea Levy, *Fruit of the Lemon* (London: Review, 1999).

14. Baldeosingh, "Writing from the Caribbean," *Writing Life,* 48.

15. I discuss this novel in more detail in "Diasporic Roots: Imagining a Nation in Earl Lovelace's *Salt,*" *SAQ* 100, no. 1 (Winter 2001): 259–86.

16. Baldeosingh, *Ten Incarnations,* 431.

17. Glissant, *Poetics,* 71–72.

18. See my discussion of this novel in chapter 2.

19. Walcott, "The Antilles," *What the Twilight Says,* 69.

20. Scott, *Refashioning Futures,* 12.

21. Ibid., 203.

22. "For Sale: Europe Begs Its Former Vassals for a Bailout," accessed April 21, 2012, http://www.slate.com/blogs/the_reckoning/2011/11/23/portugal_begs-former_colony_angola_for_a_bailout_.html.

Bibliography

Aching, Gerard. “Beyond Sites of Execution: Haiti and the Historical Imagination in C. L. R. James and Alejo Carpentier.” In *Sisyphus and Eldorado: Magical and Other Realisms in Caribbean Literature,* 2nd ed., edited by Timothy J. Reiss, 103–26. Trenton, NJ: Africa World Press, 2002.

Alaimo, Stacy. *Undomesticated Ground: Recasting Nature as Feminist Space.* Ithaca: Cornell University Press, 2000.

Alexander, Simone A. James. *Mother Imagery in the Novels of Afro-Caribbean Women.* Columbia: University of Missouri Press, 2001.

Allfrey, Phyllis Shand. *The Orchid House.* New Brunswick, NJ: Rutgers University Press, 1997.

Alvarez, Julia. *In the Time of the Butterflies.* Chapel Hill, NC: Algonquin Books, 1994.

Angelou, Maya. *I Know Why the Caged Bird Sings.* New York: Bantam, 1971.

Armstrong, John. *The Paradise Myth.* London: Oxford University Press, 1969.

Arnold, A. James. “From the Problematic Maroon to a Woman-Centered Project in the Literature of the French West Indies.” In *Slavery in the Francophone Caribbean World: Distant Voices, Forgotten Acts, Forged Identities,* edited by Doris Y. Kadish, 164–75. Athens, GA: University of Georgia Press, 2000.

Arnold, David. *The Problem of Nature: Environment, Culture, and European Expansion.* Oxford, UK: Blackwell, 1996.

Athill, Diana. *Make Believe: A True Story.* London: Sinclair-Stevenson, 1993.

———. *Stet: A Memoir.* London: Granta, 2000.

Atwood, Margaret. *The Blind Assassin.* New York: Anchor, 2001.

———. “*The Handmaid’s Tale* and *Oryx and Crake* in Context.” *PMLA* 119, no. 3 (May 2004): 513–17.

Bacchilega, Cristina. “Reflections on Recent English-Language Fairy Tale Fiction by Women: Extrapolating from Nalo Hopkison’s *Skin Folk.*” *Fabula* 47, nos. 3–4 (2006): 201–10.

Bakhtin, Mikhail. *Rabelais and His World.* Translated by Hélène Iswolsky. Bloomington: Indiana University Press, 1984.

Baldeosingh, Kevin. *The Ten Incarnations of Adam Avatar.* Leeds, UK: Peepal Tree, 2005.

———. "Writing from the Caribbean." In *Writing Life: Reflections by West Indian Writers,* edited by Mervyn Morris and Carolyn Allen, 17–50. Kingston, Jamaica: Ian Randle, 2007.

Barth, John. *The Friday Book: Essays and Other Nonfiction.* New York: G. P. Putnam's Sons, 1984.

Benjamin, Walter. "Theses on the Philosophy of History." In *Illuminations,* edited by Hannah Arendt, translated by Harry Zohn, 253–64. New York: Schocken, 1968.

Bennett, Louise. *Jamaica Labrish.* Kingston, Jamaica: Sangster's Book Stores, 1966.

Bergson, Henri. *Laughter: An Essay on the Meaning of the Comic.* Translated by Cloudesley Brereton. New York: Macmillan, 1928.

Bhabha, Homi. *The Location of Culture.* London: Routledge, 1994.

———. "The World and the Home." *Social Text* 7, nos. 31–32 (1992): 141–53.

Bissoondath, Neil. *Digging Up the Mountains.* London: Penguin, 1986.

Bloom, Sandra L. "An Elephant in the Room: The Impact of Traumatic Stress on Individuals and Groups." In *The Trauma Controversy: Philosophical and Interdisciplinary Dialogues,* edited by Kristen Brown Golden and Bettina G. Bergo, 143–68. Albany: State University of New York Press, 2009.

Boose, Lynda E. "The Father's House and the Daughter in It: The Structures of Western Culture's Daughter-Father Relationship." In *Daughters and Fathers,* edited by Lynda E. Boose and Betty S. Flowers, 19–74. Baltimore: Johns Hopkins University Press, 1989.

Brand, Dionne. *At the Full and Change of the Moon.* Toronto: Alfred A. Knopf, 1999.

———. "No Language Is Neutral." Interview by Frank Birbalsingh. In *Frontiers of Caribbean Literature in English,* edited by Frank Birbalsingh, 120–37. New York: St. Martin's Press, 1996.

Brathwaite, Kamau. *The Arrivants: A New World Trilogy.* Oxford: Oxford University Press, 1973.

———. *Born to Slow Horses.* Middletown, CT: Wesleyan University Press, 2005.

———. *Roots.* Ann Arbor: University of Michigan Press, 1993.

Braziel, Jana Evans. "'Caribbean Genesis': Language, Gardens, Worlds (Jamaica Kincaid, Derek Walcott, Édouard Glissant)." In *Caribbean Literature and the Environment: Between Nature and Culture,* edited by Elizabeth M. DeLoughrey, Renée K. Gosson, and George B. Handley, 110–26. Charlottesville: University of Virginia Press, 2005.

Bridges, Yseult. *Child of the Tropics: Victorian Memoirs.* Edited by Nicholas Guppy. Trinidad and Tobago: Aquarela Galleries, 1988.

Brodber, Erna. "Beyond a Boundary: Magical Realism in the Jamaican Frame of Reference." In *Sisyphus and Eldorado: Magical and Other Realisms in Carib-*

bean Literature, edited by Timothy J. Reiss, 15–24. Trenton, NJ: Africa World Press, 2002.

Brontë, Charlotte. *Jane Eyre.* Boston: Bedford Books of St. Martin's Press, 1996.

Brown-Guillory, Elizabeth. "Disrupted Motherlines: Mothers and Daughters in a Genderized, Sexualized, and Racialized World." In *Women of Color: Mother-Daughter Relationships in Twentieth-Century Literature,* edited by Elizabeth Brown-Guillory, 188–207. Austin: University of Texas Press, 1996.

Buck-Morrs, Susan. *Dreamworld and Catastrophe: The Passing of Mass Utopia in East and West.* Cambridge, MA: MIT Press, 2000.

Buell, Lawrence. *The Future of Environmental Criticism: Environmental Crisis and Literary Imagination.* Malden, MA: Blackwell, 2005.

Butler, Judith. *Precarious Life: The Powers of Mourning and Violence.* London: Verso, 2004.

Carew, Jan. *Rape of Paradise: Columbus and the Birth of Racism in the Americas.* Brooklyn, NY: A&B Books, 1994.

Carpentier, Alejo. *The Kingdom of This World.* Translated by Harriet de Onís. New York: Farrar, Straus and Giroux, 2006.

———. "On the Marvelous Real in America." In *Magical Realism: Theory, History, Community,* edited by Lois Parkinson Zamora and Wendy B. Faris, 75–88. Durham, NC: Duke University Press, 1995.

Carpio, Glenda R. *Laughing Fit to Kill: Black Humor in the Fictions of Slavery.* Oxford: Oxford University Press, 2008.

Cartey, Wilfred. *Whispers from the Caribbean: I Going Away, I Going Home.* Los Angeles: Center for Afro-American Studies, University of California, 1991.

Cassid, Jill H. *Sowing Empire: Landscape and Colonization.* Minneapolis: University of Minnesota Press, 2005.

Cassuto, Leonard. *The Inhuman Race: The Racial Grotesque in American Literature and Culture.* New York: Columbia University Press, 1997.

Cezair-Thompson, Margaret. *The True History of Paradise.* New York: Dutton, 1999.

Chanady, Amaryll Beatrice. *Magical Realism and the Fantastic: Resolved Versus Unresolved Antinomy.* New York: Garland, 1985.

Cixous, Hélène. "The Laugh of the Medusa." In *The Signs Reader: Women, Gender and Scholarship,* edited by Elizabeth Abel and Emily K. Abel, 279–97. Translated by Keith Cohen and Paula Cohen. Chicago: University of Chicago Press, 1983.

Cliff, Michelle. *Abeng.* New York: Plume, 1984.

———. "Caliban's Daughter: The Tempest and the Teapot." *Frontiers: A Journal of Women's Studies* 12, no. 2 (1991): 36–51.

———. "Contagious Melancholia." In *Everything Is Now: New and Collected Stories,* 218–22. Minneapolis: University of Minnesota Press, 2009.

———. *No Telephone to Heaven.* New York: E. P. Dutton, 1987.

Cobham, Rhonda. "Of Boloms, Mirrors and Monkeymen: What's Real and What's Not in Robert Antoni's *Divina Trace*." In *Sisyphus and Eldorado: Magical and Other Realisms in Caribbean Literature,* edited by Timothy J. Reiss, 25–56. Trenton, NJ: Africa World Press, 2002.

Condé, Maryse. *I, Tituba, Black Witch of Salem.* Translated by Richard Philcox. Charlottesville: University of Virginia Press, 1992.

Cooper, Carolyn. *Noises in the Blood: Orality, Gender, and the "Vulgar" Body of Jamaican Popular Culture.* Durham, NC: Duke University Press, 1995.

Coulthard, G. R. *Race and Colour in Caribbean Literature.* London: Oxford University Press, 1962.

Crosby, Alfred. *The Columbian Exchange: Biological and Cultural Consequences of 1492.* Westport, CT: Greenwood Press, 1972.

———. *Ecological Imperialism: The Biological Expansion of Europe, 900–1900.* Cambridge: Cambridge University Press, 1986.

Culler, Jonathan. *Framing the Sign: Criticism and Its Institutions.* Norman: University of Oklahoma Press, 1988.

Cvetkovich, Ann. *An Archive of Feelings: Trauma, Sexuality, and Lesbian Public Culture.* Durham, NC: Duke University Press, 2003.

Dabydeen, David, and Brinsley Samaroo, eds. *Across the Dark Waters: Ethnicity and Indian Identity in the Caribbean.* London: Macmillan Caribbean, 1996.

D'Aguiar, Fred. *Bill of Rights.* London: Chatto and Windus, 1998.

Daly, Brenda O., and Maureen T. Reddy. "Narrating Mothers: Theorizing Maternal Subjectivities." In *Narrating Mothers: Theorizing Maternal Subjectivities,* edited by Brenda O. Daly and Maureen T. Reddy, 1–18. Knoxville: University of Tennessee Press, 1991.

Dance, Daryl Cumber. "Matriarchs, Doves, and Nymphos: Prevalent Images of Black, Indian, and White Women in Caribbean Literature." *Studies in the Literary Imagination* 26, no. 2 (1993): 21–43.

Danow, David K. *The Spirit of Carnival: Magical Realism and the Grotesque.* Lexington: University of Kentucky Press, 1995.

Danticat, Edwidge. *Breath, Eyes, Memory.* New York: Vintage, 1995.

———. *Brother, I'm Dying.* New York: Vintage, 2007.

———. *The Farming of Bones.* New York: Penguin, 1998.

———. *Krik? Krak!* New York: Vintage, 1996.

Dayan, Joan. "Vodoun, or the Voice of the Gods." In *Sacred Possessions: Vodou, Santería, Obeah, and the Caribbean,* edited by Margarite Fernández Olmos and Lizabeth Paravisini-Gebert, 13–36. New Brunswick, NJ: Rutgers University Press, 1999.

de Abruna, Laura Niesen. "Family Connections: Mother and Mother Country in the Fiction of Jean Rhys and Jamaica Kincaid." In *Motherlands: Black Women's Writing from Africa, the Caribbean, and South Asia,* edited by Susheila Nasta, 257–89. New Brunswick, NJ: Rutgers University Press, 1992.

Defoe, Daniel. *Robinson Crusoe.* New York: Signet, 1998.

DeLoughrey, Elizabeth M., Reneé K. Gosson, and George B. Handley, eds. *Caribbean Literature and the Environment: Between Nature and Culture.* Charlottesville: University of Virginia Press, 2005.

Díaz, Junot. *The Brief Wondrous Life of Oscar Wao.* New York: Riverhead Books, 2007.

Dickinson, Emily. *The Complete Poems of Emily Dickinson.* Edited by Thomas H. Johnson. Boston: Little Brown, 1960.

Diot, Rolande. "Fate and Futility: Derision and Black Humor in *A House for Mr. Biswas.*" *Commonwealth Essays and Studies* 9, no. 1 (Autumn 1986): 72–81.

Drayton, Richard. *Nature's Government: Science, Imperial Britain, and the "Improvement" of the World.* New Haven, CT: Yale University Press, 2000.

Ellison, Ralph. *The Collected Essays of Ralph Ellison.* Edited by John F. Callahan. New York: Modern Library, 1995.

Espinet, Ramabai. "The Invisible Woman in West Indian Fiction." *World Literature Written in English* 29, no. 2 (1989): 116–26.

Fanon, Frantz. *Black Skin, White Masks.* Translated by Charles Lam Markmann. New York: Grove Weidenfeld, 1967.

———. *The Wretched of the Earth.* Translated by Constance Farrington. Middlesex, UK: Penguin, 1982.

Faris, Wendy. *Ordinary Enchantments: Magical Realism and the Remystification of Narrative.* Nashville: Vanderbilt University Press, 2004.

Ferguson, Moira. *Jamaica Kincaid: Where the Land Meets the Body.* Charlottesville: University of Virginia Press, 1994.

Foucault, Michel. *Language, Counter-Memory, Practice: Selected Essays and Interviews by Michel Foucault.* Edited by Donald F. Bouchard. Translated by Donald F. Bouchard and Sherry Simon. Ithaca, NY: Cornell University Press, 1977.

———. *The Order of Things: An Archaeology of the Human Sciences.* New York: Vintage, 1970.

Franco, Pamela R. "The Invention of Traditional Mas and the Politics of Gender." In *Trinidad Carnival: The Cultural Politics of a Transnational Festival,* edited by Garth L. Green and Philip W. Scher, 25–47. Bloomington: Indiana University Press, 2007.

French, Fiona. *Anancy and Mr. Dry-Bone.* London: Frances Lincoln, 1999.

French, Patrick. *The World Is What It Is: The Authorized Biography of V. S. Naipaul.* London: Picador, 2008.

Freud, Sigmund. *Civilization and Its Discontents.* New York: W. W. Norton, 1989.

———. *The Joke and Its Relation to the Unconscious.* Translated by Joyce Crick. London: Penguin, 2002.

———. "Medusa's Head." In *Sexuality and the Psychology of Love,* by Sigmund Freud, 212–13. New York: Collier Books, 1963.

———. "The Uncanny" [Das Unheimliche]. In *Standard Edition of the Complete Psychological Works of Sigmund Freud,* vol. 17, translated by James Strachey, 217–56. London: Hogarth Press, 1955.

Froula, Christine. "The Daughter's Seduction: Sexual Violence and Literary History." In *Daughters and Fathers,* edited by Lynda E. Boose and Betty S. Flowers, 111–35. Baltimore: Johns Hopkins University Press, 1989.

García Márquez, Gabriel. *The Autumn of the Patriarch.* Translated by Gregory Rabassa. New York: Harper Perennial, 1999.

Garebian, Keith. "The Grotesque Satire of *A House for Mr. Biswas.*" *Modern Fiction Studies* 30, no. 3 (1984): 487–96.

Gilbert, Sandra M., and Susan Gubar. *The Madwoman in the Attic: The Woman Writer and the Nineteenth-Century Literary Imagination.* New Haven, CT: Yale University Press, 1979.

Gillis, John R. "Taking History Offshore: Atlantic Islands in European Minds, 1400–1800." In *Islands in History and Representation,* edited by Rod Edmond and Vanessa Smith, 19–31. London: Routledge, 2003.

Gilroy, Beryl. "A Re-consideration of 'Breast Swingers' Past and Present." In *Swinging Her Breasts at History: Language, Body, and the Caribbean Woman's Text,* edited by Moira Inghilleri, 2–15. London: Mango Publishing, 2006.

Gilroy, Paul. *The Black Atlantic: Modernity and Double Consciousness.* Cambridge, MA: Harvard University Press, 1993.

Glissant, Édouard. *Caribbean Discourse: Selected Essays.* Translated by J. Michael Dash. Charlottesville: University of Virginia Press, 1992.

———. *Poetics of Relation.* Translated by Betsy Wing. Ann Arbor: University of Michigan Press, 2000.

Goodison, Lorna. *From Harvey River: A Memoir of my Mother and Her People.* Toronto: McClelland and Stewart, 2007.

———. *I Am Becoming My Mother.* London: New Beacon, 1986.

Grotjahn, Martin. *Beyond Laughter.* New York: McGraw-Hill, 1957.

Guha, Ranajit. "On Some Aspects of the Historiography of Colonial India." In *Selected Subaltern Studies,* edited by Ranajit Guha and Gayatri Chakravorty Spivak, 37–44. New York: Oxford University Press, 1988.

Handley, George B. *New World Poetics: Nature and the Adamic Imagination of Whitman, Neruda, and Walcott.* Athens: University of Georgia Press, 2007.

Harper, Graeme, ed. *Comedy, Fantasy, and Colonialism.* London: Continuum, 2002.

Harris, Wilson. *The Dark Jester.* London: Faber and Faber, 2001.

———. *The Ghost of Memory.* London: Faber and Faber, 2006.

———. "History, Fable and Myth in the Caribbean and Guianas." In *Explorations: A Selection of Talks and Articles by Wilson Harris, 1966–1981,* edited by Hena Maes-Jelinek, 20–42. Mundelstrup, Denmark: Dangaroo Press, 1981.

———. *Jonestown.* London: Faber and Faber, 1996.

———. "Quetzalcoatl and the Smoking Mirror." In *Sisyphus and Eldorado: Magical and Other Realisms,* edited by Timothy J. Reiss, 1–13. Trenton, New Jersey: Africa World Press, 2002.

———. *The Radical Imagination: Lectures and Talks.* Edited by Alan Riach and Mark Williams. Liège, Belgium: Liège Language and Literature, 1992.

———. "Theatre of the Arts." In *Theatre of the Arts: Wilson Harris and the Caribbean,* edited by Hena Maes-Jelinek and Bénédicte Ledent, 1–10. Amsterdam: Rodopi, 2002.

———. *Tumatumari.* London: Faber and Faber, 1968.

———. *The Unfinished Genesis of the Imagination: Selected Essays of Wilson Harris.* Edited by Andrew Bundy. London: Routledge, 1999.

———. "Wilson Harris with Fred D'Aguiar." Interview by Fred D'Aguiar. In *Writing Across Worlds: Contemporary Writers Talk,* edited by Susheila Nasta, 33–44. London: Routledge, 2004.

Hart, Stephen M., and Wen-chin Ouyang, eds. *A Companion to Magical Realism.* Rochester, NY: Tamesis, 2005.

Hawkes, Terence. "Swisser-Swatter: Making a Man of English Letters." In *Alternative Shakespeares,* 2nd ed., edited by John Drakakis, 26–47. London: Routledge, 2002.

Hayles, N. Katherine, and Nicholas Gessler. "The Slipstream of Mixed Reality: Unstable Ontologies and Semiotic Markers in *The Thirteenth Floor, Dark City,* and *Mulholland Drive.*" *PMLA* 119, no. 3 (May 2004): 482–99.

Henry, Paget. *Caliban's Reason: Introducing Afro-Caribbean Philosophy.* New York: Routledge, 2000.

Herman, Judith. "Crime and Memory." In *The Trauma Controversy: Philosophical and Interdisciplinary Dialogues,* edited by Kristen Brown Golden and Bettina G. Bergo, 127–41. Albany: State University of New York Press, 2009.

Herman, Judith, and Lisa Hirschman. "Father-Daughter Incest." In *The Signs Reader: Women, Gender, and Scholarship,* edited by Elizabeth Abel and Emily K. Abel, 257–78. Chicago: University of Chicago Press, 1983.

Hirsch, Marianne. *The Mother/Daughter Plot: Narrative, Psychoanalysis, Feminism.* Bloomington: Indiana University Press, 1989.

Hopkinson, Nalo. *Brown Girl in the Ring.* New York: Time Warner, 1998.

———. "'Making the Impossible Possible': An Interview with Nalo Hopkinson." By Alondra Nelson. *Social Text* 20, no. 2 (Summer 2002): 97–113.

———. *Midnight Robber.* New York: Warner Books, 2000.

———. *The New Moon's Arms.* New York: Warner, 2007.

———. *The Salt Roads.* New York: Warner Books, 2003.

———. *Skin Folk.* New York: Warner Books, 2001.

Hovet, Grace Ann, and Barbara Lounsberry. "Flying as Symbol and Legend: Toni Morrison's *The Bluest Eye, Sula,* and *Song of Solomon.*" *CLA Journal* 27, no. 2 (December 1983): 119–140.

Humphry, Derek, and David Tindall. *False Messiah: The Story of Michael X*. London: Hart-Davis, MacGibbon, 1977.

Jagan, Cheddi. *The West on Trial: The Fight for Guyana's Freedom*. Berlin: Seven Seas Books, 1975.

Jamal, Hakim A. *From the Dead Level: Malcolm X and Me*. London: Andre Deutsch, 1971.

Jameson, Fredric. *Archaeologies of the Future: The Desire Called Utopia and Other Science Fictions*. London: Verso, 2005.

Jefferson-Miles, Andrew. "Quantum Value in Wilson Harris's "Architecture of the Tides." In *Theatre of the Arts: Wilson Harris and the Caribbean*, edited by Hena Maes-Jelinek and Bénédicte Ledent, 177–93. Amsterdam: Rodopi, 2002.

Kanhai, Rosanne. "The Masala Stone Sings: Poetry, Performance and Film by Indo-Caribbean Women." In *Matikor: The Politics of Identity for Indo-Caribbean Women*, edited by Rosanne Kanhai, 209–37. Trinidad and Tobago: University of the West Indies Press, 1999.

Kaplan, Amy. "Manifest Domesticity." In *No More Separate Spheres!*, edited by Cathy N. Davidson and Jessamyn Hatcher, 183–207. Durham, NC: Duke University Press, 2002.

Kaplan, E. Ann. *Trauma Culture: The Politics of Terror and Loss in Media and Literature*. New Brunswick, NJ: Rutgers University Press, 2005.

Kayser, Wolfgang. *The Grotesque in Art and Literature*. Translated by Ulrich Weisstein. Gloucester, MA: Peter Smith, 1968.

Kincaid, Jamaica. *The Autobiography of My Mother*. New York: Farrar, Straus and Giroux, 1996.

———. "Jamaica Kincaid and the Modernist Project: An Interview." By Selwyn Cudjoe. In *Caribbean Women Writers: Essays from the First International Conference*, edited by Selwyn Cudjoe, 215–32. Wellesley, MA: Calaloux Publications, 1990.

———. "A Lot of Memory: An Interview with Jamaica Kincaid." Interview by Moira Ferguson. *Kenyon Review* 16, no. 1 (Winter 1994): 163–88.

———. *Mr. Potter*. New York: Farrar, Straus and Giroux, 2002.

———. *My Brother*. New York: Farrar, Straus and Giroux, 1997.

———. *My Garden (Book)*. New York: Farrar, Straus and Giroux, 1999.

———. "On Gardening." Interview by Kathleen Balutansky. *Callaloo* 25, no. 3 (2002): 790–800.

———. *A Small Place*. New York: Plume, 1988.

Kundera, Milan. *The Unbearable Lightness of Being*. Translated by Michael Henry Heim. New York: Harper and Row, 1984.

Kutzinski, Vera. "Violence and Sexual Others in Caribbean Literary History." In *Caribbean Interfaces*, edited by Lieven D'hulst, Jean-Marc Moura, Liesbeth De Bleeker, and Nadia Lie, 35–45. Amsterdam: Rodopi, 2007.

Ladoo, Harold Sonny. *No Pain Like This Body*. London: Heinemann, 1972.

Lamming, George. "The Aesthetics of Decolonisation: Anthony Bogues and George Lamming in Conversation." In *The George Lamming Reader: The Aesthetics of Decolonisation,* edited by Anthony Bogues, 183–240. Kingston, Jamaica: Ian Randle, 2011.

———. *In the Castle of My Skin.* Ann Arbor: University of Michigan Press, 1991.

———. *The Pleasures of Exile.* Ann Arbor: University of Michigan Press, 1992.

———. *The Sovereignty of the Imagination.* Kingston, Jamaica: Arawak Publications, 2004.

Lassner, Phyllis. "The Game Is Up: British Women's Comic Novels of the End of Empire." In *Comedy, Fantasy and Colonialism,* edited by Graeme Harper, 39–57. London: Continuum, 2002.

Layton, Deborah. *Seductive Poison: A Jonestown Survivor's Story of Life and Death in the Peoples Temple.* New York: Anchor, 1998.

Lee, Easton. *From Behind the Counter: Poems from a Rural Jamaican Experience.* Kingston, Jamaica: Ian Randle, 1998.

Lee-Loy, Anne-Marie. *Searching for Mr. Chin: Constructions of Nation and the Chinese in West Indian Literature.* Philadelphia: Temple University Press, 2010.

Levine, Lawrence. *Black Culture and Black Consciousness: Afro-American Folk Thought from Slavery to Freedom.* Oxford: Oxford University Press, 1977.

Lévi-Strauss, Claude. *Tristes Tropiques: An Anthropological Study of Primitive Societies in Brazil.* Translated by John Russell. New York: Atheneum, 1969.

Levy, Andrea. *Small Island.* London: Review, 2004.

Lewis, Gordon K. *"Gather with the Saints at the River": The Jonestown Guyana Holocaust, 1978.* Río Piedras, Puerto Rico: University of Puerto Rico, 1979.

Lorde, Audre. *Zami: A New Spelling of My Name.* Berkeley: Crossing Press, 1982.

Lovelace, Earl. *Jestina's Calypso.* In *Jestina's Calypso and Other Plays,* by Earl Lovelace, 1–41. London: Heinemann, 1984.

———. *Salt.* New York: Persea Books, 1997.

———. *While Gods Are Falling.* Essex: Longman, 1965.

Maaga, Mary McCormick. *Hearing the Voices of Jonestown.* Syracuse: Syracuse University Press, 1998.

MacDonald-Smythe, Antonia. "Self-Fashioning and the Libidinal Subject: *The Autobiography of My Mother* as Sexual Memoir." In *Caribbean Literature in a Global Context,* edited by Funso Aiyejina and Paula Morgan, 330–45. San Juan, Trinidad: Lexicon, 2006.

Maes-Jelinek, Hena. *The Labyrinth of Universality: Wilson Harris's Visionary Art of Fiction.* Amsterdam: Rodopi, 2006.

Maes-Jelinek, Hena, and Bénédicte Ledent, eds. *Theatre of the Arts: Wilson Harris and the Caribbean.* Amsterdam: Rodopi, 2002.

Malik, Michael Abdul. *From Michael de Freitas to Michael X.* London: André Deutsch, 1968.

Malinowski, Bronislaw. *Magic, Science and Religion and Other Essays*. Illinois: Waveland Press, 1992.

Marx, Karl. "Economic and Philosophical Manuscripts." In *Karl Marx: Early Writings*, translated by Rodney Livingstone and Gregor Benton, 279–400. New York: Vintage, 1975.

McCracken, Donal P. *Gardens of Empire: Botanical Institutions of the Victorian British Empire*. London: Leicester University Press, 1997.

Meeks, Brian. *Radical Caribbean: From Black Power to Abu Bakr*. Barbados: University of the West Indies Press, 1996.

Melville, Pauline. *The Migration of Ghosts*. London: Bloomsbury, 1998.

———. *The Ventriloquist's Tale*. London: Bloomsbury, 1997.

Miller, David Philip, and Peter Hans Reill, eds. *Visions of Empire: Voyages, Botany, and Representations of Nature*. Cambridge: Cambridge University Press, 1996.

Mootoo, Shani. *Cereus Blooms at Night*. New York: Avon Books, 1996.

Morgan, Paula. "Under Women's Eyes: Literary Constructs of Afro-Caribbean Masculinity." In *Interrogating Caribbean Masculinities: Theoretical and Empirical Analyses*, edited by Rhoda E. Reddock, 289–308. Mona, Jamaica: University of West Indies Press, 2004.

Morris, Mervyn. *"Is English We Speaking" and Other Essays*. Kingston, Jamaica: Ian Randle, 1999.

Morrison, Toni. *Beloved*. New York: Knopf, 1987.

———. *Song of Solomon*. New York: Vintage, 2004.

Naipaul, Seepersad. *The Adventures of Gurudeva and Other Stories*. Foreword by V. S. Naipaul. London: André Deutsch, 1976.

Naipaul, Shiva. *Black and White*. London: Abacus, 1981.

Naipaul, V. S. *Between Father and Son: Family Letters*. Edited by Gillon Aitken. New York: Knopf, 2000.

———. "A Conversation with V. S. Naipaul." Interview by Bharati Mukherjee and Robert Boyers. In *Conversations with V. S. Naipaul*, edited by Feroza Jussawalla, 75–92. Jackson: University Press of Mississippi, 1997.

———. *The Enigma of Arrival*. New York: Vintage, 1987.

———. *Guerrillas*. New York: Vintage, 1990.

———. *A House for Mr. Biswas*. London: Penguin, 1992.

———. *India: A Million Mutinies Now*. London: Heinemann, 1990.

———. *Literary Occasions: Essays by V. S. Naipaul*. Edited by Pankaj Mishra. New York: Knopf, 2003.

———. "London." In *The Overcrowded Barracoon* by V. S. Naipaul, 9–16. New York: Vintage, 1984.

———. "Man in a Glass Box." Interview by Linda Blandford. In *Conversations with V. S. Naipaul*, edited by Feroza Jussawalla, 50–56. Jackson: University Press of Mississippi, 1997.

———. *The Middle Passage: Impressions of Five Societies—British, French and Dutch—in the West Indies and South America*. New York: Vintage, 1981.

———. *Miguel Street*. New York: Vintage, 1987.

———. *A Turn in the South*. New York: Knopf, 1989.

———. "The Unsparing Vision of V. S. Naipaul." Interview by Scott Winokur. In *Conversations with V. S. Naipaul,* edited by Feroza Jussawalla, 114–29. Jackson: University Press of Mississippi, 1997.

———. *A Way in the World: A Sequence*. London: Heinemann, 1994.

———. *The Writer and the World*. New York: Vintage, 2003.

———. *A Writer's People: Ways of Looking and Feeling*. London: Picador, 2007.

Ngũgĩ, wa Thiong'o. *Decolonising the Mind: The Politics of Language in African Literature*. London: James Currey, 1986.

Olmos, Margarite Fernández, and Lizabeth Paravisini-Gebert, eds. *Sacred Possessions: Vodou, Santeria, Obeah, and the Caribbean*. New Brunswick, NJ: Rutgers University Press, 1999.

O'Neill, Patrick. *The Comedy of Entropy: Humour/Narrative/Reading*. Toronto: University of Toronto Press, 1990.

Paravisini-Gebert, Lizabeth. *Jamaica Kincaid: A Critical Companion*. Westport, CT: Greenwood Press, 1999.

Parkinson Zamora, Lois, and Wendy B. Faris, eds. *Magical Realism: Theory, History, Community.* Durham, NC: Duke University Press, 1995.

Parry, Benita. "Between Creole and Cambridge English: The Poetry of David Dabydeen." *Kunapipi* 10, no. 3 (1998): 1–11.

Persaud, Lakshmi. *Butterfly in the Wind*. Leeds, UK: Peepal Tree, 1990.

———. *For the Love of My Name*. Leeds, UK: Peepal Tree, 2000.

Philip, Marlene NourbeSe. *She Tries Her Tongue, Her Silence Softly Breaks*. London: Women's Press, 1993.

Pilette, Wilfrid L. "Magical Thinking by Inpatient Staff Members." *Psychiatric Quarterly* 55, no. 4 (Winter 1983): 272–74.

Pollard, Velma. *Leaving Traces*. Leeds, UK: Peepal Tree, 2008.

Powell, Patricia. *The Fullness of Everything*. Leeds, UK: Peepal Tree, 2009.

Prince, Gerald. "How New is New?" In *Coordinates: Placing Science Fiction and Fantasy,* edited by George E. Slusser, Eric S. Rabkin, and Robert Scholes, 23–30. Carbondale: Southern Illinois University Press, 1983.

Reichl, Susanne, and Mark Stein, eds. *Cheeky Fictions: Laughter and the Postcolonial*. Amsterdam: Rodopi, 2005.

Rhys, Jean. *Wide Sargasso Sea*. Edited by Judith L. Raiskin. New York: W. W. Norton, 1999.

Richter, Virginia. "Laughter and Aggression: Desire and Derision in a Postcolonial Context." In *Cheeky Fictions: Laughter and the Postcolonial,* edited by Susanne Reichl and Mark Stein, 61–72. Amsterdam: Rodopi, 2005.

Robertson, Geoffrey. *The Justice Game*. London: Chatto and Windus, 1988.

Robinson, Fred Miller. "Comic Realism and V. S. Naipaul's *A House for Mr. Biswas*." *Thalia: Studies in Literary Humor* 5, no. 2 (1982–83): 14–23.

Rodríguez, Ileana. *House/Garden/Nation: Space, Gender, and Ethnicity in Postcolonial Latin American Literatures by Women.* Translated by Robert Carr and Ileana Rodríguez. Durham, NC: Duke University Press, 1994.

Roh, Franz. "Magic Realism: Post-Expressionism (1925)." In *Magical Realism: Theory, History, Community,* edited by Lois Parkinson Zamora and Wendy B. Faris, 15–31. Durham, NC: Duke University Press, 1995.

Rohlehr, Gordon. "The Calypsonian as Artist." *Small Axe* 9 (2001): 1–26.

———. "Character and Rebellion in *A House for Mr. Biswas.*" In *Critical Perspectives on V. S. Naipaul,* edited by Robert D. Hamner, 84–93. Washington, DC: Three Continents Press, 1977.

———. "History as Absurdity." In *Is Massa Day Dead? Black Moods in the Caribbean,* edited by Orde Coombs, 69–108. New York: Doubleday, 1974.

———. "The Ironic Approach: The Novels of V. S. Naipaul." In *Critical Perspectives on V. S. Naipaul,* edited by Robert D. Hamner, 178–93. Washington, DC: Three Continents Press, 1977.

Romero, Lora. *Home Fronts: Domesticity and Its Critics in the Antebellum United States.* Durham, NC: Duke University Press, 1997.

Rothberg, Michael. "Decolonizing Trauma Studies: A Response." *Studies in the Novel* 40, nos. 1–2 (Spring and Summer 2008): 224–34.

Russo, Mary. *The Female Grotesque: Risk, Excess and Modernity.* New York: Routledge, 1994.

Ryan, Selwyn, and Taimoon Stewart, eds. *The Black Power Revolution, 1970: A Retrospective.* St. Augustine, Trinidad: ISER, 1995.

Sale, Kirkpatrick. *The Conquest of Paradise: Christopher Columbus and the Columbian Legacy.* New York: Alfred A. Knopf, 1990.

Salick, Roydon, ed. *The Comic Vision in West Indian Literature.* Marabella, Trinidad: Printex Converters, 1993.

Sangari, Kumkum. "The Politics of the Possible." In *The Nature and Context of Minority Discourse,* edited by Abdul JanMohamed and David Lloyd, 216–45. London: Oxford University Press, 1990.

Scott, David. *Conscripts of Modernity: The Tragedy of Colonial Enlightenment.* Durham, NC: Duke University Press, 2004.

———. *Refashioning Futures: Criticism after Postcoloniality.* Princeton, NJ: Princeton University Press, 1999.

Scott, Dennis. "An Echo in the Bone." In *Plays for Today,* edited by Errol Hill, 73–137. Essex: Longman, 1985.

Scott, Lawrence. *Witchbroom.* London: Heinemann, 1992.

Sedgwick, Eve Kosofsky. *Epistemology of the Closet.* Berkeley: University of California Press, 1990.

Senior, Olive. *Gardening in the Tropics.* Toronto: McClelland and Stewart, 1994.

Shakespeare, William. *Hamlet.* Edited by Susanne L. Wofford. Boston: Bedford/St. Martin's Press, 1994.

———. *The Tempest.* Edited by Peter Hulme and William H. Sherman. New York: Norton, 2004.

Sharp, James. *The Life and Death of Michael X.* Waterford, UK: UNI Books, 1981.

Sheller, Mimi. *Consuming the Caribbean: From Arawaks to Zombies.* London: Routledge, 2003.

Smith, Zadie. *Changing My Mind: Occasional Essays.* New York: Penguin, 2009.

———. *White Teeth.* New York: Vintage, 2001.

Spivak, Gayatri Chakravorty. *A Critique of Postcolonial Reason: Toward a History of the Vanishing Present.* Cambridge: Harvard University Press, 1999.

Stierstorfer, Klaus. "Laughing Caribbean: Humour in Caribbean Literature and Culture." In *Reading the Caribbean: Approaches to Anglophone Caribbean Literature and Culture,* edited by Klaus Stierstorfer, 315–37. Heidelberg: Universitätsverlag Winter, 2007.

Suleiman, Susan Rubin. "Writing and Motherhood." In *The (M)other Tongue: Essays in Feminist Psychoanalytic Interpretation,* edited by Shirley Nelson Garner, Claire Kahane, and Madelon Sprengnether, 352–77. Ithaca, NY: Cornell University Press, 1985.

Suleri, Sara. *The Rhetoric of English India.* Chicago: University of Chicago Press, 1992.

Tambiah, Stanley Jeyaraja. *Magic, Science, Religion, and the Scope of Rationality.* Cambridge: Cambridge University Press, 1990.

Tate, Greg. Interview by Mark Dery. "Black to the Future: Interviews with Samuel R. Delany, Greg Tate, and Tricia Rose." *SAQ* 92, no. 4 (Fall 1993): 735–38.

Taussig, Michael. "The Language of Flowers." *Critical Inquiry* 30, no. 1 (Autumn 2003): 98–131.

———. *Shamanism, Colonialism, and the Wild Man: A Study in Terror and Healing.* Chicago: University of Chicago Press, 1987.

Thaler, Ingrid. *Black Atlantic Speculative Fictions: Octavia E. Butler, Jewelle Gomez, and Nalo Hopkinson.* New York: Routledge, 2010.

Thompson, Alvin O. *The Haunting Past: Politics, Economics, and Race in Caribbean Life.* Armonk, New York: M. E. Sharpe, 1997.

Thomson, Philip. *The Grotesque.* London: Methuen, 1972.

Tinsley, Omise'eke Natasha. *Thiefing Sugar: Eroticism Between Women in Caribbean Literature.* Durham, NC: Duke University Press, 2010.

Voltaire. *Candide.* Translated by Lowell Bair. New York: Bantam, 1959.

Walcott, Derek. "The Caribbean: Culture or Mimicry." *Journal of Interamerican Studies and World Affairs* 16, no. 1 (February, 1974): 3–13.

———. *Remembrance and Pantomime.* New York: Farrar, Straus and Giroux, 1980.

———. *What the Twilight Says: Essays by Derek Walcott.* New York: Farrar, Straus and Giroux, 1998.

Walker, Alice. *In Search of Our Mother's Gardens: Womanist Prose.* San Diego: Harcourt Brace Jovanovich, 1983.

Warnes, Christopher. *Magical Realism and the Postcolonial Novel: Between Faith and Irreverence.* New York: Palgrave Macmillan, 2009.

Warren, Karen J., ed. *Ecological Feminist Philosophies.* Bloomington: Indiana University Press, 1996.

Weber, Max. *The Protestant Ethic and the Spirit of Capitalism.* New York: Charles Scribner's Sons, 1930.

Welsh, Sarah Lawson. "Experiments in Brokenness: The Creative Use of Creole in David Dabydeen's *Slave Song.*" In *The Routledge Reader in Caribbean Literature,* edited by Alison Donnell and Sarah Lawson Welsh, 416–24. London: Routledge, 1996.

Wiggan, Katherine. "Comedy and Creole in Selvon's London Stories." In *The Comic Vision in West Indian Literature,* edited by Roydon Salick, 19–30. Marabella, Trinidad: Printex Converters, 1993.

Williams, John L. *Michael X: A Life in Black and White.* London: Century, 2008.

Wood, James. *The Irresponsible Self: On Laughter and the Novel.* New York: Farrar, Straus and Giroux, 2004.

Works Project Administration. *Drums and Shadows: Survival Studies among the Georgia Coastal Negroes.* Athens: University of Georgia Press, 1940.

Index